The marginalist theory of the corporation or firm, whose character-istics were formally developed in the 1930s, represents a major change in the development of traditional economic theory. In this book, Pro-fessor Schrader, a philosopher of economics, discusses the rise of the marginalist conception of the firm in the context of economic thought over the past two centuries, and explains why economists continue to defend a theory with demonstrable shortcomings: The marginalist view of the firm retains its support not through any comparative advantage in empirical or predictive power, he argues, but by virtue of its being a part of the broader marginalist economic program.

The clear problems that beset the marginalist approach to the firm signal a general dilemma for economic theory as a whole. Although economists generally remain committed to both a methodological in-dividualism and a preference for nonintentional coordination of eco-nomic endeavor, Schrader observes that the modern corporation by its very nature is both a social collective and a locus of intentional coordination of economic activity. An economic theory that does jus-tice to a world in which managerial corporations are among the key agents of production and distribution must generate a theory of col-lective action to bolster the theory of individual action that forms the present basis for most economic thinking.

T0312152

The corporation as anomaly

The corporation as anomaly

David E. Schrader

CAMBRIDGE
UNIVERSITY PRESS

CAMBRIDGE UNIVERSITY PRESS
Cambridge, New York, Melbourne, Madrid, Cape Town, Singapore, São Paulo

Cambridge University Press
The Edinburgh Building, Cambridge CB2 2RU, UK

Published in the United States of America by Cambridge University Press, New York

www.cambridge.org
Information on this title: www.cambridge.org/9780521412414

© Cambridge University Press 1993

First published 1993
This digitally printed first paperback version 2006

A catalogue record for this publication is available from the British Library

Library of Congress Cataloguing in Publication data
Schrader, David E., 1947–
The corporation as anomaly / David E. Schrader.
p.   cm.
Includes bibliographical references and index.
ISBN 0-521-41241-2
1. Corporations.   I. Title.
HD2741.S43   1993
338.7′4 – dc20   92–13629
                                        CIP

ISBN-13 978-0-521-41241-4 hardback
ISBN-10 0-521-41241-2 hardback

ISBN-13 978-0-521-03375-6 paperback
ISBN-10 0-521-03375-6 paperback

To Gene and Joyce

Contents

Preface

This book is the product of the confluence of a number of distinct philosophical interests and is, accordingly, a product that leaves me indebted to a great number of people and institutions. In particular, I have had a long-standing professional interest in both the philosophy of science and ethics. My interest in the philosophy of science has led me, because of a number of close friendships with colleagues in the discipline of economics, into a great many discussions of theory justification in economics. At the same time, my own theoretical commitments in the area of ethics have led me to feel a deep frustration with the dominant economic view of human rationality as necessarily leading to maximizing behavior.

Roughly a decade ago I undertook to develop a course in Business Ethics in cooperation with my late colleague, Lee Van Zant (Economics, Austin College). That course brought me face to face with the modern managerial corporation in a way that I had not previously experienced. The more I examined the managerial corporation, the more I became convinced that many of the claims that seemed to be made about it by professional economists seemed appropriate claims to make about individual entrepreneurial businesses, but not about large corporations. As a result, I found myself becoming increasingly interested in theories of the firm.

Quite naturally, that interest lent a new direction and a new set of problems to my previous interest in the issue of theory justification in economics. This book is the product of that new direction and new set of problems.

Many people have helped me in the process of developing the ideas that now comprise this book. My late colleague Om P. Batish (Economics, Loras College) first engaged me in discussion about theory justification in economics. Professor Batish, whose life was tragically cut short in 1983, was a dear friend who would undoubtedly have disagreed with most of what I have to say in this book. Yet it was his forceful advocacy of what I increasingly came to regard as a mistaken position that provided the initial impetus for my study of the philosophy of economics.

As is true of all of the work that I have done on the intersections of philosophy and economics over the past decade, this book could not have emerged without the encouragement, support, and criticism of Lee Van Zant. Professor Van Zant patiently read all the earliest drafts of the material that now forms this book. Without his assurance that I was doing something worthwhile in this work, it would undoubtedly have died in a very early stage. The entire manuscript, in an earlier form, was also read by Norman E. Bowie (Carlson School of Management, University of Minnesota). Professor Bowie's careful criticism has helped me to eliminate a great many mistakes from the pages of this book. Parts of earlier drafts of the manuscript were also read and criticized by Hugh Garnett (Economics, Austin College), Larry Laudan (Philosophy, University of Hawaii), and John C. Winfrey (Economics, Washington and Lee University).

Institutional support for this project has likewise come from a number of sources. My initial research into the philosophy of economics was started with the support of a grant from the National Endowment for the Humanities in 1981 to attend a summer seminar on "Distributive Justice: Economic and Philosophic Aspect," under the direction of Royall Brandis (Economics, University of Illinois). The tightening of my focus on theoretical problems in understanding the managerial corporation was supported by another grant from the National Endowment for the Humanities, this time to attend a summer seminar in 1985 entitled "Agreement and Disagreement in Science," under the direction of Larry Laudan (at that time Director of the Center for the Study of Science and Society, Virginia Polytechnic Institute and State University). During the fall semester of 1986, Austin College granted me a sabbatical leave, during which I worked full time on this manuscript, while enjoying the facilities of the Center for the Study of Values at the University of Delaware, at that time directed by Norman E. Bowie. I am grateful for the support of the National Endowment for the Humanities and of Austin College, as well as for the help provided by all of the above-named individuals.

Finally, I want to express my sincere appreciation to Scott V. Parris, economics editor for Cambridge University Press, and his predecessor, Matthew N. Hendryx, both of whose patience and cooperation have helped greatly in bringing this book to completion. I am also immeasurably indebted to Daniel M. Hausman and to three anonymous referees for Cambridge University Press. Thanks to their careful criticisms, I am much more pleased with this book than I was with the version that I initially submitted. I must also thank Kluwer Academic Publishers for permission to reprint part of the material in Chapter 7, which previously appeared in my "The Corporation and Profits," *Journal of Business Ethics*, Vol. 6 (1987).

Much as I owe to all of those whom I've mentioned above, their contributions to this book would have been to no avail had it not been for the constant love and encouragement I received from my wife, Sandy, and our daughters, Sara and Tami, as I wrote and revised this manuscript. It goes without saying, of course, that those defects which remain in this book are mine and mine alone.

August 1992
Washington, Pennsylvania

Introduction

There is perhaps nothing in U.S. society that is both more pervasive and yet less understood than the business corporation. In popular discussion of the modern business corporation the loudest voices seem to assume an almost religious fervor. The detractors, or "corporation beaters," see the corporation as something akin to the devil incarnate in the modern world. They see the business corporation as the new leviathan, a huge, artificially created monster, trampling all in its path – people, environment, political institutions, and so on – showing no regard for anything beyond its own insatiable appetite for money and power. On the other side of the debate we see an almost religious devotion to the corporation. It is viewed as the master creation of modern society, a vehicle by which human society has become capable of creative power never before imagined, the natural outgrowth of the marvelous market mechanism whose "invisible hand" coordination of human economic activity guarantees both the highest possible level of production and the most optimal patterns of distribution and allocation.

Unfortunately, all the impassioned pleas that we hear in the public forum about "protecting people and the environment from the giant corporations" or about "getting the government off business's back" fail to reflect an understanding of the modern business corporation matching their passion. These pleas serve relatively little purpose. Understanding the corporation, however, is crucial for the well-being of contemporary society. No amount of corporation beating will make the large business corporation go away. Corporations have become a thoroughly established part of our social and economic environment. Unless we should move into a completely socialistic economy, in which case the government would come to assume the various roles played by corporations in our present society, the corporation will continue to be with us.

The corporation beaters, however, are little worse off than the corporation devotees. While it is clear that the corporation is with us to stay, it is also clear that it is an institution in turmoil. Whether we read in our newspapers about the balance-of-payments problem and

1

the noncompetitiveness of U.S. business in world markets, about corporate takeovers, junk bonds, and the savings and loan disaster; any of the large number of best-selling books written since the mid-1970s on the "crisis" in American management; or the more theoretical discussions of management theory that have emerged among management scholars, it is clear that a large number of corporations have not been operating particularly well. The economic performance of a significant number of corporations has been no better than what the critics of corporate business claim the social performance of corporations has been. Most commentators who go beyond reciting depressing statistics seem to agree that we simply don't understand the business corporation very well.

By this I do not mean to say that we lack any theoretical framework within which to place the corporation. Rather, the problem is quite the reverse. We have a number of conflicting and contradictory theoretical frameworks within which different people and groups place the business corporation. The resulting theoretical disagreement creates confusion. Moreover, the theoretical framework for the corporation that has been most dominant in framing public policy relative to the corporation and has also been most dominant in forming the general public's perspective on the business corporation is an economic-theoretical framework that is woefully inadequate to the task of providing a sound understanding of the managerial corporation.

Most discussion of the U.S. economic system generally, as well as most discussion of the role and obligations of business corporations within U.S. society, appears to be premised on the view that corporations are simply artificial persons and that their behavior in the market is substantially the same as that of other persons. Given the dominant economic view that individuals invariably act as maximizers of their utility, this translates into a view of the business corporation as an individual acting in the market to maximize its utility. Customarily, the utility of the business corporation is held to be money profits. This view claims to descend from the economic works of Adam Smith, written now over 200 years ago. There is a sense in which that view does descend from the economic theory of Smith. Yet despite that fact, most economic theorists prior to this century viewed the modern form of corporate business, a form in which business control is exercised by salaried executives, as either unworkable or incompatible with the working of a free market economy.

In spite of that fact the economic tradition that arose out of Smith's work has evolved over time to include a view of the business corporation as simply another kind of economic individual, governed by the same self-interest that it claims governs all economic individuals. That same tradition has also come to dominate our thinking and guide our policy making about economic issues in general. As a corollary, public policy makers and much of the general public have come to accept the now traditional economic view of the corporation as well.

Yet while it may seem to be plausible for economists, policymakers, and a significant part of the general public to view the business corporation as just a bigger and more powerful individual agent in the market, it is clearly not plausible for business managers and for management theorists to so view the corporation. Whatever may be said for the view that the market brings about an invisible hand coordination of economic activity apart from any conscious economic planning on the part of the larger society, the name of the game in business management is conscious coordination of the economic activity of those who make up the business enterprise. Managers and management theorists, therefore, have tended to recognize that the business corporation is an institution composed of many and varied interests, which interests it is the job of the manager to coordinate into a coherent pattern of business activity. This recognition has given rise to a number of emerging alternative theoretical approaches to the business corporation.

The result of the advocacy of such a wide variety of theoretical perspectives on the business corporation has been little short of mass confusion. Not only does this confusion infect the theoretical understanding of the business corporation as various sorts of academics attempt to understand the corporation, it also infects our collective view of the appropriate role of the business corporation in contemporary society as that role is shaped by policymakers in response to a variety of public pressures. This book is an attempt to provide some general direction toward the resolution of that confusion.

The project that I pursue in this book is primarily the development of a case study in the philosophy of science. I shall be concerned to look at the managerial business corporation as it has been treated in theory. While organizational and management theorists have had a great deal to say about corporations recently, it still remains that the dominant theoretical perspective on the business corporation is that which is developed within traditional economics. This is not surprising, because the business corporation is most immediately an economic institution. Moreover, a large part of public policy as it relates to business corporations is economic policy. Yet perhaps most importantly, the discipline of economics is simply far better established and is far broader in scope than are the disciplines of management science and organizational science. Because of the entrenchment of the economic discipline and the esteem in which economics is held by most policymakers, it is quite natural that the view of the corporation which emerges from economic theory should exercise a greater impact than the views of the corporation which come from far newer and less well established disciplines. Likewise, it is also quite natural that policymakers who accept a general theory about economic phenomena should equally accept the part of that theory that deals with the business firm.

Unfortunately, the view of the corporation that arises from traditional economic theory is woefully inadequate. Both the inadequacy of that view and the reason for its continued dominance can best be understood by examining the way in which it has developed as a part of the economic tradition. That examination thus leads me into an exercise in the history and philosophy of economic science.

The basic point I wish to make is that the development of the modern business corporation has presented a significant anomaly to traditional economic theory. As Alfred Chandler notes:

Those institutional changes which helped to create the managerial capitalism of the twentieth century were as significant and as revolutionary as those that accompanied the rise of commercial capitalism a half a millennium earlier....
The appearance of managerial capitalism has been, therefore, an economic phenomenon.[1]

Unfortunately, the mainstream of contemporary economic theory has carried on its theoretical endeavors as if this "economic phenomenon" didn't really constitute anything fundamentally new in the economic world. I shall argue that the way in which traditional economic theory has attempted to accommodate itself to the existence of the corporate form of business operation has been unsuccessful, and that a fairly radical revision of economic theory is required if economic theory is to be able to give a satisfactory and comprehensive explanation of economic phenomena in a world in which corporations are among the chief economic agents.

The first step in this phase of the project is to show that the development of the marginalist theory of the firm, now so widely accepted among economists, did in fact constitute a very significant, albeit generally unrecognized, change in the character of the economic tradition that has come down to us from Smith. The development of a theory of the firm was not simply a natural outgrowth of the economic doctrines presented in *The Wealth of Nations*. Rather, it constituted a serious attempt to accommodate the old economic theory to a significantly different kind of economic phenomenon. In Chapter 1 I contrast the views of earlier economic theorists (up to John Bates Clark writing in the early twentieth century) who saw the corporate form of business either as something that shouldn't be expected to work or as something that contravened the fundamental laws of the operation of the free market, with the contemporary economic view that takes the corporation as a perfectly natural part of the economic landscape. This in itself should suggest that the firm recognized by contemporary economists as so natural a component of their later theory was viewed by earlier economists as a creature quite alien to their earlier stages of economic theory. I then go on to identify the fundamental character of the theoretical change that occurred in the transition and explain why it has not generally been recognized as a significant change.

The second step is to show that the assimilation of the managerial corporation into economic theory has not been very successful. In order to do this I need to trace out that process of assimilation. Yet that tracing itself requires a set of categories for analysis.

Because economic theory has been developed into such a highly systematic body, I shall assume that the general categories which have been developed for the analysis of the history and philosophy of science can be fruitfully applied to give us an understanding of the history of economic theory. Given this, I argue in Chapter 2 that the history of economic theory can best be understood from the perspective of Larry Laudan's "reticulated model of scientific justification." Most discussion of the history of economic theory thus far has been carried out, first, from the perspective of Sir Karl Popper's evolutionary view of knowledge; later, from the perspective of Thomas Kuhn's notion of science as a "paradigm-bound" activity; and most recently, from the perspective of Imre Lakatos's "methodology of scientific research programmes." I argue in Chapter 2 that each of these earlier approaches suffers from weaknesses that are remedied in Laudan's approach. Armed with Laudan's methodological approach, I give in Chapter 3 a thumbnail sketch of the history of economic theory since Smith, focusing on fundamental changes in the explanatory aims and methods of economic theory and on those aspects of theory that are relevant to the eventual development of the modern theory of the firm.

While the economic tradition as it has descended from Smith is often presented as more or less of a monolith or, in Kuhnian terms, a "single paradigm," by the end of Chapter 3 it should be clear that while we can make some sense of the notion of an ongoing tradition, there are clearly significant and discontinuous changes within that tradition. In Chapter 4 I examine the extent and location of agreement and disagreement within the economic tradition. I argue that the elements of agreement are far more modest than the customary presentation of economics would have us believe. In particular, I argue that the points of agreement within the tradition are limited to three: a commitment to a methodological individualism that views all economic activity as some kind of arithmetic function of the behavior of individual agents, a commitment to the view that human economic activity is generally self-interested, and a commitment to the preferability of invisible hand or unconscious coordination of economic activity. The first and last of these three points prove particularly troublesome in the attempt to understand the operation of an economy dominated by managerial-corporate coordination of business activity.

In Chapter 5 I narrow my focus to look at three major approaches to theories of the firm, noting in particular how behavioral and managerial theories differ from the dominant marginalist theory of the economic tradition. I go on in Chapter 6, then, to explore the chief points of weakness in the marginalist approach to the firm. Most significantly, I argue that the marginalist theory of the firm suffers from a very narrow explanatory scope and does so primarily because it fails to account for the collective character of the modern business corporation.

Given what emerges as the clear inferiority of the marginalist theory of the firm in the face of its major theoretical rivals, it may initially seem that such a theory could only be held on the basis of some form of collective irrationality, perhaps, as some have charged, a commitment based on political ideology rather than scientific critical objectivity. I conclude Chapter 6 by arguing that there are very good theoretical reasons for the continued dominance of the marginalist theory of the firm. In particular, the marginalist theory of the firm is a part of the broader and more comprehensive marginalist program in economics. As a result, the marginalist theory of the firm must be judged not merely as a theory of the firm, but also as a part of a comprehensive economic theory. It is on this latter ground that the dominance of the marginalist theory of the firm must be understood. While there are other theories of the firm that are both well articulated and clearly preferable to the marginalist theory, there is no general economic theory that is both well articulated and clearly preferable to the general marginalist economic theory. The marginalist theory of the firm remains dominant, then, not because it is a good theory of the firm, but because it is a part of a fairly serviceable and more comprehensive theory that has no well-developed and serious rival.

This explanation of that dominance should hardly be very satisfying to the advocate of the marginalist theory. Thus, the final step in this project is to argue that a fairly radical revision of economic theory is required if it is to be able to give a satisfactory and comprehensive explanation of economic phenomena in a world in which managerial corporations are among the chief economic agents. If the marginalist theory of the firm is an inadequate theory of the firm and if it is a consequence of the more comprehensive marginalist theory of economics, it would seem that the inadequacy of the theory of the firm should eventually force some modification of the more comprehensive theory of which it is a part. This is precisely what I argue in the last two chapters of this work. In Chapter 7 I identify those characteristics of the managerial corporation that most render it anomalous for marginalist economic theory. In particular I note the role that profits play in corporate decision making, the role of various "stakeholder" or constituent groups in the functioning of the corporation, and the importance of corporate organization.

In Chapter 8 I argue that the central fact about the modern business corporation that makes it an anomaly for traditional economic theory is that the corporation is a genuine collective entity that features a very conscious "visible hand" type of coordination of economic activity. Such an entity must invariably prove anomalous to an economic theory committed to a reductive individualistic mode of analysis and to the ideal of unconscious invisible hand coordination of economic activity. A recognition of the collective and consciously coordinating character of the modern business corporation must sooner or later force a modification in economic theory, and do so in the direction of a theory that can include an account of collective as well as individual action, and a fortiori provide as important a place for conscious coordination of economic activity as for unconscious coordination.

While I think it is inevitable that the presence of corporations in our society must force economic theorists to develop a sound theory of collective action, and hence provide society with a theoretical understanding of the economy that makes good sense of business corporations, it is important to note that we do not need to wait for such a revision of economic theory before moving our public thinking about the corporation away from the individualistic invisible hand model of traditional economics. As I noted earlier, there is and has been for some time an emerging body of literature, mostly coming from business schools, that takes seriously the collective, institutional character of business corporations. Some of this literature has focused on the appropriate role of business corporations in twentieth-century U.S. society. Some has focused simply on sound principles of business management. Whichever focus has been taken, the general recognition is that corporate business cannot in the long run be viable, either socially or economically, if it does not pay serious attention to its own institutional character.

Unfortunately there is no single institutional theory of the business corporation that has gained even close to as widespread an acceptance within any community of business scholars as the marginalist theory of the firm has within the community of professional economists. This, however, surely need not constitute an insuperable barrier to developing a public understanding of the corporation that would pay serious attention to the collective and institutional character of the corporation.

A recognition of what the modern business corporation really is – a social institution, a locus of collective action in which the varied interests of a number of individuals and groups are brought together and transformed into a more or less coherent pattern of group behavior in pursuit of at least partially convergent purposes – requires a number of changes in the ways in which we think about the economic world in general and about business corporations in particular. At the theoretical level, we must develop analytical tools that will allow us to explain collective economic action as well as we can currently explain individual economic action. More practically, the corporation can no longer be regarded as a purely economic agent (on the model of economic agency given in traditional marginalist economic theory) or perhaps even a purely economic institution. Rather, it becomes necessary to regard the business corporation as a political institution as well (if indeed a clear distinction between economic and political institutions is itself ultimately tenable). It must clearly follow from this that a rethinking is required of the appropriate relationship between society in general and the business corporation. (It is not at all clear that this applies equally to individual-entrepreneurial businesses.)

Equally it follows that we have a clearer basis for addressing the social roles and responsibilities of corporate business as we come to see corporations not merely as economic agents, but also as semipublic political and social institutions. Finally, a recognition of the political dimension of corporate business must lead us as well to a rethinking of appropriate forms of corporate governance. If the corporation is a "semi-public power," as John Bates Clark suggests,[2] then it is surely plausible to suggest that its governing structure should provide for the input of a broader range of constituencies than is now the case.

The directions in which I have been pointing, of course, carry well beyond the scope of this present book. Yet it has always been a fundamental commitment of the economist that theory serves practice, or, more particularly, policy. I am firmly convinced that a more satisfactory theoretical understanding of the managerial corporation as a component of a general economy must go hand in hand with a changed view of the appropriate place of the managerial corporation in society as a whole.

My central thesis in this book is that the key to rethinking the place of the corporation both in theory and in actual practice is to understand the corporation as a locus of collective action. It is my hope that this book will provide at least a modest step toward that rethinking.

CHAPTER 1

The hidden change in economic theory

The mainstream of economic theory is very often presented to us as a largely continuous and progressive development of a unitary general approach or 'paradigm', to use a term about which I shall have more to say later, dating back to the work of Adam Smith. A. W. Coats, for example, has claimed that economic theory has been "dominated throughout its history by a single paradigm – the theory of economic equilibrium via the market mechanism."[1] Similarly, D. Gordon has claimed that "Smith's postulate of the maximizing individual in a relatively free market...is our basic paradigm.... economics has never had a major revolution; its basic maximizing model has never been replaced."[2] While one does hear talk among economists of "the marginalist revolution," "the Keynesian revolution," "the monopolistic competition revolution," and so on, no one, I think, would claim that these so-called revolutions have altered the foundations of the way in which people have looked at the economic world in the same manner in which the Copernican revolution altered the foundations of the way in which people looked at the arrangement of the heavens. If political metaphors are at all apt, the above-noted changes in economic theorizing would better be viewed as changes in the ruling party in a widely popular and accepted constitutional democracy.

Whatever one might wish to say about the usefulness of Thomas Kuhn's notion of "paradigm" in the attempt to understand the history of economic thought, it is clear at least that there has been something of a common thread running through the major developments in economic theory since the work of Smith. Yet it is equally clear that economic theory has undergone significant changes during the centuries that have passed since then.

Undoubtedly the changes in economic theory wrought by Jevons, Menger, and Walras (the "marginalist revolution"); the changes wrought by John Maynard Keynes; and those by Robinson and Chamberlin (the "monopolistic competition revolution") have given contemporary economic theory a face that Adam Smith would have recognized only in outline. Yet I want to claim that there has been another kind of change in economic theory of equal or greater magnitude that has remained largely unrecognized as a theoretical change. That change with which I am here concerned has been wrought not by insight in the mind of an economic theorist, but by change in the operation of the economic world since the time when Smith gave modern economics its basic shape – the evolution of the modern business corporation. I do not, of course, want to suggest that this has been the only significant change in the operation of the economic world. While I am not concerned to debate the relative magnitudes of these various changes in economic theory or in economic life, I am centrally concerned to claim that the rise of the corporation as the most significant type of agent of production in the contemporary Western world has generated a highly significant modification in economic theory. Moreover, I want to argue that for quite understandable reasons, this modification has been largely unrecognized as a theoretical modification. The neoclassical theory of the firm has generally been, quite incorrectly, presented as a simple consequence of the original insights of Smith.

The corporation and earlier economic theory

Perhaps the best way to make it clear that economic theory has changed in response to the development of the modern business corporation is to start by looking at what some of the great economic theorists of the past have had to say about the corporate organization of business activity.

1. Adam Smith:
    The trade of a joint stock company is always managed by a court of directors. . . . The directors of such companies, however, being the managers rather of other people's money than of their own, it cannot well be expected, that they should watch over it with the same anxious vigilance with which the partners in a private copartnery frequently watch over their own. . . . Negligence and profusion, therefore, must always prevail, more or less, in the management of the affairs of such a company. . . . They have, accordingly, very seldom succeeded without an exclusive privilege; and frequently have not succeeded with one.[3]
2. Alfred Marshall:
    It is true that the head of a large private firm undertakes the chief risks of the business, while he entrusts many of its details to others; . . . If those to whom he has entrusted the buying or selling of goods for him take commissions from those with whom they deal, . . . [i]f they show favouritism and promote incompetent relations or friends of their own, or if they themselves become idle and shirk their work, or even if they do not fulfil the promise of exceptional ability which

induced him to give them their first lift, he can discover what is going wrong and set it right.

But in all these matters the great body of the shareholders of a joint stock company are, save in a few exceptional instances, almost powerless; . . . It is a strong proof of the marvellous growth in recent times of a spirit of honesty and uprightness in commercial matters, that the leading officers of great public companies yield as little as they do to the vast temptations to fraud which lie in their way.[4]

3.   John Bates Clark:

The field for business enterprise has been open to individuals, partnerships, and corporations; they have entered it fearlessly, and a free-for-all competition has resulted. This free action is in process of being repressed by chartered bodies of capitalists, the great corporations, whom the law still treats somewhat as though in its collective entirety each one were an individual. They are building up a semi-public power – a quasi-state within the general state – and beside vitiating the action of economic laws, are perverting governments. They trench on the freedom on which economic laws are postulated and on civic freedom also.

. . . Prices do not conform to the standards of cost, wages do not conform to the standard of final productivity of labor, and interest does not conform to the marginal product of capital. The system of industrial groups and subgroups is thrown out of balance by putting too much labor and capital at certain points and too little at others. Profits become, not altogether a temporary premium for improvement, – the reward for giving to humanity a dynamic impulse, – but partly the spoils of men whose influence is hostile to progress.[5]

Note at the outset that each of the three economists cited recognizes a certain tension between the operation of the large managerial corporation and the laws of classical economic theory. Smith and Marshall see a conflict between the interests of the owners of a business and those of its salaried managers. Each sees the owners as interested in the profits of the business, that part of the business's return which, at least in theory, returns to the owner. Yet salaried managers of business, at least if they are economically self-interested agents, will have their own quite independent sets of interests. They will, of course, be interested in the level of their salaries. They will, in many cases, also be interested in leisure, the well-being of friends and relatives (who may be quite unknown to the owners of the business), and so on. The various factors involved in the meeting of these divergent interests in the running of a managerial corporation have been of significant interest to writers in the areas of business ethics and management science. They have also long been of interest to the courts that have had to render decisions on the legal priority of interests within the managerial corporation. Yet they have been re-markably little touched upon by economic theorists.

Clark, by contrast, recognizes a related, but clearly distinct problem. Like Smith and Marshall, he recognizes that the managerial corpo-ration, unlike the individual entrepreneur, is not simply an individual in the market, with a unique self-interest that is molded by the free market mechanism into a socially beneficent force. Yet Clark also recognizes, as Marshall seems also to have done in his *Industry and Trade*, the additional problem of the market power of the large man-agerial corporation. That power enables the corporation to contra-vene the impersonal (and beneficent) forces of the market mechanism itself.

Smith's remarks, of course, were written before the modern busi-ness corporation had become the dominant, or even a very significant, component of the economy. What Smith reflects primarily is simply a very strong doubt that corporations (and I am talking here about not owner-controlled corporations but rather managerial corpora-tions) could succeed in a market economy. Smith starts by noting that in a corporation or "joint stock company," as it was called in his time, control falls in the hands of "directors," not the owners; that is, there is separation of ownership and control. Smith claims, presumably as a direct consequence of his fundamental view that economic agents are and *should be* self-interested, that nonowning "directors" cannot be expected to tend to the business owners' interests as well as the owners themselves would. Thus, according to his theory, non-owner-managed businesses should be at a competitive disadvantage as against owner-managed businesses. This leads him to suspect that non-owner-managed businesses, managerial corporations, should tend to be driv-en from the market. He also notes, and this as a matter of observation, that such businesses have not, in his own time, very often succeeded unless given some form of protection by government.

Marshall was writing nearly a hundred years later, at a time when, as he observed, "the joint-stock companies in the United Kingdom do a very great part of the business of all kinds that is done in the country."[6] Smith's contention that corporate management of business simply wouldn't work in a market economy was no longer tenable in Marshall's time. Experience had proved otherwise, no matter what one's theoretical proclivities might incline one to say.

Yet Marshall clearly shows an awareness of those theoretical im-plications that led Smith to deny that corporate business could work. Marshall acknowledges that the separation of control from ownership places the upper-level managers, "the leading officers," of corporations in a position in which they are subject to a collection of natural tendencies (if one maintains that human beings are generally self-interested) or "temptations" that would lead to behavior counter to the interests of the owners (and presumably of the firm itself). He acknowledges an inclination to "take commissions from those with whom they deal." This is presumably a kind of behavior that one might expect if the manager is more interested in his or her own financial return than that of the firm. Marshall acknowledges an inclination to "show favouritism and promote incompetent relations or friends of their own." This would surely be another form of behavior that we might expect of managers who were concerned with their own utility (in this case various forms of nonfinancial return) more than that of the firm. Finally, Marshall acknowledges an inclination to "become idle and shirk their work." Here again, Marshall is simply noting that if managers were to be more interested in their own total utility than in that of the firm, we should expect to find what we find with people generally, that some of them would reach a point where they show a preference for increased leisure over increased financial return. Moreover, Marshall is astute enough to notice that managers are not prevented from falling to such temptations because of their fear of the power of the shareholders. Rather, he notes that "in all these matters the great body of shareholders of a joint-stock company are . . . almost powerless."

Note that Marshall has given us a partial catalog of the kinds of "negligence and profusion" that Smith claimed were endemic to managerial control of business, and that he claimed should lead to the failure of that mode of business. Marshall, too, seems to recognize that Smith's dire expectations of managerial behavior are more or less what all of us would expect of primarily self-interested economic agents if not restrained by fear of penalty.

Marshall's explanation of the success of the managerial corporation involves what is surely a wonderful bit of irony: "It is a strong proof of the marvellous growth in recent times of a spirit of honesty and uprightness in commercial matters, that the leading officers of great public companies yield as little as they do to the vast temptations to fraud which lie in their way." Marshall makes no comment on the matter of whether the managerial corporation could succeed if its officers did yield to the temptations noted. Yet the manner in which he explains their failure to so yield, while consistent with his own view that noneconomic motives must be attended to in economics, is seriously at variance with the motivational assumptions that have come to dominate mainstream economic theory, including the dominant theory of the firm.

The self-interest assumptions on which the economic tradition since Smith rests would lead one to expect that managers should attempt to maximize their own long-range utility. The only factors that might reasonably be expected to lead managers to pay high regard to the interests of the owners would be those of the following four kinds: (1) John Stuart Mill, writing about seventy years after Smith, notes that "there are modes of connecting more or less intimately the interests of the employees with the pecuniary success of the concern."[7] Devices such as stock options, bonuses, and so on, can be used to make the success of the firm a *component* of the economic well-being of the manager. (2) Although Marshall notes that the shareholders are "almost powerless," there may yet be a small amount of fear in the manager that if he or she goes beyond a certain point in ignoring the interests of the shareholders, they may discover that fact and find it worth their effort to mobilize what little power they do have against management. (3) Managers may be concerned with public approval, and hence find the kind of public disapproval that might be brought to bear on them for neglect of the firm's interests an element of disutility within their own system of preferences. (4) Finally, there may be effectively enforceable law requiring a certain level of good stewardship among managers. It is worthy of note that seventy-five years after Marshall first published his *Principles of Economics*, R. Joseph Monsen, Jr., and Anthony Downs wrote "A Theory of Large Managerial Firms," which claimed that managers do seek their own self-interest, not the interest of the firm, and that they do so subject to the kinds of constraints previously noted, a theme that is echoed with certain variations in both the "contract view" of the firm put forward by Eugene Fama and the "managerial theory" of the firm developed by Oliver Williamson.[8]

What Marshall claims leads managers to work for the interests of the shareholders – and hence allows Marshall to maintain that managerial firms as well as owner-controlled firms are profit maximizers – is "a marvellous growth in recent times of a spirit of honesty and uprightness in commercial matters." Marshall appears to be claiming that even without the kinds of constraints noted by Monsen and Downs, the upper-level managers of his day were motivated by a newly increased kind of altruistic concern to serve the interests of the shareholders. It would, of course, be open to Marshall to claim that this kind of altruistic activity created happiness for the managers of his day, and that it was therefore incorporated as a part of their own self-interest. The real problem with Marshall's account, however, is that it would imply that his theory of the firm could apply to managerial firms only in periods in which such a "marvellous . . . spirit of honesty" was pervasive. Since Marshall clearly suggests, in claiming this spirit to be of recent origin, that not all periods are governed by such an attitude, there would remain a very significant question about how the managerial firm might be expected to operate (and survive) in periods of lower virtue.

Whether it be that the United States at the turn of the century was simply a less virtuous place than the United Kingdom, or for some other reason, John Bates Clark, writing only a few years later than Marshall but on this side of the Atlantic, noted no such spirit. Clark, an enthusiastic advocate of private enterprise, saw the modern corporation as a kind of "semi-public" enterprise, "vitiating the action of economic laws" and "perverting governments." Clark held that economic science consisted of the discovering of those "natural laws" that govern the creation and use of wealth by human individuals.[9] The chartering of corporations, however, created a new kind of economic creature. This creature was a large collective organization, "a quasi-state," yet still generally treated as an individual. This established the corporation as a unique kind of economic agent, one with a level of power that went beyond that which could be had by genuine individual economic agents and whose actions in the market could not, therefore, be constrained by the same "natural laws" that constrained the actions of genuine individual economic agents. Thus, for Clark the corporation undermined the operation of the free market and constituted a fundamental challenge to economic theory.

I have selected Smith's, Marshall's, and Clark's comments on the corporate operation of business for two reasons. In the first place, each of the three occupies a uniquely important position in the development of mainstream economic theory. Smith, of course, is the father of economic theory. His position in establishing the main tradition should be clear from what I said at the outset of this chapter. Marshall's *Principles* stands out as one of the seminal works in the establishment of the marginalist theory of the firm. Indeed, Kenneth Boulding has said that "there was no theory of the firm in economics before Marshall."[10] Moreover, Marshall was one of the first great economic theorists to write at a time in which the corporation was a significant part of the economy. Finally, Clark was not only the first American economic theorist of note, but as well one of the pioneer developers of the "marginal productivity theory," which has played a very important role in a number of justifications of free market distribution of wealth.

In the second place, the comments made by Smith, Marshall, and Clark on the corporate operation of business seem to be quite typical of what other significant economic theorists have had to say on that issue prior to the twentieth century. Writing, as they do, at different times and places, these three theorists say somewhat different things about the corporate organization of business. Smith claims that corporations can't succeed very well in a market economy. Marshall seems to find it surprising that they do succeed and attributes a significant role in that success to the aforementioned "spirit" among business persons in his time. Clark sees that corporate business has succeeded and finds that fact a serious threat to the working of the whole economy.

While having different things to say about corporate business, the three theorists share one very important view: The successful operation of the managerial corporation fits poorly with classical and even marginalist economic theory. Smith thinks that the truth of classical economic theory should rule out the successful operation of the managerial corporation. Marshall finds the success of the managerial corporation a surprising fact that requires explanation. Both of them, of course, find the root of the problem in the managerial corporations' separation of the function of management from the risks and rewards of ownership. Finally, Clark sees the obvious successful operation of the managerial corporation as seriously undermining the operation of economic laws. This arises from the fact that the new corporate mode of organizing capital provides for the generation of market power in the hands of individuals, a phenomenon clearly assumed not to arise in classical theory. One and all, they see the managerial corporation as something that either doesn't or only strangely fits with the dominant tradition in economic theory.

The corporation in contemporary economic theory

Today the economic theory descended from Smith's work continues to hold a position of dominance (within the economics departments of colleges and universities, within government circles, and within the economics profession generally) that is seldom effectively challenged. Moreover, today the managerial corporation thrives as never before in history. The world we live in belies Smith's belief that managerially controlled business operations would "very seldom succeed without an exclusive privilege." Very, very few economic theorists and even fewer teachers of economic theory would be prepared to say, with Clark, that the success of the managerial corporation has come at the cost of "vitiating the action of economic laws." Nor, for that matter, does it appear that *anyone* would wish to claim, with Marshall, that the success of managerial-corporate business is at least in significant measure due to a "marvellous... spirit of honesty and uprightness in commercial matters." Rather, it appears that most economic theorists and surely the vast majority of business people and person-in-the-street defenders of market capitalism see the managerial corporation as a natural and normal component of a free market economy.

People in such applied economic disciplines as management science or operations research have, of course, generally treated the managerial firm as a richly complex and multifaceted creature, one to be distinguished sharply from the individual business person of classical theory. Nevertheless, the thousands upon thousands of students of economics who have been brought up on Paul Samuelson's field-dominating textbook, *Economics,* have been told that, "generally speaking, there will be no clash of goals between the management and stockholders. Both will be interested in maximizing the profits of the firm."[11] Even of those economics student who weren't introduced to the discipline through Samuelson's book, a considerable majority were taught precisely the same view of the corporation.

This view of business as carried on by undifferentiated profit-maximizing monoliths has been firmly entrenched among economists for some time. As early as 1933, Frank Knight was able to write:

A business unit, or enterprise, is made up of individuals (among whom the man who sells to or buys from it may himself be included) but is distinct from these individuals and constitutes a fictitious person, company, a firm or typically a corporation. Production is now commonly carried out by such units. They are, of course, controlled by natural persons, but these "officers" act for the organization and not as individuals.
It is a fact familiar to every reader of such a book as this [my emphasis] that in the modern world economic activity has typically been organized in this form: *business units* buy productive services and sell products; *individuals or families* [Knight's emphasis] sell productive services and buy products.[12]

Note that Knight does not, as did Smith, Marshall, and Clark, see any need to distinguish between managerially controlled and owner-controlled business units. All businesses are undifferentiated simply as maximizers of profits.

It is important to note here that economic theorists over the past half century or so have not simply failed to see a distinction that was terribly obvious to their predecessors. Knight himself acknowledges the difference between economic organizations (corporations) and traditional economic agents just a few pages before his above-noted collapse of that distinction: "the organization as a whole has no value in itself or purpose of its own...but exists solely to promote the interests of its members."[13] In fact, Nobel laureate James Buchanan argues that "Knight's intellectual honesty forced him to the very edges of a shift in vision, but he was never able to escape the maximizing vision which his own early work, in part, helped to impose on the whole discipline."[14]

Rather, as Buchanan's comment might suggest, what we have is, I think, a kind of adaptation of the existing economic theory to deal with a new kind of reality. It would appear that economic theory, after the time of Marshall and Clark, was faced with something like the following choice: (1) Economic theorists could continue to maintain, along the lines of Smith, that the corporate organization of business could not be very successful. Yet that alternative would make the economic theorist appear ludicrous. It would be a bit like saying that because the bumblebee is aerodynamically unsound it cannot *really* fly. Clearly bumblebees do fly, and clearly corporate organization of business is successful. (2) The economic theorist could follow out the obvious implication of Clark's ominous assessment. The theorist could say that those laws discovered by previous generations of economic theorists to govern the interrelations of individual agents simply failed to be operative in a world in which a significant number of economic agents were corporate in nature. This would, of course, have involved the abandonment of existing economic theory as a very useful tool for analyzing a broad range of economic phenomena. While I shall discuss in Chapter 6 the reasons why it would have been unreasonable for the economics profession collectively to have followed this alternative, it is surely not surprising, on intuitive grounds, that economic theorists failed to make such a concession. (3) Finally, economic theorists could find a way of modifying their theory in such a way that it could make sense of the existence and success of the managerial corporation. As we should expect, this is exactly what they did.

One can, I think, find no better explanation of the way in which the needed modification was made than that given by Andreas Papandreou in "Some Basic Problems in the Theory of the Firm":

The concept of the firm which is employed by economists in their teaching and research clearly reflects the frame of reference they have selected in dealing with the problems of their discipline. This frame of reference has been aptly called [by Talcott Parsons in *The Structure of Social Action*] the *action* frame of reference.... The norm postulated by the economist is that of rationality. The agent is conceived as engaging in action which maximizes a utility index (an ordinally structured preference system), given the constraints inherent in the situation.

The concept of the firm has been built to fit the specifications of this frame of reference. This has been accomplished through the postulation of the concept of the entrepreneur, which to all intents and purposes displaces that of the firm in analysis. This result is attained in a fairly simple manner. The firm emerges as soon as the owners of productive services sell them to an entrepreneur for a definite price. When this set of transactions is consummated the owners of the productive services cease to be of analytic concern to us. We then turn to the entrepreneur, who thus becomes our sole object of analysis as far as the behavior of the firm is concerned. This tour de force enables the economist to retain his schema of an acting individual agent, even in the case of the firm, which may legitimately be regarded as a "collective" of some sort.[15]

Received economic theory has been designed to talk about individual agents. The key, then, to giving it the ability to explain the operation of corporate businesses is to find a way of treating the corporation as an individual, not as a collective entity. Thus, contemporary economic theory talks about two different kinds of individuals: what we might call "natural individuals," and what Knight spoke of as "fictitious" individuals. Perhaps a better term to apply to this second type of individual would be "analytical individuals," as the corporation has come to be treated as an individual simply to meet the demands of economic analysis. Yet once economic theory has made the move to treat the corporation as an individual, the corporation takes on the appearance of a component of the free market economy so natural that it appears always to have been there. This makes it perfectly natural for economic theorists and historians of economic thought to see the present-day theory of the firm as substantially there in approximation in such early works as Lardner's *Railway Economy* (1850)[16] and Cournot's *Recherches sur les principes mathématiques de la théorie des richesses* (1838, English translation by N. T. Bacon entitled *Researches into the Mathematical Principles of the Theory of Wealth*, 1897)[17].

A number of things should be clear at this juncture. In the first place, the vast majority of economic theorists would agree, and I think more or less justifiedly so, that economics has been dominated by what Coats called "the theory of economic equilibrium via the market mechanism" and what Gordon referred to as "Smith's postulate of the maximizing individual in a relatively free market" since shortly after Smith's publication of *An Inquiry into the Nature and Causes of the Wealth of Nations* in 1776. Second, earlier economic theorists – like Smith himself, Marshall, Clark, and generally, I would say, those who wrote prior to about 1920 – saw the existence and success of the managerial corporation as more or less at odds with received economic theory. Finally, most contemporary economic theorists see the existence and success of the managerial corporation, as explained by the marginalist theory of the firm, as more or less implicit in received economic theory from a relatively early date, a date surely well before the time of Marshall and Clark.

It must be granted that contemporary economic theorists do not want to make the clearly absurd claim that there was a theory of the firm from the beginning. As I already noted, Boulding makes the claim that "there was no theory of the firm before Marshall." Moreover, Mark Blaug notes that Stanley Jevons, writing between 1862 and 1882 and clearly influenced by the above-cited works of Cournot and Lardner, never developed a theory of the firm, presumably because "he showed no awareness of the need for a theory of the firm."[18] Fritz Machlup claims that the theory of the firm "had only come into being in the 1930's."[19]

Yet while economic theorists do recognize that the theory of the firm is not nearly as old as economic theory generally, they do not appear to see it, in itself, as constituting a significant change in the shape of economic theory. Rather, what appears to be the case is that economic theorists have generally seen the development of the theory of the firm as simply a natural outgrowth of two of the "revolutions" noted at the beginning of this chapter. The explicit mathematical notion of *maximization* arises with the so-called Marginalist revolution. It is here, as well as in Marshall's development of the idealized "representative firm" (replaced in Pigou by the "equilibrium firm"), that economic theorists find the roots of the theory of the firm in Marshall's *Principles* and the early mathematical work of Cournot. Similarly, when Machlup dates the theory of the firm from the 1930s, he appears to be identifying it as a child of the discussions that arose from the so-called monopolistic competition revolution of that period.[20] In this direction also we can trace some roots of the theory of the firm back to Cournot's discussion of monopoly and duopoly.

What I wish to argue in the remainder of this chapter is that the development of the theory of the firm has constituted a crucially significant, verging on revolutionary, modification of the economic theory of economic equilibrium via the market mechanism. I want also to provide an account of why economic theorists have generally failed to recognize the independence and significance of this modification.

The hidden change

Let us start by noting what most economists understand to be the nature of theory. I take it that Milton Friedman's "The Methodology of Positive Economics" has become almost canonical on this point:

> The ultimate goal of a positive science is the development of a "theory." ...
> Such a theory is, in general, a complex intermixture of two elements. In part, it is a "language" designed to promote "systematic and organized methods of reasoning." In part it is a body of substantive hypotheses designed to abstract essential features of complex reality.
>
> Viewed as a language, theory has no substantive content; it is a set of tautologies. Its function is to serve as a filing system for organizing empirical material and facilitating our understanding of it; ...
>
> Viewed as a body of substantive hypotheses, theory is to be judged by its predictive power for the class of phenomena which it is intended to "explain."[21]

Friedman's division of a theory into a language and a body of substantive hypotheses is a perfectly acceptable starting point, but requires yet further breakdown if we are to be clear on the character of the modification in economic theory brought on by the development of the theory of the firm. What Friedman speaks of as "a language" must be further broken down into a purely formal language and its interpretation. The formal language is composed of a set of terms and predicates, a set of rules telling us what concatenations of these terms and predicates are to count as legitimate formulas for the theory. This much is purely formal. What we have thus far is basically a set of interrelated assertions, none of which has any concrete meaning.

Only with an interpretation of the formal language does the language of the theory come to have any meaning. The interpretation must start out with a domain, a specification of what different things can be the possible referents of the terms of the language – and what different kinds of things can serve as values for the theory's terms. Let us call this the theory's ontology. From that point, the interpretation will associate certain elements of the theory's domain with certain terms of the language, specify the intended meanings of the language's predicates, and thereby give concrete meaning to the language.

While I do not want to raise such philosophically contentious issues as whether there are such things as "natural kinds," it does seem to me quite clear that corporations, or at least managerial corporations, are a very different kind of creature from human individuals. There is a similarity in kind that holds between any other human individual and me that does not hold between, say, General Motors and me. Given that a theory's ontology tells us what things and kinds of things the theory is capable of talking about, it clearly follows that a fundamental change in the ontology of a theory constitutes a modification of major proportions in the theory. It is equally clear that an expansion from an ontology that includes only natural human individuals to one that includes natural human individuals and firms – the latter collection of objects including such diverse entities as the small-town insurance agency and the giant, multinational managerial corporation (or even more extremely, analytical "economic persons" and analytical "maximizing firms") – is a fundamental change in a theory's ontology. It is for this reason, then, as well as the fact that earlier and more recent economic theorists have spoken so differently about the managerial firm and its prospects, that I claim that the development of the theory of the firm has constituted a *major* change in the tradition of economic theorizing that has come down to us from Adam Smith.

My final concern is to explain why a change in economic theory that I see as so monumental should have remained predominantly hidden to economic theorists. The answer, I think, is relatively simple. The change in ontology brought about by the development of the theory of the firm was a change in an area of theory to which economic theorists have paid little explicit attention in their methodological discussions. Let me be clear that I do not mean to suggest that the development of the theory of the firm has been unproblematic to economic theorists. Quite to the contrary, at least from the first discussions of theories of monopolistic and imperfect competition onward, the theory of the firm has been at the center of a great deal of methodological controversy among economists. That controversy, however, has not really drawn much focus on issues of theoretical ontology.

If we look at Friedman's two components of theory, we see that the development of the theory of the firm has not brought about any real change in either of those parts. Looking first at that part of theory that is a "body of substantive hypotheses," the development of marginal analysis certainly created some modification in both the kinds and precision of substantive hypotheses that economic theory generated. Similarly, the discussions of the 1930s and later about imperfect and monopolistic competition generated some modification (precisely how much modification is a hotly debated point among economists) in the kinds of substantive hypotheses that economic theory might generate. In terms of substantive hypothesis, however, the development of the theory of the firm was, in fact, little more than a natural outgrowth of marginalism and the monopolistic competition discussions.

Similarly, if we look at the "language" component of theory, at least as it is characterized by Friedman, the development of the theory of the firm created no real change. Although the new term 'firm' crept into the economist's vocabulary, because 'firm' was, as already noted, effectively defined by Papandreou as a synonym for the old and familiar 'entrepreneur', its introduction constituted no real change in the language. Both the terms used and the ways in which economic theory put those terms together remained virtually unchanged with the development of the theory of the firm.

Before I bring this chapter to a close, there is one possible misunderstanding of my claim that I would like to dispell. I do not wish to claim that the earlier tradition in economics didn't leave room for talk about corporate entities. Clearly, the claims from Smith, Marshall, and Clark with which I started the chapter are precisely talk about such things. From the very beginning, we find Smith giving detailed discussion to trade corporations as well as to both "regulated" and "joint-stock companies." My claim has been rather that the earlier economic theorists did not see such corporate entities as a natural part of the ontology of economic theory, and certainly did not see them as *simple* agents. They saw these corporate entities, instead, as anomalous. By contrast, that is not the case with more recent economic theorists.

Unfortunately, the understanding of theory that most economic theorists bring to their work is such that it never uncovers the level at which the real change took place as the theory of the firm emerged. Economic theorists' discussions simply don't include ontology. For this reason it is not altogether surprising that even a fundamental change in ontology should fail to be recognized by economic theorists as a change at all.

Yet recognized or not, I hope that the arguments of this chapter succeed in showing that the expansion of the ontology of economic theory to include corporations, especially managerial corporations, did indeed constitute a very significant change in economic theory, perhaps even, as I am inclined to think, a change of revolutionary proportions.

CHAPTER 2

Four views of scientific change

In the last chapter I argued that the development of the modern theory of the firm constituted a major change in face of the economic tradition dating back to Adam Smith's *Wealth of Nations*. In the remainder of this book I shall be centrally concerned to do three things: (1) to set the change in economic theory that I identified in Chapter 1 into the broader context of the development of economic theory since the time of Smith; (2) to examine the major theoretical alternatives to the traditional marginalist theory of the firm and argue that taken simply as a theory of the firm, the marginalist theory suffers from significant weaknesses; and (3) to argue that the need for economists to adhere to a preferable theory of the firm also places pressure on economic science to develop a somewhat different comprehensive theory of the economy as a whole than that which has dominated the tradition since Smith.

The central argument that I shall develop depends crucially on my being able to apply the general kinds of analytical frameworks that have been developed for the analysis of scientific change to the analysis of change in economic theory. I do not regard this as a very controversial application. There is little to dispute in the claim that economic theory has, over the past two centuries, been developed to a high level of systematicity. Likewise, it is hardly controversial to claim that there has been a course of theoretical changes and modifications in economic theory over that same time. This history of systematic change in economic theory renders economic theory and its history amenable to the application of analytical tools developed by philosophers of science. At the same time, the history of economic theory since 1776 may itself serve as an interesting test case for theories of scientific change. Thus, it will also follow that my comments will have some significance as part of a general evaluation of the adequacy of current theories of scientific change.

Before briefly glancing in Chapter 3 at a few of the major developments in the history of economic theory since Adam Smith, it is important to examine some of these theoretical perspectives on the general phenomenon of scientific change, as well as to introduce some terminology that will help us come to a better analytical understanding of that history. To that end I want to identify four important and different views on the character of scientific change. In addition, I shall make a few brief comments on what I see as the central virtues and shortcomings of each of these perspectives for understanding the historical development of economic theory.

Writing in the mid-1970s, Mark Blaug offers these comments on the interpretation of the history of economic theory:

In the 1950s and 1960s economists learned their methodology from Popper. Not that many of them read Popper. Instead, they read Friedman and perhaps a few of them realized that Friedman is simply Popper-with-a-twist applied to economics. To be sure, Friedman was criticized, but the "Essay on the Methodology of Positive Economics" nevertheless survived to become the one article on methodology that virtually every economist has read at some stage in his career....

All that is almost ancient history, however. The new wave is not Popper's 'falsifiability' but Kuhn's 'paradigms'. Again it is unlikely that many economists have read *The Structure of Scientific Revolutions*, but that is neither here nor there.... Recently, however, some commentators have expressed misgivings about Kuhnian methodology applied to economics, throwing doubt in particular on the view that 'scientific revolutions' characterize the history of economic thought.... [The] notion that theories come to us, not one at a time, but linked together in a more or less integrated network of ideas, is however better conveyed by Lakatos's 'methodology of scientific research programmes'.[1]

While I think that Blaug, like a number of other economic commentators including Friedman himself, overestimates the similarities between Karl Popper's view on the evaluation of scientific theories and Friedman's methodology, with that caveat Blaug's reflection on recent history seems to be well taken. Moreover, Blaug is, I think, also correct in finding Imre Lakatos's view of scientific change preferable to that of Thomas Kuhn. Yet I want to argue that we can do even better in understanding the changes that have occurred in economic theory over the past couple of centuries by looking at those changes in terms of what Larry Laudan calls "the reticulated model of scientific rationality."[2] Thus, the four views of scientific change that I shall consider in this chapter are those of Popper, Kuhn, Lakatos, and Laudan. For both historical and systematic reasons I shall treat them in that order.

Popper and evolutionary epistemology

In an essay entitled "The Aim of Science," Popper gives us a brief characterization of what he takes science to be about:

I suggest that it is the aim of science to find *satisfactory explanations*, of whatever strikes us as being in need of explanation. By an *explanation* (or casual explanation) is meant a set of statements by which one describes the state of affairs to be explained (the *explicandum*) while the others, the explanatory statements, form the 'explanation' in the narrower sense of the word (the *explicans* of the *explicandum*).

We may take it, as a rule, that the *explicandum* is more or less well known to be true, or assumed to be so known. For there is little point in asking for an explanation of a state of affairs which may turn out to be entirely imaginary. ... The *explicans*, on the other hand, which is the object of our search, will as a rule not be known: it will have to be discovered. ...

The *explicans*, in order to be satisfactory (satisfactoriness may be a matter of degree), must fulfill a number of conditions. First, it must logically entail the *explicandum*. Secondly, the *explicans* ought to be true, although it will not, in general be known to be true; in any case, it must not be known to be false even after the most critical examination. If it is not known to be true (as will usually be the case) there must be *independent* evidence in its favor. In other words, it must be independently testable; and we shall regard it as more satisfactory the greater the severity of the independent tests it has survived.[3]

This much should serve to drive a very clear and large wedge between Popper's methodological position and that of Friedman. Popper claims that truth, or more accurately truthlikeness ("verisimilitude") is the goal of scientific explanation; and that an *explicans* should be true, or at least not known to be false, and should be supported by *"independent"* evidence. Friedman, however, claims that scientific theories are simply instruments for the generation of predictions, and that the truth of the *explicans* (assumptions) is irrelevant. While it has not always been recognized as such, a number of recent economic writers have come to recognize Friedman's methodological position as an instrumentalist position.[4] Far from being sympathetic to such a position, Popper's views on scientific method are clearly at odds with instrumentalism. Moreover, in an essay entitled "Three Views Concerning Human Knowledge," Popper gives a very explicit exposition and criticism of the instrumentalist view.[5] If there is any truth to Blaug's claim that "Friedman is simply Popper-with-a-twist applied to economics," it must be added that the twist is one of nearly 180 degrees.

While it is important to distinguish Friedman's methodological position from Popper's, that is nevertheless somewhat ancillary to my central concern here to explicate Popper's view of the course of scientific change. For Popper, "It is not the accumulation of observations which I have in mind when I speak of the growth of scientific knowledge, but the repeated overthrow of scientific theories and their replacement by better or more satisfactory ones."[6] Popper sees the course of scientific change as a progressive course, with theory replaced by theory, in the direction of greater and greater truthlikeness. It is a course, to use words from one of Popper's titles, of "conjectures and refutations." A theory is proposed (conjectured). Its implications are drawn out and given the most severe and critical tests that the scientific community can devise. Then, when it is discovered to have been in error at points (refuted), as scientific theories invariably are sooner or later, it is replaced by a new and presumably "truer" theory.

Three points in Popper's position are particularly relevant to my present purposes: (1) The *scientific theory* is the unit of scientific change in Popper's framework; (2) the aim of scientific theorizing is truthlike explanation; and (3) scientific change is almost always progressive.

1. In saying that scientific change is a process of theory being replaced by theory, Popper identifies the basic unit of scientific change as the theory. Unfortunately, taking the theory to be the basic unit of scientific change does not help us very much if we are concerned to understand the actual history of a given science. Looking at science as composed of theories may well be useful for a number of purposes, but it does not help us understand the process of scientific change for the simple reason that it provides no way for us to distinguish among different degrees of change or different kinds of change. The notion of a theory is simply too formal.

A theory is a consequence class of a set of statements (ideally a set of formal axioms). The problem is this: If we keep the same set of starting statements (or axioms), we must always continue to have the same theory. The notion of consequence class is a purely logical notion, not in any way contingent on human discovery or any other human process. Accordingly, any change in the theory involves some change in the set of starting statements. Popper provides no way of distinguishing more from less fundamental changes in theory. Given the formal mechanisms that Popper sets up, one might be inclined to say that he can meet this problem in terms of the amount of the content of one theory that is contained in another. Yet Popper's view of the progressive character of scientific theorizing commits him to the claim that "a theory which has been well corroborated can only be superseded by one of a higher level of universality; that is, by a theory which is better testable and which, in addition, *contains* [Popper's emphasis] the old, well corroborated theory – or at least a good approximation of it."[7] Partial or degrees of containment will not do, according to Popper.

In looking at the history of a science, we may oftentimes want to identify a broad tradition of theorizing, one that includes a number of revisions of some basic insight. I take it that this is clearly the case in economics, where most theorizing done over the past two centuries involves revision and further revision of the basic insights of Smith. Yet Popper's analytical framework tells us only that a theory is a theory is a theory. It provides no basis on which we might be able to say that marginalist economic theory is related to classical Smithian economic theory in a way in which neither of them is related to mercantilism. Or if the example is judged to be inapt on the ground that mercantilism does not actually constitute a theory, we would still like to say that marginalist economics is related to classical economics in a way in which Newton's physics is not related to Aristotelian physics. It seems important, then, to find a way of explaining scientific change that is somewhat richer than simply seeing theory as replacing theory.

2. While Popper does acknowledge that "different scientists have different aims, and science itself (whatever that may mean) has no aims,"[8] he still wants to claim that the aim of science (whatever that may mean in light of the above disclaimer) is to produce truthlike theories. Clearly Popper's acknowledgment that different scientists have different aims should tell us that he does not intend his claim about the aim of science to be a simple descriptive claim about what scientists in fact do. Yet Popper claims in that same text that scientific activity is a rational activity and that rational activity must have some aim. (Of course, it does not follow that science is a single rational activity, or that even if it is a single rational activity it must have a single aim.)

It appears that Popper's claims about the aim of science are pre-scriptive claims; that science ought to aim at truthlike theories, or that science, when it is really being *scientific*, aims at truthlike theories. Yet there is a touch of arrogance in proclaiming what science ought to aim at, apart from what scientists have actually aimed at in the course of the history of science. Moreover, it is not at all clear that all of those scientific episodes that we have come over the years to regard as science at its best have invariably had the production of truthlike theories as their aims. At the very least, Popper's claims on this point should prove unpalatable to most contemporary economic theorists with their Friedmanian upbringing.

Yet even beyond this, it is important to note that a single episode of scientific investigation may involve a number of coexisting aims. Perhaps there is a hierarchy. It may even be that the production of truthlike theories is usually at the top of that hierarchy. Yet it is still valuable as we attempt to examine the history of a science to pay heed to whatever other operative aims there may be. Prior to the time of Kepler, for example, it was clearly a very important aim of astronomers to explain in terms of circular motion. This aim surely did not follow from the aim to produce truthlike theories. Equally, it did not, on its face at least, conflict with that aim. Similarly economists, at least since the time of Jevons, have taken it as a fairly central aim of their theorizing to explicate economic relationships in mathematical terms. I take it, again, that such an aim is neither a part of nor in conflict with truthlikeness. In sum, we should, I think, like to have a bit more flexibility in our discussion of scientific aims than is allowed by Popper's framework.

3. Finally, Popper's claim that the course of science must always be progressive in the sense of building upon the truth content of older theories seems to be troublesome on a number of counts. First, it does not appear to be true of the history of science, even in its best moments. Nor should we expect it to be. Popper's own emphasis on problems as the motivating force behind scientific theorizing should probably lead us to expect that as the problematic interests of a scientific community change over time, a theory of high explanatory value in the problem area of concern might legitimately come to succeed a theory whose explanatory value in that area is not as great, but whose explanatory value in some problem area that is no longer of crucial interest to the investigating community is somewhat greater than that of the succeeding theory. Second, as I already noted, Popper's progressivity claims have exacerbated the problem of distinguishing among different kinds and degrees of scientific change. All in all, while we probably do want to claim that the course of scientific investigation has some kind of long-term progressivity to it, we surely do not, as we shall see shortly in considering Lakatos, want to make the kind of rigid and invariant progressivity claim for scientific change that we find in Popper.

On all three of these counts, then, Popper's philosophy of science proves to have significant shortcomings as a vehicle for helping us come to an understanding of the history of science. Popper's position has its very clear merits, especially in making clear the role that criticism plays within the scientific community. As Bruce Caldwell points out in reviewing the influence of Popper on methodological discussions in economics, "Popper, unlike many philosophers, deals with issues that go to the heart of the problems that actually trouble practicing scientists (economists among them)."[9] Yet Popper's position also has a clear weakness in its tendency to be ahistorical.

Kuhn and self-contained paradigms

If Popper can legitimately be criticized for paying inadequate attention to science as a historical enterprise, the same can surely not be said of Thomas Kuhn. The first chapter of Kuhn's most important work, *The Structure of Scientific Revolutions,* is entitled "Introduction: A Role for History." As titles such as *The Structure of Scientific Revolutions, The Copernican Revolution,* and *The Essential Tension* clearly indicate, Kuhn's central concern is with large-scale change in the history of science. The question is not whether he pays adequate attention to the history of science, but rather whether he interprets it correctly and whether the analytical categories that he develops for the interpretation of scientific history are adequate.

Kuhn sees science as operating in alternation between two different kinds of episodes, "normal science" and "scientific revolutions." What distinguishes the two is that in a period of normal science, the scientific community operates with a shared "paradigm," while a revolutionary period is one that is host to competing paradigms. Two of Kuhn's terms have gained immense popularity in discussions of the history and philosophy of science, 'paradigm' and 'revolution'. The term 'revolution' is, of course, a word that conjures up a host of exciting images. This probably accounts for a part of its popularity. Yet it also has come to perform the very useful task of helping us to distinguish major changes in the development of a science from those kinds of minor adjustments and fine tunings that are still *changes in* theory. The revolutionary terminology is still troublesome, however, since changes in theory are not neatly separable into major and minor. Thus, we see commentators disagreeing over whether a particular change is or is not revolutionary. At the beginning of Chapter 1, I noted the Coats and Gordon claim that economics has never witnessed a "major revolution." Yet at the same time, economists and economic historians talk of the "marginalist revolution," the "Keynesian revolution," and others. Some would say that these are minor revolutions. Others would simply call them revolutions. Whatever one might say about these changes, neither of them is a change in theory of the magnitude of the Copernican revolution. Even so, Kuhn's schema leaves no room for distinguishing major from minor revolutions. For Kuhn, either we have a revolution or we have normal science.

What distinguishes between those two periods, again, is the absence or presence of a dominating paradigm, the notion which is the key to Kuhn's entire framework. The paradigm terminology has, if anything, become even more popular than the revolutionary terminology in the years that have elapsed since the publication of *The Structure of Scientific Revolutions*. The notion of paradigm has been useful in facilitating the identification of broad traditions of theorizing. It has also, I suspect, tended to be popular in part because its high level of ambiguity allows it to mean so many different things to so many different people.[10]

This ambiguity makes it difficult to say what a paradigm is within Kuhn's framework. Nevertheless, certain basic points about paradigms have emerged through the discussions of his work over the years. Two of these points are particularly important for my present purposes. In the first place, a paradigm, Kuhn's basic unit of scientific change, is much broader in its scope than just a theory. It includes a whole view of the scientific enterprise. As Kuhn says:

In learning a paradigm the scientist acquires theory, methods, and standards together, usually in an inextricable mixture. Therefore, when paradigms change, there are usually significant shifts in the criteria determining the legitimacy both of problems and of proposed solutions.[11]

By contrast with Popper – who sees the basic standards or aims of science, as well as its method, remaining constant while theories change – Kuhn sees theory, method, and aims all bound together in a paradigm. Because of the fact that the paradigm includes its own aims and standards of justification, it will tend to be self-justifying. This leads to the second important point, namely that scientific change is not the result of rational inquirers reaching a common assessment of rival scientific structures based upon commonly agreed-upon and objective standards. Rather, scientific change is a result, primarily, of persuasion (perhaps conversion would be better), intellectual fashion, and political power (opponents of the favored paradigm don't get tenured). Both points will be discussed in more detail it what follows.

1. In taking the paradigm to be the basic unit of scientific change, Kuhn offers us a promising starting point. The notion of paradigm, as I previously noted, appears to provide for the possibility of identifying a large, broad-ranging tradition of research in a way that the notion of theory clearly cannot. Within economics there has been a largely continuous tradition since Smith that is worthy of identification as a continuous tradition. Unfortunately, the promise of the paradigm soon turns sour. The key problem is that Kuhn sees the paradigm as such an indivisible whole. The fact that he never explicates the relationship between the paradigm and its constituent parts, theories, methods, aims, and so on makes it difficult, if not impossible, to ac-

count for modest change within a paradigm.[12] If the paradigm is the sole unit of scientific change, then it would seem that all scientific change is revolutionary. If this is the case, then the development of marginal analysis in economics is indeed a revolution, but unfortunately it would become revolutionary only at the cost of our being unable to speak of a continuous paradigm operative since Smith.

As Kuhn talks of a paradigm's including theory, methods, and aims, there is an initial promise of being able to distinguish these various elements in the scientific enterprise. In acknowledging that methods, and even aims, are not invariant, he seems to be giving us a clear advance beyond Popper. When he tells us that the theories, methods, and aims or standards come bound together in an "inextricable mixture," however, the advantage disappears. Suddenly it seems that we cannot identify any change in theory, methods, or aims that is not a change in the entire paradigm.

Surely we want to grant that aims, methods, and theories all are mutually interrelated, that one can exercise a significant influence on the others. To acknowledge this much, however, should not preclude the ability to recognize continuities amid changes. Kuhn's holistic conception of paradigm leaves us, in the end, with much the same problem that we found with Popper's "theories." Scientific change seems to become an all-or-nothing phenomenon. We cannot separate out the elements of change in a piecemeal fashion. Yet we clearly need to be able to do just that if we are to be able to distinguish different kinds and levels of scientific change.

It had seemed, at the outset, that the whole appeal of Kuhn's notion of paradigm was that it should give us the ability to examine small and even intermediate-sized changes within an overarching continuity of some sort. If, however, the notion of paradigm, as Kuhn develops it, cannot do that, one is left wondering what useful purpose it does serve. Perhaps Mark Blaug's suggestion that "the term 'paradigm' ought to be banished from economic literature [as well as the literature of other sciences], unless surrounded by inverted commas,"[13] is not such a bad idea.

2. My other point concerns Kuhn's view of scientific change as a predominantly nonrational process, at least as compared with our usual understanding of rational processes:

Paradigm debates are not really about relative problem-solving ability, though for good reasons they are generally couched in those terms. Instead, the issue is which paradigm should in the future guide research on problems many of which neither competitor can yet claim to resolve completely.... A decision of that kind can only be made on faith.[14]

Kuhn can start out with the nearly universally accepted claim that observation is theory-laden, influenced by the conceptual categories and anticipations set out by the theory that the investigator has in mind going into the context of observation. Thus, in a sense, advocates of rival theories "see things differently." Kuhn, however, makes the rather large move from that to the claim that observation can provide no help in adjudicating among rival paradigms.

Kuhn can also start with the claim that the meanings of theoretical terms are shaped by the semantic web of the theory. Yet he moves from that obvious truth to the claim that advocates of rival paradigms cannot communicate with each other because their theoretical languages are incommensurable. Finally, Kuhn can start with the claim that standards of evaluation are not everywhere agreed upon and invariant. Yet he moves from that to the claim that rival paradigms have so incorporated into themselves their own standards of evaluation that advocates of rival paradigms can never find any common standards on which to base interparadigm evaluations.

Again, all of this makes for serious difficulties in the attempt to understand the course of development in a given science. Kuhn's "incommensurability thesis" makes it nearly impossible to trace out continuities within scientific change. If the term 'economic agent' means some kind of flesh-and-blood individual (as it surely appears to, to Adam Smith) and yet also means some kind of analytical individual (perhaps a household or firm, as it appears to, to Milton Friedman), then Kuhn will have the two economists speaking what are effectively different languages. What we had hoped to be able to make sense of as a single paradigm of a "maximizing individual in a relatively free market" ceases to be a single paradigm. Rather, it very much appears that economic theory since the time of Smith has been characterized by ongoing revolution. Ricardo's development of the labor theory of value was revolutionary. The development of marginal analysis was revolutionary. Indeed, we would not be far off the track in claiming that every genuinely great economic theorist produced his or her own revolution, modifying in some way the views that had been handed down, and hence produced a unique paradigm incommensurable with the views of both previous and subsequent great economic theorists.

This, of course, might simply be taken as good evidence for the claim that economics had not in fact ever had a dominating paradigm, and that it is therefore not really a science at all, given Kuhn's claim that the possession of a paradigm is an absolutely requisite condition for a discipline's legitimate claim of scientific status. Yet I think that such a conclusion would be premature. It would be premature precisely because virtually the same thing could be said of physics, biology, or any of the disciplines that provide us with our "paradigm" cases of science. One would like, I take it, to make sense of both the originality and significance of Newton's work in physics, while at the same time being able to note the ways in which he built on the more than 200 years of work done by such predecessors as Copernicus, Kepler, and Galileo. Rather, I think the conclusion we ought to draw from all of this is that Kuhn's holistic and self-enclosed notion of paradigm leaves us with a situation in which all scientific change is revolutionary change, and that such a result renders Kuhn's schema seriously inadequate as a vehicle for understanding scientific change.

Lakatos and the "methodology of scientific research programmes"

As I said at the outset of this chapter, it seems to me that Blaug is clearly correct when he says that Imre Lakatos's "methodology of scientific research programmes" does a better job of accounting for the fact "that theories come to us, not one at a time, but linked together in a more or less integrated network." If Popper pays inadequate attention to the integration of the network, Kuhn fails to note at all that the network may be *more or less* integrated. For Kuhn the network is always totally integrated.

Lakatos, unlike Popper and Kuhn, identifies several different levels at which scientific change may occur. The most comprehensive category in Lakatos's analysis is the "scientific research programme." The notion of a research program is intended to do the same kind of work as Kuhn's paradigm was supposed to, that is, to designate a broad-ranging collection of scientific work that somehow manages to comprise a continuous tradition. Thus, while I have argued that "the theory of economic equilibrium via the market mechanism" could not, because of the kinds of changes that have occurred in that theory since the time of Smith, constitute a Kuhnian paradigm, it clearly could constitute a Lakatosian research program. While the paradigm's character as an "inextricable mixture" does not seem to allow for small changes within a given paradigm, at least beyond drawing new implications and making new applications, the various parts of a research program are not so inextricably intertwined. Some of those parts are indispensable to the program. Others, however, are quite dispensable.

A research program "consists of methodological rules: some tell us what paths of research to avoid (*negative heuristic*), and others what paths to pursue (*positive heuristic*)."[15] The negative heuristic identifies those theories (or perhaps parts of theories), methods, aims, and the like that are essential to the program. A researcher who abandoned a part of the program's "hard core," as Lakatos colorfully calls this essential component of the program, would no longer find him- or herself working within the same research program. The hard core, in other words, serves to identify the research program and to distinguish it from other, perhaps rival, research programs. The negative heuristic identifies the hard core by setting out methodological rules that tell the researcher that a particular part of the program is not subject to refutation. Given the "Duhem–Quine thesis" that any theory or hypothesis can be saved from refutation simply by rejecting not the theory or hypothesis, but one or more of the background assumptions that were operative in the derivation of the denial of the theory or hypothesis, what the negative heuristic does is to tell the investigator which propositions, among the many possible candidates for refutation in the course of research, are to be regarded as "protected" from refutation.

By contrast with the hard core, those elements within the program that can be suitably modified in order to explain that which the scientist wants to explain, while at the same time saving the hard core of the program, are called the "protective belt." This process of modifying that part of the program which is subject to modification is governed by the positive heuristic, which "consists of a partially articulated set of suggestions or hints on how to change, develop the 'refutable variants' of the research-programme, how to modify, sophisticate, the 'refutable' protective belt."[16] Scientific change, then, can occur at either of two levels for Lakatos, at the grand level, with one scientific research program superseding another, or it may occur within the protective belt of a single research program.

This distinction between the hard core and protective belt of a research program is a clear advance beyond the categories that Popper and Kuhn give us for examining scientific change. Moreover, the notion of an irrefutable hard core surely helps to explain the way in which the course of change actually develops in science.

My sole complaint with Lakatos's views on the units of scientific change is that they need to go further in the direction of dissecting these units. Much as I criticized Kuhn for ignoring the relationship between a paradigm and its constituent parts – the theories, methods, aims, and other components – in like manner Lakatos has very little to say about the relationship between the constituent parts of either the hard core or the protective belt. It seems that the constitution of a research program's hard core may very well vary or at least that it might involve nothing other than a set of methods, the entire theoretical content belonging to the protective belt. Perhaps a hard core may consist of nothing more than a part of a theory, or perhaps even just a single crucial proposition around which whole theories may be constructed. In short, it is not at all clear to me that we can identify a set of necessary constituent parts of a program's hard core.

However, there do seem to be certain components that must be a part of the protective belt, and I take it that a hard core must include at least one, most likely more than one, thing from this constellation. Clearly a positive heuristic must include at least some of the subsidiary aims of the program – the modifiable part of the program's conception of legitimate scientific methods and a succession of theories that are developed within the program. While Lakatos has very little to say about the precise interrelations among these various components within the protective belt, within the hard core, or within the research program as a whole, it seems to me that those interrelations are important if we are to come to a clear understanding of the course of scientific change.

A second and final aspect of Lakatos's philosophy of science that is significant for our present purposes is the framework for the evaluation of scientific change that he develops. Lakatos sees the developments that occur within a research program as a series of modifications made in response to the anomalies and other problems that arise in the life of the program. The line of development within a research program may be either "progressive" or "degenerating," and both of these on either a theoretical or an empirical level. Here again, the general idea of what Lakatos is trying to accomplish is very helpful. Some research traditions seem to progress, to produce new and exciting ideas, to predict phenomena that we could not have predicted earlier, or to tie together large ranges of previously unrelated data. Other research traditions seem to stagnate into a kind of sterile scholasticism concerned with little more than self-perpetuation and the development of sophisticated tools that seem to produce very little of interest to anyone outside of the program itself. Of course, these judgments of progression and degeneration within research programs must always be somewhat tentative, at least when those judgments are made during a period in which the program is still living. Yet these tentative judgments are still valuable as both scientists and interested outsiders attempt to reach decisions about which programs are worth spending their time and money on.

Lakatos characterizes these notions of progression and degeneration as follows:

Let us take a series of theories, T_1, T_2, T_3, . . . where each subsequent theory results from adding auxiliary clauses to (or from semantical reinterpretations of) the previous theory in order to accommodate some anomaly, each theory having at least as much content as the unrefuted content of its predecessor. Let us say that such a series of theories is *theoretically progressive* (or *'constitutes a theoretically progressive problemshift'*) if each new theory has some excess empirical content over its predecessor. . . . Let us say that a theoretically progressive series of theories is also *empirically progressive* (or *'constitutes an empirically progressive problemshift'*) if some of this excess empirical content is also corroborated. . . . Finally, let us call a problemshift *progressive* if it is both theoretically and empirically progressive, and *degenerating* if it is not.[17]

The problem here is that Lakatos's conditions for scientific progress are too rigid. In order for a move from one theory to another to be an instance of progress, the new theory has to explain everything that the old theory explained and more. There clearly are cases in history, such as the Priestly–Dalton–Lavoisier controversy in chemistry – and if there were not such cases we could surely construct them – in which there is a change in theory for which the succeeding theory can explain a good many things that the older theory cannot, but for which there are a few things (judged by the scientific community to be relatively unimportant) that the older theory, but not its successor, could explain. It certainly seems inappropriate to judge such shifts as degenerating. If we attend to Popper's very crucial insight that scientific work begins with the recognition of a problem situation, it seems unduly restrictive to require each new theory, if we are to call the change a progressive one, to address all the problem situations of earlier days.

Again, I want to emphasize that Lakatos's framework for understanding scientific change is clearly an advance over the views of either Popper or Kuhn. His distinction between the hard core and the protective belt elements of a research program is a step in the direction of being able to make the distinctions we would like to make as to the various levels of fundamental change. Moreover, his distinction between progressive and degenerating problem shifts within research traditions is a useful tool to begin the evaluation of scientific change.

Yet on neither of these counts does Lakatos give us all that he might. As I suggested, it would be very helpful to have a schema that paid greater attention to the constituent parts of both the hard core and the protective belt of the research program, one that would enable us to see with more clarity the kind of changes that occur within a scientific tradition. Moreover, his characterization of progression and degeneration is simply too rigid. It would seem to characterize most actual instances of scientific change as degenerative. This surely seems undesirable. An adequate characterization of scientific progress (and I am firmly committed to the position that we want to be able to characterize a notion of progress in science) should not require each new theory to be able to do all the good things that its predecessors were able to do before we call it a case of genuine progress.

Laudan and the reticulated model of scientific justification

Both the kind of additional dissection of the units of scientific change and the more modest view of the requirements for scientific progress for which I have argued are found in the works of Larry Laudan. Also, there is in his schema a category in which to include the large historical scientific tradition, Lakatos's scientific research program, and what seems to be intended by Kuhn's paradigm. Yet Laudan's view of the research tradition is rather more flexible than that of Lakatos. This also is positive.

Laudan's "reticulated model of scientific justification" involves the recognition of three kinds of elements in the structure of justification – theories, methods, and aims. In most previous work in the philosophy of science, Laudan maintains, these three elements were seen as arranged in a hierarchy, with scientific aims at the top dictating scientific methods, which fell in the middle of the hierarchy and in turn dictated scientific theories, which formed the lowest level of the hierarchy. Justification of an element at any level of the hierarchy was accomplished by appealing to elements at the next higher level. This, of course, would naturally lead to a problem of justification at the highest level.[18]

Popper, as I noted early in this chapter, seems to think that there is *an* aim (not aims) of science, and that that aim, fully explicated, drives the whole course of scientific change. Joining Kuhn and Lakatos against Popper on this point, Laudan sees science as involving a number of possible aims, and in such a manner that the aims of a scientific community may change from time to time. Yet unlike Kuhn, Laudan does not see scientific aims as being so inextricably bound up with a particular set of methods and theories, thereby forming a wholly self-contained paradigm, that one element in the group cannot change without the entire constellation or paradigm changing. Moreover, since Laudan does not see the three kinds of elements as comprising a hierarchical structure – with aims at the top of the hierarchy and, hence, nothing above aims in terms of which the aims themselves can be justified – he does not accept the position, which appears implicit in the work of Kuhn, Popper, and most other philosophers of science, that aims are simply given or stipulated, maybe subject to disagreement, but never subject to rational assessment.

Instead, Laudan sees these three levels of scientific commitment as comprising a justificatory network. Schematically, we can view the three elements as the three corners of a triangle, with the sides of the triangles symbolizing the justificatory relationships that hold among the three elements.[19] Of course, Laudan recognizes the traditional justificatory relationships. The aims of science justify scientific methods, and the methods, in turn, justify scientific theories. Yet Laudan also recognizes other kinds of relationships involved in the justificatory network. Scientific aims, for example, must exist in a kind of harmonious relationship with the dominant scientific theories of the day. Laudan provides a helpful example at this point. At the time of Newton, scientists and natural philosophers generally held as an aim of scientific work the production of conceptually clear explanation (explanation in terms of what Descartes called "clear and distinct ideas"). The notion of action at a distance was singled out as a paradigmatically obscure idea. Yet of course, Newton's gravity was precisely a species of action at a distance. In this historical instance, the fact that a particular and important aim of scientific theorizing stood in conflict with a particular theory did not lead to the abandonment of the theory. Rather, it led to the revision of the aim.[20] Moreover, I take it that, at least in retrospect, most of us would agree that it was both reasonable and progressive in this instance for the aim to give way rather than the theory.

Another element in the justificatory network is that connecting methods and theories. While methods clearly serve to justify theories, theories also exercise a constraining role with respect to methods. Again, Laudan illustrates from the influence of the theory of gravity. At and even well after the time of Newton, the dominant conception of scientific method was inductivist. The "method of hypothesis," or the hypotheticodeductive method, was seen as fuzzy headed and a flight to metaphysics. Scientists were to limit themselves to what is given in experience, rather than positing unobserved theoretical forces or entities. At least one of the nails in the coffin of inductivist method involved George Lesage pointing out, well after the acceptance of Newton's work, that in accepting Newton's theory, scientists had in fact abandoned the methodological position of inductivism.[21]

The final relationship within the network of scientific justification is that between methods and aims. Of course, the aims of science serve to justify its methods. Yet equally, Laudan claims, methods must be able to exhibit the realizability of scientific aims. If a given set of methods cannot accomplish a given set of aims, that does not automatically mean that the methods need revision. Perhaps it is the aims that are problematic or simply unrealizable. The crucial point to note is that the conflict can be resolved by revision at either end of the line.

Thus, Laudan claims not only that the aims of science are variable and subject to discussion and negotiation, but that they can be assessed from either of two angles. One may argue, starting from the scientific methods available to the investigator, that a given aim or set of aims is simply utopian or unrealizable. One may also argue, starting from well-accepted theory, that a given aim is at variance with the implied collective theoretical judgments of the scientific community.[22]

Laudan's rejection of unrealizable goals should, I think, at least raise a note of reservation. In other areas we do not automatically reject a goal because it is unrealizable. Many of us still regard virtue in our private lives and justice in the life of society as fundamentally important goals. Yet clearly, neither of those goals is completely realizable. There is an interesting kind of tension here. In the realm of politics as well as that of science, there is a certain kind of utopianism that is, I think, legitimately criticizable. Various kinds of utopian political schemes have been subject to criticism over the centuries because they are not realizable in a world populated by human beings. Moreover, few of us are inclined to reject any political program simply on the grounds that it contains minor elements of injustice. Yet many of us continue to hold justice as a goal. We tend to assess political programs more or less on the basis of whether, within the limits of the realizable, they tend to increase or diminish justice. The fact that perfect justice is not realizable seems not to diminish the role that justice can play as an aim of society. If there is any parallel between science and society, then we need to exercise more caution here than Laudan does.

Laudan identifies three kinds of utopianism. "Demonstrable utopianism" is characteristic of goals that "cannot possibly be achieved, given our understanding of logic or the laws of nature."[23] "Semantic utopianism" is characteristic of goals that cannot be characterized "in a clear and cogent way."[24] "Epistemic utopianism" is characteristic of goals such that their "advocates cannot specify (and seem to be working with no implicit form of) a criterion for determining when the value is present or satisfied and when it is not."[25] I suspect that the political aim of justice, in those instances in which we find it objectionably utopian, is demonstrably utopian, while that aim, in the sense in which most of us are likely to regard it as the fundamental aim of society, is more or less semantically utopian. The latter, it should be noted, would seem to be a matter of degree, since clarity and cogency are themselves matters of degree, rather than all-or-nothing concepts. The scientific aim of truth or truthlikeness, in contrast, seems to be epistemically utopian. If my political analogy is not inappropriate, not all of these kinds of utopianism are equally objectionable.

This point aside, however, Laudan does provide us with a schema for understanding scientific change that is far richer than those offered by either Popper or Kuhn, and at least preferable in terms of its dissection of the units of change to the schema given by Lakatos. As I mentioned above, one still needs to have some category for the large, ongoing scientific tradition, a category comparable to Lakatos's scientific research program. Laudan does not neglect such a category. Yet his research tradition is a rather more flexible creature than Lakatos's scientific research program. Laudan identifies the following traits of a research tradition:

1. Every research tradition has a number of specific theories which exemplify and partially constitute it; some of these theories will be contemporaneous, others will be temporal successors of earlier ones;
2. Every research tradition exhibits certain *metaphysical* and *methodological* commitments which, as an ensemble, individuate the research tradition and distinguish it from others;
3. Each research tradition (unlike a specific theory) goes through a number of different, detailed (and often mutually contradictory) formulations and generally has a long history extending through a significant period of time. (By contrast, theories are frequently short-lived.)[26]

Unlike Lakatos's research programs, which are individuated by their essential hard cores, Laudan's research traditions are individuated by a more flexible "ensemble" of metaphysical and methodological commitments. It does not appear that this ensemble must contain one or more elements that remain a part of the ensemble for its entire existence any more than an orchestra must have one or more of the same members in order to be the same orchestra.

I am inclined to think that it is a wise move to reject the essentialism involved in Lakatos's notion of a hard core. It is not at all clear that there needs to be some class of things that are essential for all stages of a scientific research tradition to possess in order still to belong to that tradition. It seems more plausible that a scientific tradition may be better characterized in terms of the rope analogy with which

Wittgenstein spoke of language. There need not be one continuous thread running through the whole tradition, but rather the tradition may be made up of shorter strands that come and go, but that are intertwined in such a way to make a recognizable continuous whole. This weakness in Lakatos's position, of course, has been clearly recognized by Axel Leijonhufvud.[27] It provides as well the inspiration for E. Roy Weintraub's idea of a "hardening of the hard core," in his attempt to provide a Lakatosian appraisal of general equilibrium analysis.[28] Laudan's schema still allows us to speak of research traditions, but it does not at least appear to commit us, as does Lakatos's schema, to the view that each tradition has an essence. As we shall see in Chapter 4, this denial of essentialism will count heavily in favor of a Laudan-style analysis of the history of economics. It will enable us far better to identify a research tradition going back to the work of Adam Smith than would either Lakatos's notion of a scientific research program or Kuhn's notion of a paradigm.

Finally, Laudan also gives us the more flexible view of progress that seems necessary if we are to recognize progress in the actual history of science:

Knowledge of the relative weight or the relative number of problems can allow us to specify those circumstances under which the growth of knowledge can be progressive even when we lose the capacity to solve certain problems.[29]

There is clearly a view of progress. Assessment of progress, however, does not depend on a strictly cumulative ability to solve more and more problems (all the while never losing the ability to solve old ones). It does not even depend on the purely numerically assessable ability to solve a greater number of problems than earlier theories. Rather, it involves a reflective assessment of both the weight and number of problems that successive theoretical formulations within a common research tradition are able to solve. This view of progress doesn't promise an algorithm by means of which to determine whether progress has occurred. It does, however, present a view according to which it is possible for there to be progress and for us to be able to recognize actual instances of progress in the history of science. It also *leaves open* the possibility of some progress in economic theory since the time of Smith. This is surely what we would like it to be able to do.

I would conclude then by claiming that in Larry Laudan's views on scientific change, we find a position that is clearly preferable to the views of Popper, Kuhn, and Lakatos, the views of scientific change that have most commonly been used in examining the historical development of economic theory. Therefore, in the remainder of this book it will be Laudan's schema in terms of which I will look at the development of economic theory and what I see as the unique theoretical problems connected with the theory of the firm and the rise of the modern managerial corporation.

CHAPTER 3

A glance at the history of economic theory

When one looks at what economists and historians of economics have had to say about the history of economics it becomes increasingly clear why the Kuhnian language of paradigm and revolution is ill suited to shed much light on the history of economics. It is not clear, speaking in that terminology, whether economics has never had a revolution or whether it has been in a constant state of revolutionary warfare. As I noted at the outset of Chapter 1, A. W. Coats and Donald F. Gordon have claimed that there has never been a significant revolution in economics. By contrast, just a very cursory review of literature written by authors who like to use the revolutionary terminology reveals at least seven revolutions and a major counterrevolution. Among those economic theorists who are sometimes called the fathers or mothers of revolutions are the following: Adam Smith, David Ricardo (sometimes along with James Mill), John Stuart Mill, Stanley Jevons (usually along with Leon Walras and Karl Menger as joint fathers of the "marginal" or "marginalist revolution"), Alfred Marshall, John Maynard Keynes, and Edward Chamberlin and Joan Robinson (joint parents of the "monopolistic competition" or "imperfect competition revolution").[1] At the same time, A. C. Pigou, Frank Knight, and (most recently) Milton Friedman are frequently seen as leaders of a significant counterrevolution. There is, I think, more than a touch of irony in the fact that this list of "revolutionaries" does not include Karl Marx. It also leaves out Thorstein Veblen, John Commons, and Wesley Mitchell. If talk of revolutions were appropriate in the history of science, these latter three would surely have to be ranked as leaders in a revolution, even if that revolution has not proven successful in giving rise to a dominating paradigm.

As this should make clear, talk of revolutions and paradigms is not very helpful. Thus, I will abandon such language in the remainder of this chapter. Instead, I shall look at change in economic theorizing in a piecemeal manner as suggested by Laudan's position as explained in the last chapter. Accordingly, I shall attend not only to changes in *theory* and *method*, both of which have been examined at great length in any of a number of works on the history of economics, but I shall also attend to changes in the *aims* that different economic theorists have set for their work and their discipline. In order to break up the more than 200 years of tradition since Smith into reasonably manageable units, I shall divide that tradition in what I take to be a fairly customary manner. I shall first look at roughly the first century of modern economic theorizing, that phase of development often labeled "classical political economy." The second phase of my discussion will focus on the developments from the rise of marginal analysis in the 1870s through the mid-1930s developments in the theory of imperfect competition. The third phase will focus on the view of Keynes, and the fourth on the anti-Keynesian reaction centering around the "Chicago school."

I shall make no significant mention in this chapter of Marx or of the American institutionalist tradition. While I shall note those traditions in passing in Chapter 6 in my assessment of the reasons for the dominance of the mainstream tradition, I am only concerned in this chapter with the development of the presently dominant research tradition in economics. Marxism and institutionalism both fall outside that development of tradition. I should hasten to add that my comments in this chapter will tend to focus on those aspects of the development of economic theory that relate to the eventual emergence of a theory of the firm.

Classical political economy

I shall limit my discussion of the classical English tradition of political economy to three thinkers, each of whom made significant contributions to that tradition: Adam Smith, David Ricardo, and John Stuart Mill.

Adam Smith. Like the Bible and the works of Shakespeare, the works of Adam Smith seem to be more frequently quoted than read. Perhaps because of its position as the first book to give something like a theoretical foundation for market capitalism, Smith's *Wealth of Nations* has come to take on something of the aura of a holy book for many of today's ideological partisans of the capitalist system. It has, for example, been featured alongside the Bible on a quasi-political advertisement aired from Dallas, Texas, as a book with which every "good Christian" and "good American" (the two being, in the eyes of the advertiser, more or less synonymous) should be familiar.

As everyone knows, Smith's *Wealth of Nations* provides a general argument for a political policy of laissez-faire. It is important to note, however, that Smith's defense of laissez-faire is radically different from that given by many, if not most, twentieth-century libertarians. The aim of Smith's economic theory is not primarily to argue for an economic system that protects a particular conception of freedom. Rather, Smith's title, like that of so many seventeenth- and eighteenth-century British scholarly works, tells us precisely what is the aim of his work: *An Inquiry into the Nature and Causes of the Wealth of Nations.* Smith is concerned to uncover the natural laws governing the acquisition of wealth by the society as a whole. He seems to be rather little concerned with questions of economic distribution, the pattern of which he sees as determined by natural laws of the market. Just as the unrestricted and free play of the market will generate the greatest wealth for the nation, so also will it generate a system of distribution that will prove most beneficial to at least the landed and laboring classes in society. Note, however, that Smith's primary aim is to explain the generation of wealth.

The well-known heart of Smith's economic theory is his "invisible hand" view of social coordination. Smith sees economic movement, not coincidentally I think, within the same model that the Newtonian physicists of his day saw physical movement. Just as the movement of a large mass was an arithmetic function of the movements of the various points of mass that composed it, so was the economic movement of the nation an arithmetic function of the economic movement of the individuals who composed it. Thus is the invisible hand – if each individual pursues his or her own best economic interests in the market, each will thereby contribute, not by design but through the market mechanism, to the economic best interest of the nation.[2] This is not to say, however, that Smith is an advocate of profit maximization for the firm or utility maximization for the consumer. There is in his work no developed notion of utility. Moreover, while each economic agent always prefers more to less, to ascribe to Smith a notion of maximization would ignore the fact that the mathematics in terms of which that notion is cast had simply not yet been developed in Smith's time. Perhaps he might have been perfectly happy with the notion of profit maximization if it had been presented to him. Perhaps if he had written a century later, he might even have used the language of profit maximization himself. However, Smith wrote in 1776, not 1876, nearly a century before maximization was to become a piece of economic theoretical currency. As a result, it would be simply anachronistic to attribute the modern notion of profit maximization to him.

This is also not to say, as so many of Smith's modern-day adapters seem to claim, that "what's good for General Motors is good for the USA." Smith recognizes three classes in society: landowners, laborers, and businesspersons. This division is consequent on his claim that, in any nonprimitive society, price is composed of three parts: labor, rent, and profit. Labor is, in a sense, primary in that Smith claims that the "real value of all the different component parts of price...is measured by the quantity of labor which they can...purchase or command."[3] Of these three classes, only two, the landowners and the laborers, have class interests that are congruent with the economic well-being of the nation. The class interests of business, by contrast, are in part antithetical to the economic well-being of the nation. This is not to say that Smith sees the business class as a negative force in the total economy. Quite to the contrary, he sees it as providing the real impetus for economic growth. Rather, Smith's claim is that an increase in national aggregate wealth coincides with an increase in the wealth of both the landowning and laboring classes. By contrast, the narrow class interests of the business class could be most strongly advanced by the institution of governmental policies some of which would have a negative impact on the generation of national wealth. In the conclusion of Book 1 of *Wealth of Nations,* Smith argues that any increase in the overall wealth of the nation will be tied to an increase in the real level of rents. This will happen because of both an increased productivity in land and an overall decrease in the price of manufactured goods.[4] Similarly, an increase in the overall wealth of the nation will likewise tend to increase the real wage of labor. This will occur because of an increased demand for labor as the national economy grows faster than the available supply of labor.[5] By contrast, the rate of profit tends to be "naturally low in rich, and high in poor countries, and it is always highest in countries which are going fastest to ruin."[6] The reason for this, according to Smith, is that growth in an economy will generate an increase in competition. This in turn will generate a reduction in prices for manufactured goods. Thus:

The interest of the dealers...in any particular branch of trade or manufactures, is always in some respects different from, and even opposed to, that of the publick. To widen the market and to narrow the competition, is always the interest of the dealers. To widen the market may frequently be agreeable enough to the interest of the publick; but to narrow the competition must always be against it, and can serve only to enable the dealers, by raising their profits above what they naturally would be, to levy, for their own benefit, an absurd tax upon the rest of their fellow-citizens.[7]

For Smith, the clear signs of a healthy economy are high rents, high wages, and low profits.

If we combine with this Smith's claim that the business class has a knowledge of the working of economic forces that is superior to that of either the landowning class (because of landowners' tendency toward indolence) or the laboring class, and that gives it a persuasive advantage in the determination of public policy, it becomes clear that his advocacy of the pursuit of self-interest does not extend to the realm of politics. Again unlike many of Smith's present-day adapters, he would not be a fan of interest group politics.

The final point I want to note with respect to Smith is that the modern notion of the profit-maximizing firm would have been quite foreign to him. As long as the government allowed for the free play of the market, profits, along with wages and rents, were strictly determined by the natural forces of the economy. Competition would ensure that profits would be low. As Spiro Latsis has pointed out:

There seems to be a persistent failure to notice that the behavior of the seller under perfect competition is over determined and that a weaker assumption [than profit maximization] could do the same job: namely, the assumption that the firm avoids bankruptcy.[8]

Smith's view was that a growing economy spawned ever-increasing competition. Some firms survived. Others didn't. For those that survived, the freedom of entry into the market would ensure continuing competition and continuing low profits. While that level of profit, strictly determined by market forces, could be spoken of as a maximum, there is, as Latsis suggests, something seriously misleading about that way of speaking. Then, of course, there is also the problem I previously noted about the anachronistic character of attributing the language of maximization to Smith. Virtually the only way that businesspersons could increase profits above that low level would be by using their persuasive power to gain protectionist or trade-restraining policies from the government. These policies, however, would be purchased at the expense of the national well-being, coming "from an order of men, whose interest is never exactly the same with that of the publick, who have generally an interest to deceive and even to oppress the publick, and who have, upon many occasions, both deceived and oppressed it."[9]

Moreover, as we have already seen in Chapter 1, Smith was convinced that the managerial corporation simply wouldn't succeed without government help. His position was that the separation of business control from the profit motivation attached to ownership would produce an allocation of business resources that would make it very unlikely that such a corporation could survive in a genuinely competitive environment.

I might add that it is by no means obvious that Smith was wrong in these views. It is not at all obvious that the modern managerial corporation emerged in a competitive environment and a free market. Rather, there is considerable reason to believe that it emerged with a great deal of help from government policy and in markets that were far from competitive.

In any case what I want most importantly to note about the economic theory of Adam Smith is that it aimed primarily at explaining the production of wealth, and that it was a theory which took human individuals as its domain. The behavior of any aggregate, be it nation, class, joint stock company, or the like, required explanation in terms of the behavior of the individuals that made it up. The 'firm', in the modern sense of that term which fails to differentiate between the large managerial corporation and the small owner-operated business firm, could never have stood as a primitive element in the ontology of Smith's theory.

David Ricardo. A brief examination of Ricardo's *Principles of Political Economy and Taxation* reveals one profound difference from Smith's *Wealth of Nations.* Ricardo, unlike Smith, is primarily concerned with distribution. In his preface to the *Principles,* Ricardo claims that "to determine the laws which regulate this distribution, is the principal problem in Political Economy."[10] Thus, at the outset we see Ricardo adopting an aim for his work in economic theory quite different from that adopted by Smith. This shift in concern may have, at least in part, stemmed from Ricardo's practical bent. By contrast with Smith, a lifelong academic, Ricardo was a successful stockbroker, occasional pamphleteer, and member of Parliament.

The particular issue that kindled Ricardo's passions was the Corn Law, designed to guarantee a high price for English wheat. These laws, Ricardo became convinced, would hasten the eventual collapse of the English economy by channeling an increasing proportion of the nation's wealth into the hands of the landowners, the one class who did nothing in return for their gain. Land was scarce in England. Landowners inherited their land and got large rents simply for being there. Similarly, the high prices of wheat would drive up the cost of labor, because the cost of keeping a laborer alive, which was determined by the price of wheat, set a floor under the wages of labor. This increase in the cost of labor would not create any real advantage for the laboring class since their expenses would go up accordingly. Yet the increase would have the effect of diminishing profits, driving them with increasing rapidity to their natural limit point – zero. Ricardo agreed with Smith that the natural tendency of profits in a free economy is to remain low. Ricardo, however, went beyond Smith to claim that they would tend to diminish over the long term to zero, leaving the economy in a "stationary state." In such a state investment produces no profits, and the whole economy would come grinding to a halt. This process is hastened if the price of wheat, the base determinant of the price of labor, is held artificially high. The process can be reasonably abated as long as the price of wheat is held low.

The full extent to which the aim of economic theory is changed from production to distribution in Ricardo's work is perhaps best revealed by noting that more than two-thirds of his *Principles of Political Economy and Taxation* is devoted to a discussion of various forms of taxation, attending especially to their ultimate incidence and their distributional effects. It is a central claim in Ricardo's theory that these distributional effects are the primary determinants of the long-range prospects of a national economy.

Other innovations in theory have also been attributed to Ricardo. It is at least debatable, however, to what extent these are genuine innovations. Ricardo, in the popular view of the history of economics, is generally regarded as the father of the "labor theory of value." Yet as I noted, Smith tends to see labor at least as a primary determinant of value, although he clearly does not generally hold to a monofactor view of that value. However, as Blaug has noted, "If [Ricardo] adhered to the labor theory at all, he did so only as a rough approximation and because it served as a convenient device for expounding his model."[11]

Ricardo is also often recognized for his sharp distinction between "natural price" and "market price."[12] Yet it is surely arguable that this is little more than a tying together of the implications of a labor theory of value (to the extent that Ricardo did hold such a theory) and the distinction between "use value" and "exchange value," which he adopted from Smith and with which he opens the *Principles*.

While Ricardo says nothing in the *Principles* about joint stock companies or anything else that might seem akin to the modern managerial corporation, it is clear that Ricardo's economic theory is based on the same kind of ontology of human individuals as is Smith's. There is no mention in the *Principles* of any kind of collective other than the nation. Moreover, given Ricardo's views on profits, there is every reason to believe that he would wholeheartedly agree with Smith's claims about the prospects for managerial organization of business.

John Stuart Mill. Mill's *Principles of Political Economy* was first published in 1848 (as was Marx and Engels's *Communist Manifesto*), the same year in which social revolutions sprang up all around Europe. This was a time when the newly developed industrial system was under attack on grounds that it failed to distribute appropriately the goods that it produced. These attacks undoubtedly influenced the aims of Mill's theory of political economy. Writing in that time, Mill could hardly have failed to attend in his writings on political economy to questions of both production and distribution. Thus, Mill says, at the end of the preliminary remarks to the *Principles,* "the laws of Production and Distribution, and some of the practical consequences deducible from them, are the subject of the following treatise."[13]

While Smith attended primarily to an explanation of production and Ricardo to an explanation of distribution, nevertheless both of Mill's great predecessors seemed to be of the opinion that the laws governing production and distribution were of the same kind and went hand in hand. Mill, however, departed from tradition on this point:

Unlike the laws of Production, those of Distribution are partly of human institution: since the manner in which wealth is distributed in any given society, depends on the statutes or usages therein obtaining. But though governments or nations have the power of deciding what institutions shall exist, they cannot arbitrarily determine how those institutions shall work. The conditions on which the power they possess over the distribution of wealth is dependent, and the manner in which the distribution is effected by the various modes of conduct which society may think fit to adopt, are as much a subject for scientific inquiry as any of the physical laws of nature.[14]

There is surely a sense in which what Mill says about the laws of distribution is obvious. Had Smith and Ricardo lived later than they did and been confronted by Mill's claim, I cannot doubt that they would have agreed with it. Both of them, after all, advocated positions of public policy that they saw as having influence on the distribution of the nation's wealth. Yet Mill recognized a kind of independence of production and distribution that had not struck his predecessors. The reason for this, I think, is twofold. First, Mill, writing thirty years later in the development of industrial capitalism observed, as his predecessors could not have, that the life of the laboring class, unlike the business class, was not improving with the advances of the capitalist economy. By Mill's time, as both the social revolutions and the contemporary writings of Marx illustrate, that problem had become widely apparent. Thus, Mill devotes the first book of his *Principles* to production, and the second to distribution.

The second reason springs from one of the most fundamental innovations in Mill's theory, his utilitarian theory of value. It is particularly worthy of note that Mill starts out his treatment of distribution with two chapters on property, since his understanding of the basis of property rights constitutes one of his sharpest points of divergence from his predecessors. Smith, for example, appears to be heir to the Lockean tradition that property rights are natural rights based on an initial investment of labor; as he says, "the property which every man has in his own labour . . . is the original foundation of all other property."[15] Ricardo, surprisingly, gives no explicit treatment of property in his *Principles*. Mill, by contrast, writes of property rights as we would expect of perhaps the greatest of utilitarian moral theorists: "Private property, as an institution, did not owe its origin to any of those considerations of utility, which plead for the maintenance of it when established."[16] While Mill claims that the origins of private property come from giving legal effect to "first occupancy," he claims that the subsequent justification of property rights must be on grounds of utility. As such, property rights are not natural rights, rights that exist antecedent to governmental convention, but rather institutional rights that are based on and limited by governmental grant. This new view of property rights allows Mill to see legitimate property arrangements as dependent on government policy, not natural law – hence, his view of the laws of distribution is as institutional law, not natural law.

Of special interest here is Mill's treatment of rent, which he claims is the effect of a natural monopoly. English land was and continues to be very scarce. The landowning class of Mill's day inherited the land, and it provided landowners a way of garnering a large income without expending any effort. Moreover, virtually the only way in which land changed possession was through inheritance. The fact that Mill viewed property rights as actually grounded on a legalization of first occupancy and not on an initial investment of labor clears the way for Mill to say, "Landed proprietors are the only class, of any numbers or importance, who have a claim to a share in the distribution of the produce, through their ownership of something which neither they nor any one else have produced."[17]

This should serve to illustrate how Mill's understanding of the central economic concept of property provided the theoretical underpinning for Mill's claim, also supported by his observation of life under industrial capitalism, that the laws of distribution are by no means laws of nature in the same manner as are the laws of physics. Very simply, the institution of property is one of political society, not of nature, and is grounded in social utility, not the value-creating capacity of labor.

A second major development in Mill's economic theory is the large step he takes in the direction of a theory of the firm in recognizing what he calls the "wages of superintendence" as a special component of business expense.[18] This provides an initial recognition that the superintendence of business is, in theory, separable from the ownership of business. While the customary pattern in Mill's day was for businesses to be owner managed, he does note that:

Sometimes the capital is supplied and the risk incurred by one person, and the business carried on exclusively in his name, while the trouble of management is made over to another, who is engaged for that purpose at a fixed salary. Management, however, by hired servants, who have no interest in the result but that of preserving their salaries, is proverbially inefficient, unless they act under the inspecting eye, if not the controlling hand, of the person chiefly interested: and prudence almost always recommends giving to a manager not thus controlled, a remuneration partly dependent on the profits.[19]

Mill, then, recognizes the separability in principle of business control or supervision from business ownership or investment. Along with Smith, he recognizes a fundamental divergence (potentially a conflict) between the interests of those who have invested their money in a business enterprise and the paid managers of such an enterprise. While recognizing that divergence, Mill, unlike Smith, suggests that management-controlled business may be made feasible if the owners take advantage of the available means of tying the economic interests of the managers to the economic interests of the owners.

Mill did not posit anything like the firm of present-day theory as a unitary entity. Rather, he saw the forerunner of the managerial corporation as a voluntary association between an owner-employer and a manager-employee. The two have different interests, divergent to some extent, but interests that can be made increasingly convergent. What is crucially important, however, is that Mill analyzes the managerial firm not as a single individual in the market, but as an association of flesh-and-blood individuals, the kind of individuals that constitute the domain of his theory.

I see in Mill's economic theory, then, three things of fundamental importance. In the first place, he separates the laws of distribution from those of production. This is made necessary by his experience of the world, but, what is *theoretically* more important, it is made possible, I think, by his new, utilitarian conception of property, and more generally of economic value. In the second place, Mill draws a separation in theory between the managerial function in business and business ownership. Finally, Mill maintains the same kind of ontology of human individuals that had been maintained by all his predecessors.

As Mill's *Principles* served as the standard canon of economic theory for nearly fifty years after its initial publication, I close my discussion of the classical tradition of political economy with an analysis of that work.

Marginal utility theory and measurement

In looking at some of the significant developments in economic theory from the initial development of marginal analysis up to the discussions of imperfect competition during the 1930s, I shall focus on five figures in that development: W. Stanley Jevons, Alfred Marshall, John Bates Clark, and Edward Chamberlin and Joan Robinson.

W. Stanley Jevons. In drawing my focus on Stanley Jevons at this point, I do not mean in any sense to slight the work of Karl Menger or Leon Walras. The centrally important idea of constructing economic theory on the basis of the notion of "final utility" or marginal utility was developed at roughly the same time (between 1871 and 1874) and quite independently by all three. Menger, however, differed from Jevons and Walras in certain fundamental respects relating especially to the aims and methods of economic science. Of the three, Walras is particularly identified as the initial developer of the idea of general equilibrium analysis, the attempt to develop an explanatory model that takes account of all markets within the economy simultaneously. Nevertheless, as the English member of the marginalist triumvirate, Jevons's work is easier to place within the traditions, both before and after, that I am trying to trace in this chapter.

The central innovations of Jevons (along with Walras) were in the areas of the aims and methods of the science of economics. The actual changes in theory were largely consequent upon these former innovations. The change in the aim of economic science was undoubtedly the most fundamental. For Smith the problem of economics was how to increase the wealth of the nation, for Ricardo how to distribute the nation's growing wealth in such a way as to keep the economy from grinding to a halt. For Mill, both the productive and distributive concerns were there, but the subject matter of economics still involved an explanation of the dynamic processes. For Jevons, by contrast, the problem of economics was: "Given, a certain population, with various needs and powers of production, in possession of certain lands and other sources of materials: required, the mode of employing their labor which will maximize the utility of the produce."[20] Notice, by the way, that this is the first time we have run across the term 'maximize'.

The change in aim is really quite radical. Earlier theorists had not assumed that anything was static. Population might grow or diminish. In fact, Thomas Malthus had, in 1789, developed a whole theory of population dynamics that came to be an accepted part of economic theory. The nation's supply of resources might grow or diminish. Virtually all of the classical writers treated the issue of colonization as an issue relating both to the supply of resources and to the availability of markets. These issues of growth and diminution were regarded as central facts to be explained by the economist. With Jevons, however, all that changed. Assuming a given population and set of productive resources, he asked how society allocates those resources in such a manner as to create the greatest utility for the members of the society.

In addition to the fact that Jevons set out to explain a different process than his predecessors, he also set out to explain a new phenomenon, utility. "The theory here given [in the *Theory of Political Economy*] may be described as *the mechanics of utility and self-interest*."[21] Granted, economists since Smith had spoken in terms of self-interest. Yet the major issue of concern to earlier economists was wealth. While the term 'utility' does turn up in the writings of Hume and other eighteenth-century British moral theorists, there simply was not a well-developed principle of utility at the time of Smith's writing. While Ricardo did write his *Principles* nearly thirty years after Bentham had given a carefully developed theory of utility, Ricardo's general tendency to ground value in labor clearly foreclosed any attempt to give utility a very large role in his economic theory. Only in the work of John Stuart Mill do we see the notion of utility start to play a significant role. Yet Mill's notion of utility, surely a far less mathematical notion even than that of Bentham, clearly could not have provided the ground for the development of a "mechanics of utility."

This phrase, "mechanics of utility," leads us directly into Jevons's central change in method. Yet even here we find an additional element of a change in aim. Jevons claimed that "economy, if it is to be a science at all, must be a mathematical science."[22] Mathematization of economics became for Jevons and the marginalists (with the exception of those who followed Menger's lead) not just a scientific method, but a fundamental aim of science as well, much as giving explanation in terms of circular motion was an aim in astronomy prior to Kepler. Of course, if a mathematical exposition of utility became the fundamental aim of economics, it follows that economic theory would need to develop a notion of utility that was mathematically characterizable. Jevons acknowledged that Bentham's idea of utility, with its attendant "moral calculus," was not so suitable.[23] The solution was to look for utility "in the margin," at that point in any economic process at which additional inputs fail to generate a net increase in utility. Jevons says,

"I never attempt to estimate the whole pleasure gained by purchasing a commodity; the theory merely expressed that, when a man has purchased enough, he would derive equal pleasure from the possession of a small quantity more as he would from the money price of it."[24] This move to analysis at the margin has provided the basic method for most of economics since the beginning of the present century. It provides the basis for a mathematically clear notion of utility. In particular, it generates the underpinning for the method of equilibrium analysis so basic to most of contemporary economic theory. As a result of this new mathematical clarity, for the first time it becomes natural, almost necessary, to see maximization of utility (or profits) as a goal for economic agents. It has allowed economics to become the mathematical science that Jevons desired it to be.

The central modifications that Jevons made in economics are three-fold. He abandoned the explanation of wealth in a dynamic context in favor of an explanation of utility maximization in a static context. He abandoned any hint of a labor theory of value in favor of a notion of purely subjective utility. Finally, he transformed economics into a thoroughly mathematical science. I should add that I can find no discussion at all in Jevons's work that would seem to relate to the managerial corporation. In general, he seems not to distinguish managerial from other forms of labor, and seems not to give an explicit consideration to entrepreneurship.

Perhaps as a footnote, it is worth mentioning that the shift in the aims of economic theory in the work of the early marginalists, and the consequent shift in theory, led the new marginalist economic theory to abandon the Malthusian theory of population. While it appears that the early marginalist economists generally thought that Malthus was substantially correct, their construction of economic theory left no room for population dynamics as a part of economics. In the sense, then, that economic theory lost a theory of population dynamics, it thereby became, if we were to stick to Lakatos's rather rigid characterization of scientific progress, a theoretically degenerating research tradition. I take it, however, that the chief lesson to be learned from this, in light of the fact that the shift was generated by a redefinition of the scope of the discipline, is that Lakatos's characterization of progress is simply too rigid. By contrast, given Laudan's characterization of a research tradition, as noted in the last chapter, there is no particular problem identifying the early marginalists as part of a common research tradition started by the classical political economists. Laudan's characterization of a research tradition requires that there be some continuity of "metaphysical and methodological commit-

ments." It will be the task of the next chapter to identify those continuities that will serve to identify the research tradition that continues
from Smith through the early marginalists and into the present day.

   Alfred Marshall. As Mill's *Principles of Political Economy* proved
to be the canon of economics during most of the last half of the
nineteenth century, so Marshall's *Principles of Economics* proved to be
equally dominant from its first publication in 1890 until well into the
twentieth century. In the preface to the First Edition, he sums up
very well what he wished to do in his presentation of economic theory:
"the present treatise is an attempt to present a modern version of old
doctrines with the aid of the new work, and with reference to the new
problems, of our own age."[25] Marshall had a broader conception of
the aims of economics than did Jevons. Far from seeing economics
as a "mechanics of utility and self-interest," he spoke disparagingly
of the attempts that had "been made to construct an abstract science
with regard to the actions of an 'economic man', who is under no
ethical influences and who pursues pecuniary gain warily and ener-
getically, but mechanically and selfishly."[26] For Marshall, "economics
is a study of men as they live and move and think in the ordinary
business of life, but it concerns itself chiefly with those motives which
affect, most powerfully and most steadily, man's conduct in the business part of his life."[27]

   Marshall lists, in some detail, the major questions that he sees economic theory as addressing:

What are the causes which, especially in the modern world, affect the consumption and production, the distribution and exchange of wealth; the organization of industry and trade; the money market; wholesale and retail
dealing; foreign trade, and the relations between employers and employed?
How do all these movements act and react upon one another? How do their
ultimate differ from their immediate tendencies?[28]

Obviously there is much here that reminds one of the broad view of
economics that we find in Mill, as opposed to Jevons's "mechanics of
utility and self-interest." Yet the stamp of Jevons's view of utility is
left indelibly on Marshall. There is no hint in Marshall's work, for
example, of a labor theory of value. Wealth is characterized in terms
of subjective utility, the "satisfying of wants."[29] This of course leads
Marshall to place his analysis of demand at the very center of his
economic theory. As his tendency is to examine the various issues
within economics in a more or less piecemeal fashion, limiting himself
to partial equilibrium analyses and paying little heed to the interre-

lations among those issues, it becomes very easy for him to hold various factors as stable and go on to apply the tools of marginal analysis to a wide range of economic issues. While Marshall tends to leave much of his mathematical exposition in footnotes, due to the audience that he perceived for his work, the basic method of analysis is clearly in the marginalist mode of Jevons.

I noted Boulding's claim, in Chapter 1, that "there was no theory of the firm in economics before Marshall." From the perspective of this study, perhaps the most important single innovation in theory in Marshall's work was in his discussion of the firm. In his *Principles,* he devotes five chapters of treatment to the topic of industrial organization. There is also a chapter on the "theory of monopolies," and two chapters on "profits of capital and business power." In addition to the treatment in the *Principles,* Marshall wrote a volume of equal size called *Industry and Trade.*[30] In that work, he devotes over 200 pages to "dominant tendencies of business organization."

Marshall's discussions of the firm involve two points of particular interest. Marshall sees business firms as having something like a life cycle. They are born with great energy, go through periods of growth and decline, and eventually die. His concern to pay attention to the facts of real-world economic relationships led him to recognize a wide variety of business operations as well as different stages and modes of organization. In Marshall's time the managerial firm had started to become a dominant mode of doing business. As I noted in Chapter 1, he was fully aware of the tendency for the interests of managers to conflict with the interests of the shareholders. I cited him there as giving a regular catalog of the major ways in which a relentless pursuit of self-interest by the managers would lead them to abuse the interests of the shareholders. I noted at that time that his explanation for the fact that, as he saw it, managers did not generally thus abuse their power within the firm to pursue their own interests at the expense of the shareholders was a moral explanation, not a strictly and narrowly economic one. While this explanation was surely consonant with Marshall's own view of human motivation and the operations of the economic world, it is equally an explanation that most contemporary heirs to the marginalist tradition would find at odds with their most basic professional assumptions about both.

Moreover, Marshall saw other aspects of the conflicts of interest built into the structure of the managerial firm as contributing to the degeneration of the firm. In an address delivered in 1896 entitled "The Old Generation of Economists and the New," Marshall observed:

Everyone is aware of the tendency to an increase in the size of individual businesses, with the consequent transference of authority and responsibility from the owners of each business to its salaried managers and officials.... [Marshall goes on about how an increase in honesty has made this possible.]

And indeed this tendency to an increase in the size of businesses introduces an ever-growing discord into industry. The owner of a business, when contemplating any change, is led by his own interest to weigh the whole gain that it would probably bring to the business against the whole loss; but the private interest of the salaried manager or official draws him in quite another direction. For the trouble of a new experiment will come largely on him. If it fails, he will have to bear much of the blame; and, if it succeeds, only a very small part of the consequent gain will accrue to him. So the path of least resistance, of greatest comfort and least risk to himself is generally that of not striving for improvement himself, and of finding plausible excuses for not trying an improvement suggested by others, until its success is established beyond question.[31]

Thus, Marshall does recognize the composite nature of the managerial firm, a combination of conflicting interests. He also recognizes how this fact forces the economic theorist away from anything very much like a pure profit-maximizing assumption. Yet because of the need to generalize about the variety of actual world firms, from small, owner-managed firms to large firms run by salaried managers, Marshall is driven to posit what he calls "the representative firm," which, as Blaug notes, is not representative with respect to size or stage of development. It is not an arithmetically average firm, but rather purely an abstraction, a firm with "average costs" and "normal profits."[32] Yet it is in terms of this representative firm that talk of profit maximization starts to make sense, especially as it comes to be replaced by what Pigou called the "equilibrium firm," following criticisms lodged against Marshall's notion by A. C. Pigou and Lionel Robbins in 1928.[33] Marshall's notion of the representative firm is the second point in his treatment of business institutions that is of interest for our present purposes. It seems, then, that among Marshall's most significant developments in economic theory were his reexpansion of the scope of economics, broadening the aim of the discipline from that given to it by Jevons, and his explicit treatment of business organization.

John Bates Clark. John Bates Clark clearly does not rank with Smith, Ricardo, Mill, Jevons, and Marshall among great economic theorists of the past. Yet in addition to being the first American economic theorist of any note, he did make contributions to economic theory on two points that I think are worth noting. In the first place, Clark was one of the initial developers (at the same time as, but independently of, Philip Wicksteed and Knut Wicksell) of marginal productivity theory, the point of which is well expressed in the first sentence of the preface to Clark's *Distribution of Wealth:*

It is the purpose of this work to show that the distribution of the income from society is controlled by a natural law, and that this law, if it worked without friction, would give to every agent of production the amount of wealth which that agent creates.[34]

Marginal productivity theory asserts that a competitive economy allows for the identification of the "marginal product" of each factor in the productive process. That marginal product can be identified with the component of the productive process which that factor contributes to production. In a free market it turns out that the marginal product of any factor in the productive process is identical to the portion of the proceeds from the production which that factor receives.

Clark also contributed importantly in recognizing that there was a difference between "factoral" and "personal" distribution. The same person, as a laborer, could receive a part of the marginal product of labor, and, as a shareholder, receive part of the marginal product of capital. It is surely worth noting at this point that Clark's treatment of factoral distribution, as well as Marshall's invention of the representative firm, constituted some of the initial steps in the process of including analytical individuals along with natural individuals within the domain of economic theory. Yet all in all, the upshot of marginal productivity theory was to show that in a competitive capitalist economy, every person got what he or she deserved (at least if we take desert to be based simply on contribution). The theory, then, constituted for many one of the fundamental underpinnings in a defense of capitalism against the charge of distributive injustice.

Yet while Clark wants to maintain that "the creation and use of wealth are everywhere governed by natural laws, and these, as discovered and stated, constitute the Science of Economics,"[35] he also notes, as did Mill, that society plays a large role in the determination of distribution:

The civilized society creates its wealth cooperatively, by the joint action of its various members; that is, it proceeds by means of a division of labor and an exchanging of products....

When we say that production has been [thus] socialized, we mean something very far-reaching. We mean that an organization has grown up in which men are members or parts of members, and that this great organization has undertaken to do the productive work for all the individuals that compose it. ... Economic independence gives way to interdependence, because the fortune of each man is largely dependent, not merely on his own efforts, but on the relations which he sustains to other men. Simple laws of nature still largely control his income, but social laws also have a certain control over it.[36]

Clark recognizes the need to attend to industrial organization.

His second important contribution involves the recognition that the development of the large managerial corporation has created a new kind of problem. The managerial corporation is, on the one hand, a social organization; on the other hand, it is in many instances treated by the law as an individual. As I noted in Chapter 1, Clark sees this as creating a kind of economic superagent, with "powers and abilities far beyond those of mortal men." I use language drawn from the introduction to the old television show "Superman" because, just as Superman was not bound by the laws of nature that constrained the action of "mortal men," so the modern managerial corporation is not bound by the economic laws that constrain the economic behavior of lesser creatures. Clark claims then, as I noted in Chapter 1, that these "chartered bodies of capitalists, great corporations . . . [build] up a semi-public power, . . . vitiating the action of economic laws."

All of this is not to say, of course, that there may not be some analytical value in a theory of the firm that treats the firm as an individual, but it is to claim that there is a serious danger to both human individuals and the economy at large if public policy toward such corporations is premised on viewing them substantially as legal individuals.

Thus, the two important contributions of Clark come together in an interesting way. The natural laws governing the distribution of wealth in a competitive, free market economy guarantee a fair distribution of that wealth, but the existence of large managerial firms, treated by the law as though they were economic individuals, destroys the economic basis on which market distribution can be argued to be just. It does this by destroying the delicate balance of economic power that characterizes the free, competitive market. In amassing the collective economic power of a multitude of individuals, the large corporation negates the crucial assumption of free market determination of distribution that no one participant in the market has the power to influence either prices or wages. Yet the moment agents in the economy come to have that kind of power, the central tenet of marginal productivity theory – namely, that the return to each factor of production is determined by purely economic forces in the market – fails to hold. The central implication of this, I take it, is that a theory of the firm that fails to recognize the social, collective nature of the

large managerial firm has *very* limited value as a tool for the determination of public policy.

Edward Chamberlin and Joan Robinson. The final pre-Keynesian
episode in the development of marginalist economic theory is the
development of theories of imperfect and monopolistic competition
in the 1930s. Edward Chamberlin's *The Theory of Monopolistic Competition* and Joan Robinson's *The Economics of Imperfect Competition* were
both published in 1933. In fact, Chamberlin's preface and Robinson's
foreword were both written in Cambridge (Massachusetts in Chamberlin's case and England in Robinson's) in October of 1932. There
has been a good deal of debate since 1933 over whether Chamberlin,
Robinson, and others made significant modifications in economic theory, and even whether the theories propounded by Chamberlin and
Robinson were one basic theory or two different theories.[37] Whether
one or two, the theories of monopolistic competition and imperfect
competition have generally been treated as arising from a common
basic aim, to explain the operation of firms in markets that are neither
perfectly competitive nor wholly monopolized. The existence of such
markets in a modern economy is an outgrowth of Clark's problem
(also recognized, as I have noted, by Marshall) of corporate power.
Markets that include a modest number of large corporations, unlike
those that include a multitude of insignificantly small individual entrepreneurs, are imperfectly or monopolistically competitive markets.

Whether these theories of imperfect or monopolistic competition
constituted significant revisions in theory or not, they clearly did not
make any revision in the basic marginalist method of analysis that had
proved dominant since the work of Jevons and Walras. Indeed, as I
noted in Chapter 1, Machlup, in his famous defense of the marginalist
theory of the firm, cites Chamberlin's and Robinson's works as among
the first versions of the marginalist theory of the firm. Spiro Latsis
has even gone so far as to criticize Chamberlin for "pretend[ing] to
handle imperfect competition with tools only applicable to perfect
competition."[38]

Whatever one wishes to say about these points of controversy, there
are two points I wish to make about the early work in the analysis of
imperfect and monopolistic competition. In the first place, these early
writers on imperfect and monopolistic competition recognize a fact
about the world that had not been attended to by earlier economic
theorists. The need to explain the effects of this fact – that there are,
especially in an economic world dominated by managerial corporations, significant markets that are neither perfectly competitive nor

perfectly monopolized – led to at least some revision in the aims (perhaps simply by addition) of economic theory.

The second point is somewhat more important. The early work in theories of imperfect and monopolistic competition contributed significantly to solidifying the change in the ontology of economic theory begun by Sraffa, Pigou, and Robbins,[39] which was my chief reason for maintaining in Chapter 1 that the emergence of the modern theory of the firm constituted a radical change in economic theory. I will use Robinson's work to illustrate my point. In laying out her "assumptions" in the first chapter of *The Economics of Imperfect Competition*, she says, "the fundamental assumption is that each individual acts in a sensible manner, in the circumstances in which he finds himself, from the point of view of his own economic interests."[40] Note that Robinson starts out by claiming that her theory is assumed to be talking about individuals.

She then defines the firm in such a manner that it can be treated as an individual:

A *firm* is a concern very similar to the firms in the real world, but which produces only one commodity, and is controlled by a single independent interest.

The controlling interest of a firm is an *entrepreneur*. For long-period problems the entrepreneur is conceived to require a certain reward, sufficient to induce him to continue in business, which is independent of the amount of his output. [Robinson's emphases][41]

Robinson's characterization of the firm denies very explicitly the internal conflicts of interest that were universally recognized from Smith to Clark. She claims that the firm is controlled by a single interest, that of the entrepreneur. (She also makes the theoretically unimportant, but practically very important claim that her theoretical firm is "very similar to the firms in the real world.") In this process of collapsing the concept of the firm into that of the entrepreneur, Robinson is led to view the firm as a maximizer of profits, just as marginal analysis had traditionally assumed the entrepreneur to be such a maximizer.

Since Robinson's view of the firm rules out the separate recognition of the role of management, a role we now see recognized quite clearly since the work of Mill, she has no way of even raising the questions about managerial behavior that were raised so clearly by Marshall. Moreover, even if she had been able to raise those questions, Robinson would have had to reject Marshall's answer for the simple reason that he appeals to action that is not aimed at economic self-interest.

It is important to note here that we ought not to conclude that

Robinson simply missed something about corporate producers that was perfectly obvious to so many other economic theorists. Especially given her familiarity with all of Marshall's work, it is far more reasonable to see her as making a methodological choice to ignore the problem of managerial self-interest in order to examine the full implications of the problem of corporate power. In effect, Robinson is making the claim that *even if* we see no internal blocks to profit maximization in the managerial corporation, there still remains this problem of power, the problem that imperfectly or monopolistically competitive markets cannot be expected to produce the same level of efficiency as perfectly competitive markets.

It should be clear, then, that the work of those who developed the theories of imperfect and monopolistic competition made a significant contribution to the development of economic theory simply in leading to a consideration of the kinds of markets with which they were concerned. Perhaps most significant of all, however, they helped to fashion a very great change in economic theory by the way in which they worked to merge the many and varied interests that comprise the managerial firm into a single-minded pursuer of profit maximization. In the hands of Robinson and Chamberlin, of course, the consequence of such single-minded pursuit implied a policy move away from a totally unrestricted market. Under imperfect or monopolistic competition, the invisible hand of the free market required the aid of policy.

Keynes and the possibility of aggregate analysis

In the history of economic theory, Keynes probably looms as a larger figure than anyone except Adam Smith. Given this, it may seem surprising that I shall have very little to say about him. Monumental as were the changes in economic theory advocated by Keynes, those changes do not bear very much relevance to the development of the theory of the firm.

Like Smith before him, Keynes gives us a title that tells us very clearly what he is trying to develop: *The General Theory of Employment, Interest, and Money*. The central aim in his theory was to explain how society could affect "the volume of employment and the national income (or national dividend) measured in wage-units."[42] The variables in terms of which Keynes's theory explained these quantities were "the propensity to consume, the schedule of the marginal efficiency of capital and the rate of interest."[43] To illustrate with a particularly important issue, Keynes held, contrary to most of his more traditional contemporaries, that employment would not be significantly increased by a reduction of wages. Rather, he held that what was needed instead to increase employment was an increase in demand. Such an increase in demand could be generated by an additional injection of spending power by the government into the economy if such an injection was not forthcoming from the private sector of the economy. It should be clear from this example that the policy implications of Keynes's theory were as enormous as they were controversial.

While he had very, very little to say about the economics of the firm (the term 'firm' does not even appear in the index to the *General Theory*), there is one aspect of his modification of economic theory that is of immense relevance to the concerns of this book. Keynes, in contrast with most of those economic theorists who preceded and followed him, went some, albeit a small, distance toward an easing of methodological individualism, the view of method that requires economic theory to treat aggregate economic phenomena as simple arithmetic functions of the individuals who make up those aggregates. Keynes's "propensity to consume," as Blaug has noted, "is not derived from individual maximising behavior; it is instead a bold inference based on the known, or at that time suspected, relationship between aggregate consumer expenditure and national income."[44] While Keynes's claims about aggregates may well be reducible to claims about their constituent individuals, nevertheless his laws of aggregate behavior are neither justified nor justifiable, as Blaug says, "not derived from" any laws of individual behavior.

This point is well illustrated in J. W. N. Watkins's treatment of Keynes in his 1952 article, "Ideal Types and Historical Explanation."[45] Watkins correctly notes Keynes's claim that

the fundamental psychological law, upon which we are entitled to depend with great confidence both *a priori* from our knowledge of human nature and from the detailed facts of experience, is that men are disposed, as a rule and on the average, to increase their consumption as their income increases, but not by as much as the increase in their income.[46]

Watkins goes on to suggest that the propensity to consume can be deduced from this "fundamental psychological law."[47] Yet on Keynes's account of the propensity to consume, that "fundamental psychological law" is only one of a number of factors determining that propensity:

The amount that the community spends on consumption obviously depends (i) partly on the amount of its income, (ii) partly on the other objective attendant circumstances, and (iii) partly on the subjective needs and the psychological propensities and habits of the individuals composing it and the principles on which the income is divided between them.[48]

Among the "principle objective factors which influence the propensity to consume," Keynes cites several, perhaps the most important of which, for my present purposes, is "changes in fiscal policy."[49] This characterization of Keynes's propensity to consume should make it clear that Blaug is correct in finding in Keynes's work some modest departure from methodological individualism, as I have characterized it already and as I shall in more detail in the next chapter.

While Keynes did not go on to apply any kind of aggregative analysis to firms, the fact that his work does make at least a modest break with the practice of theorizing purely from an ontology of only individuals is at least significant. Keynes himself seemed to think of firms as individuals, but at least he acknowledged that economic theory could involve other kinds of analyses as well.

Chicago economics and the affirmation of individualism

At the same time that Chamberlin and Robinson were developing theories of monopolistic and imperfect competition, and that Keynes was bringing in small elements of economic analysis in terms of aggregates, another group of economists, identified almost from the beginning with the University of Chicago, steadfastly maintained that all important work in economic theory could be carried on from the perspective of an individualistic analysis and with an assumption of perfectly competitive markets. While the Chicago tradition has produced a number of eminent economic theorists, including Frank Knight, Jacob Viner, Henry Simons, Milton Friedman, George Stigler, any number of whom could be treated here, I will concern myself with two of the Chicago economists in particular. Frank Knight did much of his most important work during the same period in which Chamberlin and Robinson and Keynes produced their most important works. Knight was surely one of the first great economic theorists of the Chicago tradition, and Milton Friedman has been the dominant figure of the Chicago tradition from the 1950s through the 1980s, his work profoundly influencing a whole generation of American public policy makers. I shall therefore confine my discussion of Chicago economics to the work of Knight and Friedman.

Frank H. Knight. As I noted in Chapter 1, Nobel laureate James Buchanan has argued that Knight was "forced ... to the very edges of a shift in vision, but he was never able to escape the maximizing paradigm which his own early work, in part, helped to impose on the whole profession."[50] Knight was indeed an economist whose work was filled with tensions. While there is much in his work that foreshadowed the subsequent Chicago tradition, there is equally much that is quite at odds with it. Knight was concerned to continue in the marginalist tradition of "scientific" economics. Yet at the same time, he stoutly maintained that economics was fundamentally different from the natural sciences. He maintained that there were three importantly different kinds of knowledge: that of the natural sciences, that of logic and mathematics, and that of the social sciences or "knowledge of human conduct."[51] This threefold division of knowledge, for example, provides the basis of Knight's scathing criticisms of the positivism embodied in T. W. Hutchinson's *The Significance and Basic Postulates of Economic Theory*.[52] Similarly, while Knight wants to maintain that "economic problems . . . constitute but a small fraction of"[53] problems relating to human conduct, at the same time he wants to maintain that all human behavior has an economic aspect to it.[54]

Because of his inability to escape the "maximizing paradigm," there is really very little that is new in Knight's work, with the exception of the fact that his work provides the basis for a considerable expansion of the scope of economics and for the present Chicago view on economic methodology. In explaining the economic element in human behavior generally, he gives the following characterization of economic behavior as one aspect of "motivated, or deliberately problem-solving action":

A subject uses given means to realize given ends, only the procedure being problematical. (Taken in the strict sense, this applies only to "stationary conditions," but all deliberative behavior is economic "in so far as," and in the sense that, ends and means are given and the problem is that of procedure.)[55]

Since all decisions in human life are decisions about how to use the various (scarce) resources (including time) at our disposal to accomplish various ends, it follows that all decisions are economic ones. This has led economists of the Chicago tradition to provide reductive economic analyses of everything from marriage, divorce, and suicide, to law and justice. There is a sense in which Knight's work provides the basis for a transformation of economics into a kind of master social science.

The characterization of "behavior [that] is economic" in the previous quote, of course, leaves economic behavior, by definition, as individual behavior. Knight emphasizes time and again in a wide variety of places that although the individuals with which economic theory is concerned are analytical individuals,[56] economics is nevertheless committedly individualistic. Thus,

in its second aspect or stage, economic theory deals with social, in the sense of inter-individual, relations. But the "economic man" is not a "social animal," and economic individualism excludes society in the proper human sense. Economic relations are *impersonal* [Knight's emphasis]. The social organization dealt with in economic theory is *best pictured* [my emphasis] as a number of Crusoes interacting through the markets exclusively.[57]

While Knight does not show the same kind of disdain for the truth of his analytical assumptions that we will see in Friedman, nevertheless if those analytical assumptions can be claimed to embody "partial truths," then their predictive value can provide a general justification for those assumptions.[58]

Generally speaking, the actual theory that Knight provides is very much in the spirit of the early marginalists. In 1931 in an article entitled "Marginal Utility Economics" written for *The Encyclopaedia of the Social Sciences*, Knight makes clear his commitment to marginal utility analysis: "At the present time marginal utility analysis, in one or another of its numerous variants, is firmly established in the economic thought of all important countries."[59] Similarly, Knight seems generally to adhere to the marginal productivity theory of distribution as developed by Clark and others.[60]

Although, generally speaking, he does not share Clark's view that the basis of the marginal productivity analysis of distribution is undercut by the rise of the large corporation, he does warn that "with gross inequality in the distribution of wealth among individuals, all ethical defenses of freedom lose their validity; and ... the automatic system of control (market competition) breaks down, for competition requires a large number of units, every one of negligible size."[61]

Knight's treatment of the firm, like his methodological individualism, is a substantial bow to theoretical "partial truth." By the time of Knight's writing, of course, the large managerial firm was a well-established item in the real economic world. Writing in 1921, he notes: "The typical form of business unit in the modern world is the corporation. Its most important characteristic is the combination of diffused ownership with concentrated control. In theory the organization is a representative democracy, of an indirect type."[62] Note that Knight does not pay great attention to the conflict of interests within the corporation that had been noted by his marginalist predecessors, Marshall and Clark. Note also, however, that Knight does not simply gloss over the conflict, as Robinson seems to do, albeit for her own analytical purposes. Rather, he sees the corporation in theory as a democracy. This provides his resolution to the conflict. It is important to realize that he is not suggesting that the corporation works that way in the real world, but rather is claiming that the corporation can be treated that way in theory. This allows Knight to claim that "on the whole we must say that the discussion of profit in relation to wages of management has been greatly overworked."[63] This is because, in Knight's theory, unlike Marshall's reality, the owners of a firm do have a kind of ultimate power to hire and fire managers.

All of this provides the basis for the following characterization of economic activity under free enterprise:

A free enterprise organization is one in which the economic activity of a large number of individuals is organized through the medium of "productive units" each made up of one or more individuals and each of which, acting as a unit, buys the use of economic means in the competitive market from individuals in exchange for "money," and sells "products" in a competitive market, to individuals, for money.[64]

Knight does note, and here is where he verges most closely on the "shift of vision" noted by Buchanan, that such a productive unit "as a whole has no value in itself or purposes of its own . . . but exists solely to promote the interests of its members."[65] Yet Knight's view of the corporation as a democracy permits him, for purposes of analysis, to ignore the interests of those corporate members in favor of the interests of the productive unit as an analytic individual.

It is important to note that there is very little in the basic economic theory of Knight that is very new. The theory is one of individual agents in a free market economy (going back to Smith) maximizing their subjective utility (going back to Jevons). What is genuinely novel in the work of Knight, and sets the basis for the direction carried on through the Chicago tradition, lies in the area of method and aim. The chief modification in aim, as I noted, was in Knight's claim that every deliberative action has an economic aspect, a claim that paved the way for an expansion of the scope of economics to the point where it constituted a universal science of human behavior. The concern to provide thoroughly mechanistic explanations also constituted a shift in aim from some of his predecessors, although a continuation of the view of others (e.g., Jevons). Also, of course, Knight's explicit concern for prediction, paving the way for Friedman's methodological position about which I shall speak, began a significant change in aim from the positions of most previous economists. In the area of method, the very explicit embrace of partial truth in one's theory and the concern for predictive efficacy that I just mentioned was Knight's chief novelty. It was, however, a novelty that was, in a less cautious form, soon to come to dominate the methodological view of the larger part of the economics profession.

Milton Friedman. Within the areas of our concern, Friedman's work constitutes the further development of several of the themes that emerge in Knight's view of economics. He also gives applications of Knight's approach to issues that have largely arisen since the time of Knight's work. Far and away the most important contribution of Friedman's in these areas concerns economic method. Clearly the most forceful and influential expression of the methodological position – that the sole point of economic theory is to generate predictions and not to be concerned with the "realism" of the theory's "assumptions" – has been, as I noted in Chapter 2, Friedman's "Methodology of Positive Economics."[66] The views on scientific method in economics expressed in that essay have clearly dominated the field since the time of its publication.

Friedman's views on the firm seem to be substantially the same as those of Knight's. The firm is treated as an individual in the market, because so treating it provides a simple model for predicting market behavior:

Specialization of function and division of labor would not go far if the ultimate productive unit were the household. In a modern society, we have gone much further. We have introduced enterprises which are intermediaries between individuals in their capacities as suppliers of services and as purchasers of goods....
Despite the important role of enterprises and of money in our actual economy, and despite the numerous and complex problems they raise, the central characteristic of the market technique of achieving co-ordination is fully displayed in the simple exchange economy that contains neither enterprises nor money. As in that simple model, so in the complex enterprise and monetary exchange economy, co-operation is strictly individual and voluntary provided: (a) the enterprises are private, so that the ultimate contracting parties are individuals and (b) that individuals are effectively free to enter or not to enter into any particular exchange, so that every transaction is strictly voluntary.[67]

While Friedman's views on the aims and method of economic theory pick up on themes that appear in Knight's work, they also drop other of Knight's themes. In Friedman's hands, Knight's concern with the predictive efficacy of theory becomes an exclusive concern. Likewise, Knight's emphasis that the basic postulates of economic theory are only partial truths, not the whole truth, becomes for Friedman a complete lack of concern for the truth of those postulates, as long as they succeed in generating appropriate predictions. Friedman holds to substantially the same set of theoretical commitments. Like Knight, his theory starts out with an ontology of undifferentiated individuals. Some of these individuals are flesh-and-blood persons, some are households, and some are enterprises or firms. But it is important to remember that Friedman, again like Knight, does this not because he is unaware of the importance of economic collectives in the real world, but rather because he believes that the individualistic marginalist theory of the firm remains unsurpassed in its predictive power, a claim that we shall examine more carefully in Chapters 5 and 6.

Conclusion

In concluding my brief glance at the history of economic theory I do not mean, in any sense, to suggest that these have been the only or even the most significant developments in the history of economic theory. There are, of course, the contributions of the Austrians, the institutionalists, the Marxists, and others. Likewise, I have not attended to the methodological advances of the mid-twentieth century in mathematical economics, such as the techniques developed by Kenneth Arrow, Gerard Debreu, and others, that have substantially advanced the project of general equilibrium analysis set out nearly a century earlier by Walras. In selecting from the history of economic theory as I have, I have tried to trace those broad strands of economic theory that have had the greatest impact on the state of economics in the contemporary United States. Clearly the Chicago tradition has not carried the whole field. It has both its advocates and its opponents. Moreover, its opponents constitute a diverse group in and of themselves. The influence of Keynes remains very strong in some quarters, and the verdict is still out on the significance of theories of monopolistic and imperfect competition. Moreover, the future will without doubt bring changes that none of us could have predicted.

In addition to having traced those strands in economic theory that have had the most significance on contemporary American economics, I hope also to have shown something about the piecemeal character of scientific change. We see from the time of Smith up to the present day a mélange of changes at virtually every moment in the life of economic theory. Smith sought centrally to explain growth, Ricardo and Mill to explain distribution. The marginalists were most generally concerned to explain allocation, yet some of them sought to provide in their economics a social "theory of everything." Prior to the development of marginal analysis, most economists thought that a theory of population dynamics had an appropriate place within the theory of political economy. Marginalism, however, abandoned population dynamics as a part of its proper theoretical quest. Prior to the rise of the Chicago tradition, most economists thought that science involved identifying causal laws to explain the phenomena with which they were concerned. With the rise of the Chicago tradition, the view has come to be that science is merely prediction. Then, of course, there is the change in ontology that I identified in Chapter 1. All in all, the changes in economic theory over the past two centuries have been gradual, multifaceted, and surely profound, not simply a matter of the addition of new insights and new tools. There have been theoretical losses as well as gains, in many cases generated partly by changes in the aims to which economic theorists bent their efforts. Change is surely the constant feature, but it is a change that occurred in bits and parts.

It is, I would maintain, yet sensible to make the point that Coats and Gordon, as cited at the beginning of Chapter 1, were trying to make about some kind of continuous research tradition dating back to the work of Adam Smith. It is not, I think, sensible to try to speak of that as a Kuhnian paradigm. The changes have been significant and have come in every component of the scientific enterprise: aim, method, and theory. Yet the changes have not come in self-contained wholes. There has still been a continuity. In the next chapter I shall examine the elements of agreement that have persisted through the many changes in the development of mainstream economics, and I shall also look with sharper focus at the kinds of disagreement that have arisen over the course of that development.

CHAPTER 4

Agreement and disagreement within the tradition

I began Chapter 1 by noting Coats's claim that economic theory has been "dominated throughout its history by a single paradigm – the theory of economic equilibrium via the market mechanism" and Gordon's similar claim that "Smith's postulate of the maximizing individual in a relatively free market...is our basic paradigm." If there is one single point that should be clear from the last two chapters it is that Kuhnian talk of paradigms and revolutions is simply not very helpful if we wish to understand the development of economic theory since 1776. The changes in economic theory have certainly been far too significant and fundamental to allow us to speak of that period as one of Kuhnian normal science. Yet as I noted in concluding Chapter 3, there are some continuities that have persisted in economic theory since Smith's writings. Moreover, I take it that most contemporary economists regard themselves as working in a scientific tradition that began with *The Wealth of Nations*. These factors constitute the kernel of truth that lies behind the claims of Coats and Gordon. They also set the agenda for this chapter, to identify what has remained the same in economic theory since the time of Smith and to come to greater clarity on the kinds of change that have occurred in economic theory since that time.

Agreement

If we are to speak with much precision, neither Gordon nor Coats manages to identify correctly the elements of continuity that have been maintained in economic theory since Smith. Gordon speaks of Smith's maximizing individual as a paradigm, yet Smith's individuals were clearly not maximizers, at least in anything very much like the contemporary economic use of that term. Smith does, of course, speak of individuals pursuing their own economic interests to the best of their abilities, but his economic theory lacked the mathematics that would have been required even to make sense of the notion of maximization. As should be clear from the last chapter, the notion of maximization that plays so dominant a role in contemporary economic theory only gained prominence in economics with the work of Jevons and Walras. At its very earliest (perhaps in the work of Cournot), it was not developed until well after the death of Smith. Thus, Smith's individual economic agent, while clearly self-interested, was surely no maximizer. Moreover, that economic interest which Smith's individuals pursued was not subjective utility – again made prominent in the works of Jevons, Menger, and Walras – but rather was wealth. By the individual trying to increase his or her own wealth, in relatively free markets, the wealth of the nation would thereby be increased as well.

Coats's claim about the continuity of a paradigm of economic equilibrium fares no better here. The contemporary idea of equilibrium, like that of maximization, is a characteristically marginalist notion. Frank Hahn gives a good rough characterization of economic equilibrium as

a state in which the independently taken decisions of households and firms are compatible. Thus it is a set of prices such that if they ruled there is a profit maximizing choice of firms and a preference maximizing choice of households *such that the total demand for any good is equal to the amount of it initially available, plus the amount of it produced* [Hahn's emphasis].[1]

There are two problems with the claim that any theory of equilibrium has been a continuous part of economic theory since the time of Smith. In the first place, the notion of equilibrium as defined by Hahn depends crucially on notions that did not appear in economic theory before the marginalists. He makes specific reference to maximization decisions and firms, neither of which appears in the work of Smith.

Yet even if we retreat to a more primitive notion of equilibrium, say one in which the decisions of economically self-interested producers and consumers are mutually consistent, the notion of equilibrium still seems to arise in economic theory only with the marginalists. As I noted in the last chapter, the rise of marginal analysis brought about a fundamental change in the aims of economics, in the set of problems that economic theory set itself to explain. Again to cite Jevons, the problem of economics was: "Given, a certain population, with various needs and powers of production, in possession of certain lands and other sources of materials: required, the mode of employing their labor which will maximize the utility of the produce." If this is taken as the aim of economics, then "the theory of economic equilibrium via the market mechanism" provides a potentially interesting answer. The basic claim of such a theory is that the mechanism of the market is such that the interests of the various parties interacting in the market can be jointly satisfied, at least if we cash out the notion of joint satisfaction in terms of something, like Pareto optimality, that doesn't require too much in the area of satisfaction.

Yet the problem of how to jointly maximize a certain set of individual utilities was not a central aim for economic theory prior to marginalism. Hahn starts out his article "General Equilibrium Theory" with the following claim:

In decentralized economies a large number of individuals make economic decisions which, in the light of market and other information, they consider most advantageous. They are not guided by the social good, nor is there an overall plan in the unfolding of which they have preassigned roles. It was Adam Smith who first realized the need to explain why this kind of social arrangement does not lead to chaos.[2]

Hahn's claim about Smith is subtly mistaken here; for Smith did not look at a decentralized economy in his own time, puzzle about how such a thing could work, and then set about explaining that fact. Confronting quite a different economic problem, "the nature and causes of the wealth of nations," he provided an argument for a decentralized economy. Smith did not take the explanation of a decentralized economy as the aim of his theoretical work, as Hahn suggests. Rather, he took the explanation of aggregate national wealth as the aim of his theoretical work, arguing that a decentralized economy is the best way to promote that aggregate national wealth. To claim otherwise is to misread Smith by about a hundred years.

Smith is, of course, concerned with a variety of coordination problems, such as how the market mechanism works to bring market prices into an approximation of natural prices, and also that the market mechanism can work to generate national wealth from the self-interested wealth-producing activity of individuals. These coordination problems certainly do implicitly appeal to a kind of notion of equilibrium. In this sense Hahn and Coats are both perhaps on a correct general path, yet equally they are both mistaken in their precise claims about the history of equilibrium theories.

Hahn and other "Whig historians of economic science,"[3] of course, continue to maintain that the contemporary equilibrium theorist is only "making precise a tradition which is two hundred years old."[4] In what I have said about the notion of self-interest and its role in Smith's economic theory, I surely agree with Hahn's implication that it is a good deal less precise than the marginalist notion of maximization. There is clearly a sense in which it is correct to say that the marginalist notion of maximization is a "making precise" of Smith's notion of self-interest. That claim is correct if by it we mean only that the marginalist notion of maximization is a more precise and legitimate descendant of Smith's notion of self-interest, which has developed through a series of refinements and modifications within a historical tradition of economic theorizing. If, by contrast, we mean by that claim that the marginalist notion of maximization makes precise the notion of self-interest that Smith actually held, but only expressed imprecisely (because he lacked the mathematics for a more precise expression), then Hahn's claim is surely incorrect. It would be incorrect because it would fail to account for the background context of the aims of economic theorizing on which Smith is quite explicit, and on which he quite explicitly differs from the aims espoused by marginalist theorists of a later century. If Hahn's claim is understood in this latter way, then the "Whig history of economic science" that he, Samuelson, and others pursue is "Whiggish" not in an unpejorative sense as claimed by Samuelson,[5] but in the quite pejorative sense that makes historical data almost irrelevant to the history of a science.

We might also remember, in assessing Coats's claim, that Ricardo thought that the natural condition of an economy, even a decentralized one, was not a state of equilibrium, but a state of entropy, with the economy gradually winding down, degenerating into the dreaded "stationary state." Granted, Ricardo did think that a decentralized economy would slow down the entropic process. Perhaps this might be regarded in Ricardo as a kind of bow to equilibrium. Yet there is still a major theoretical difference between a state of equilibrium and a state of slowed entropy.

So, if the continuity in the tradition of mainstream economics dating back to *The Wealth of Nations* does not consist of either the maximizing individual or economic equilibrium, of what does it consist? I think that both Coats and Gordon are quite close to identifying genuine elements of continuity in the economic tradition, even though they do both miss those elements. There are, as I see it, three basic elements of continuity within the economic tradition, two of which were, in greater or lesser degree, less fully operative in the work of Keynes than in the rest of the tradition. These three are: the method of individualistic analysis; postulates of self-interest (the more modest genuine point of continuity that lies behind talk of "maximizing individuals"); and, perhaps as a consequence of the methodological individualism, a commitment to the preferability of nonintentional coordination to intentional coordination of economic activity (likewise, the more modest genuine point of continuity that lies behind talk of "the theory of economic equilibrium"). Ironically, there seems to be no continuity at all in the aims of economics, unless it be in the aim to give a certain general type of explanation. One of my claimed points of continuity has to do with method, the other two with the broad outlines of *theory*.

Methodological individualism. With the exception of the institutionalist tradition descending from the works of Veblen, Commons, and Mitchell, economic theorizing has almost invariably been dominated by methodological individualism. As I mentioned in the last chapter, Keynes did make modest departures from this principle at significant points, yet even he developed the larger part of his theory on the basis of an individualistic analysis. In speaking of methodological individualism, I mean the methodological commitment to the view that "ideal explanations of social phenomena are to be found at an 'individual level' of investigation, concerned with individual human action."[6] There are, of course, a variety of positions that are maintained under the broad rubric of "methodological individualism." The variety of methodological individualism that I wish to identify as one of the abiding features of mainstream economics since Smith, however, is perhaps best characterized by Julius Sensat as the "asocialism" constraint:

If certain beliefs, desires, and actions are the basic constituents of a given institution or social practice, then a subject's having any of those beliefs or desires or performing any of those actions is not by itself a matter of his standing in social relations to other agents.[7]

I take this characterization of methodological individualism to be simply a more careful specification of what I characterized, in connection with my discussion of Keynes in the last chapter, as the view of method that requires economic theory to treat aggregate economic phenomena as simple arithmetic functions of the individuals who make up those aggregates.

The position as it applies in economics may best be summed up by Knight's claim, cited in the last chapter, that "the 'economic man' is not a 'social animal.'" Plato (most conspicuously) and all the premodern social thinkers saw the human being as such a social animal. In their work the human individual is always seen in terms of his or her membership in a human community. Theoretically speaking, the community provides the theoretical framework that shapes the identity of the individual as a part of the theoretical ontology. By contrast, in economic theory the bare individual is the only kind of primitive member of the theoretical ontology. Any reference to economic aggregates treats those aggregates simply as arithmetic functions of the individuals that compose them. The problems introduced by the rise of the managerial corporation are met within the constraints of methodological individualism by simply taking the "firm" as a new kind of individual.

A commitment to methodological individualism, of course, is not at all surprising in a science that came to life in the late eighteenth century. It seems to have been one of the most fundamental intellectual commitments of the classical modern period, whether in Hobbes's politics or in Newton's physics, that respectable analytical work started with the atomic, isolated individual unit and built from there.[8] By the time Smith wrote his *Wealth of Nations*, the success of Newton's physical theory had made the individualistic, atomistic method of analysis almost a mandatory aim of genuinely "scientific" work.

Smith wished to explain "the nature and causes of the wealth of nations." A scientifically minded person of the late eighteenth century would quite naturally be inclined to explain the wealth of nations as a function of the wealth of the individuals that composed the nations. Thus, just as we might see a number of units of physical mass moving in one direction combined into a larger unit of mass moving in the same direction, so Smith saw a collection of individuals each increasing his or her own wealth combined into a larger unit, the nation, working also at increasing its wealth. Given the initial success of Smith's theory – as well as the fact that, prior to Einstein's development of relativistic physics, methodological individualism stood as one of the most basic commitments of science, simply as science – it would have been terribly surprising to see any economic theorist of note depart from methodological individualism before the early part of the twentieth century.

In their treatment of the managerial firm, it is not at all surprising that economic theorists prior to the 1930s attempted to analyze the corporation as a function of the various persons and interests that went into making it. It is also not very surprising that the early attempts to look at the behavior of the firm, as an economic agent in its own right, within the market mechanism simply took the firm to be another individual. The reigning assumptions about scientific method (outside of physics) virtually required it.

In 1905 Albert Einstein's two papers introducing the special theory of relativity brought to respectability in physics the idea of analyzing the physical motion of an individual as in part a function of the placement of that individual within a particular physical system.[9] Old methodological commitments die slowly, but just thirty years later Keynes's *General Theory* brought economics its first flirtation with an analysis that took an aggregative phenomenon as basic. During the years that have followed, his move has surely proven controversial among economists. While the economic community as a whole has surely not rushed to dismiss Keynesian theory on the basis of its modest departure from methodological individualism, there are significant numbers of economists who would wish to do so. Moreover, methodological individualism is so firmly entrenched within the marginalist mode of analysis that even those who are sympathetic to Keynes's general position seem unclear about how to give it theoretical justification.

Lest I give the impression here that methodological individualism is simply a relic from the classical modern period that will be dispensed with as soon as economists discover that relativistic physics is really scientific, I should add that methodological individualism in economics is commonly defended on two different grounds, one of which has to do with scientific justification, the other to do with political ideology. In the first place, a good many economists, particularly those sympathetic to the Chicago tradition, argue that an individualistic mode of analysis is perfectly adequate to deal with the problems with which economic theory is interested. They hold that the purpose of economic theory is not to capture economic reality, but to predict economic phenomena. Just as Newtonian, nonrelativistic physics is perfectly adequate for engineers and billiard players, so an economic theory based on methodological individualism is all that is required for the purposes to which we put economic theory.

Second, political libertarianism, and this is also often associated with the Chicago tradition in economic theory, takes the individual to have a moral priority in all forms of social interaction. Since economic theory deals with social interaction, those economic theorists who are also political libertarians commit themselves to a methodological individualism as a methodological approach that will guarantee that economic systems and policies will honor that basic moral priority of the individual that lies at the basis of their politics. It is important, I should add, that these two lines of defense for methodological individualism not be confused. It is surely not unusual to find one individual who defends methodological individualism, as does Milton Friedman, on both of these bases. Yet clearly the two lines of defense are quite independent of each other.

Self-interest. Economic theory since the time of Smith has always taken economic activity to be based on self-interest. When I first noted this as a point of continuity in the tradition, I stated it as "postulates of self-interest," not "a postulate" or "the postulate of self-interest." My reason for doing so is that while economic theory has always maintained that economic activity is self-interested, the broader contexts within which that claim has been made have differed greatly. Smith, for example, did not claim that all rational human activity is self-interested. In his *Theory of Moral Sentiments* Smith claims that humans are motivated by a kind of "moral sense," which moves us in the direction not only of prudence (pursuit of self-interest), but also of propriety and benevolence. That Smith continued to hold this position even at the time of his publication of *The Wealth of Nations* should be evident from the fact that he also published a revised edition of the *Theory of Moral Sentiments* in 1790, fourteen years after he published *The Wealth of Nations*. Rather, Smith's position is that humans, in their economic productive activity, *generally* act on the basis of self-interest, and moreover that such activity *should* be ruled by self-interest because in that way the general wealth of society is increased, quite apart from any intentions on the part of the individual to increase the general wealth. It should be equally obvious from Marshall's explanation of why corporate managers failed to succumb to the many temptations that beset them that he also saw self-interest as operating in a fairly narrow economic domain.

By contrast, contemporary economic theory, at least in application, tends to see self-interest as something like an assumed universal principle of human motivation. Moreover, self-interested activity has become, with the mathematization of economic theory, maximizing activity. Mainstream contemporary economic theory attributes ordered preferences to individuals and identifies rational activity with choice of the most preferred available option. While this may be in principle consistent with altruistic motivation, in application this model of rationality normally attributes to agents purely self-interested objectives such as the maximization of the agent's consumption bundle. This is not to say that economists really believe that self-interest is the only motivation in real human activity. Rather, self-interest is assumed, for purposes of theory development (again viewing the theory simply as a predictor), as the basis of all rational human activity. This, of course, goes hand in hand with the expansion of the scope of economic activity that I mentioned in the last chapter in my discussion of the Chicago tradition of economic analysis.

Thus, there have been a number of quite different ways in which self-interest has been postulated in the economic tradition since Smith. Yet throughout that tradition, self-interest has continuously played a crucial role and been taken to be the ruling motive in purely economic behavior. Yet this is hardly radical or even novel, for even in Plato's

Republic people of the commercial class were taken to be ruled by their appetites.

Nonintentional coordination. While, as I have already argued, Coats's claim for the continuity of any theory of economic equilibrium is anachronistic at best, I take it that the perfectly legitimate point behind that claim is that there has been a general continuity in the tradition's affirmation of the possibility of nonintentional coordination of economic activity. It is important to recognize this affirmation as far more general than a theory of economic equilibrium. Equilibrium theories assert the possibility of a certain kind of nonintentional co-ordination. They are addressed, as I have already noted, to Jevons's problem. They claim that a free market mechanism, subject to certain constraints, is capable of generating an allocation of resources such that any gain in utility for one consumer or profit for one producer could only be had at the price of some loss for another consumer or producer (Pareto optimality). As Friedman observes:

The possibility of co-ordination through voluntary co-operation rests on the elementary – yet frequently denied – proposition that both parties to an economic transaction benefit from it, *provided the transaction is bi-laterally voluntary and informed.*

Exchange can therefore bring about co-ordination without coercion. A working model of a society organized through voluntary exchange is a *free private enterprise exchange economy* – what we have been calling competitive capitalism. [Friedman's emphases][10]

Few economists, I think, would be prepared to say that a situation of economic equilibrium can *only* be generated through a market mechanism. The notion of equilibrium, as characterized above, is so flexible as to be attainable in a notoriously wide variety of ways. Yet the point of most of the defenders of equilibrium theories is that nonintentional coordination of the economic plans of maximizing individuals and firms *can* be achieved through the market mechanism. This means that the economic objectives characterized by the notion of equilibrium are compatible with a set of political objectives that are embodied in a free market, as opposed to a command economy. Thus, Friedman and a great many economists before him affirm that society can be so arranged as to protect a certain rather narrowly defined conception of human freedom while at the same time accomplishing central objectives of economic efficiency. This, of course, frequently leads these economists to see a very limited role for government in the coordination of economic activity. Keynes and those economists sympathetic to his position constitute a departure, albeit a fairly modest one, from the kind of strong affirmation of the preferability of nonintentional coordination that seems to have been the dominant position among economists since the rise of marginalism.

While the economists about whom I have just been speaking assert the (political) preferability of nonintentional coordination of economic activity through the mechanism of free markets as a way of achieving an optimal allocation of social resources, earlier economists as well as some present-day ones assert the preferability of nonintentional coordination for quite different purposes. Smith, as I have already noted several times, was concerned with the promotion of aggregate national wealth. His now famous claim is,

[The individual] intends only his own gain, and he is in this...led by an invisible hand to promote an end which was no part of his intention.... By pursuing his own interest he frequently promotes that of society more effectually than when he really intends to promote it. I have never known much good done by those who affected to trade for the publick good.[11]

Smith's claim is not, then, that nonintentional coordination is the best way of bringing about an efficient allocation of the resources that society already has. Rather, it is that nonintentional coordination of economic activity is the best way to generate an increase in the aggregate wealth. His primary concern is with production, and he thinks that the presence of elements of command coordination in an economy will tend to decrease aggregate production. Smith, then, sees nonintentional coordination of economic activity as preferable for quite different reasons and for the accomplishment of a quite different end.

It is, I think, important to note at this point that many contemporary economists do also defend nonintentional coordination of economic activity on the grounds of productivity. Yet that defense is theoretically quite independent of one based on efficiency (at least when that is defined in terms of Pareto-optimal allocation). There are many possible changes in economic arrangements that could lead to increased productivity and yet not be Pareto-optimal transitions. Consider an initial state A, in which all the resources of a society are owned by one wealthy family. The laborers are paid very low wages, with no chance for an increase in wages based on increases in productivity. A change to a state B, in which the holdings of the wealthy family were broken up and distributed to the workers, would presumably lead to an increase in production. State B would be one in which increases in production would benefit the laborers, which, according to the standard motivational assumptions of economic theory, would lead them to produce more. Yet clearly the transition from state A to state B

would not be Pareto optimal, since one group of individuals in the society, the initially wealthy family, would find their economic situation worsened by the transition. In fact, given the likely loss of status that such a transition would create for the initially wealthy family, and the cost of compensating them for such a loss, it is entirely possible that the transition from state A to state B would not even be a potential Pareto improvement. Thus, while allocative efficiency is surely related to production, it is still theoretically independent of production. We continue to see two quite different ends for which we might prefer nonintentional coordination of economic activity.

Ricardo, by contrast, saw nonintentional coordination as a preferable means of accomplishing yet a third kind of end. For Ricardo the problem was how to forestall the "stationary state." That could be best accomplished by ensuring a social distribution that would not leave all of society's wealth in the hands of the landowning class, thus leaving nothing left for the laborers and, perhaps more importantly, nothing left with which the capitalist might generate continued investment.

This much should show that some economic theorists have held that nonintentional coordination of economic activity was preferable for distributive purposes, some for productive purposes, and others (generally on political grounds) for purposes of allocative efficiency. While that constitutes a very modest kind of continuity within the tradition of economic theory since Smith, it does, nevertheless, constitute a significant element of continuity. It is, moreover, the element that I think Coats had in mind when speaking of the continuity of "the theory of economic equilibrium via the market mechanism." Beyond these three points of continuity – methodological individualism, postulates of self-interest, and a commitment to the preferability of nonintentional coordination of economic activity – I see no additional elements that could reasonably be taken to provide a common thread in the mainstream economic tradition.

Disagreement

I trust that it is clear from Chapter 3 and what I have just said that there has been a great deal of disagreement within the tradition of economic theory descending from Adam Smith. In the remainder of this chapter I shall largely ignore those changes that occurred at the level of theory content. That is the most obvious level of change and also the level that is most amenable to being viewed as a simple and cumulative story of scientific progress. By contrast, I am more concerned here with those levels of change that generate significant discontinuities, those that create a genuine difference where there is an appearance of surface similarity based on a continued affirmation of the same or similar theoretical propositions, namely, changes in the aims, method, and theoretical ontology of economic science.

Aims. That the aims of economic science have changed since Adam Smith's *Wealth of Nations* should be apparent on even a fairly casual reading of the great works in economic theory to have been written since that book. Smith, of course, gave his chief aim in his title, the concern to identify the causes of national wealth. Smith, Ricardo, and Mill were not, as we have seen, concerned to explain the same thing. Smith was concerned to explain the production of national wealth. Ricardo, by contrast, had a preoccupying concern with explaining the laws of distribution, which is quite lacking in Smith. Mill, in a sense bringing together the notions of his two great predecessors, was concerned with the laws of both production and distribution.

Yet Smith, Ricardo, and Mill did at least share a common notion of what it is to explain. They all saw economic phenomena as governed by causal laws of nature, much as physical motion is governed by causal laws of nature. For Mill, as we saw in the last chapter, the laws governing distribution were in part the product of human institution, yet even these laws were in large measure the product of nature. The three great classical economists were of one mind in seeing the aim of economic science as the discovery of the natural laws governing the phenomena they wished to explain. Their concern to uncover the actual laws by which nature governs human efforts at production and distribution was very different from the more modern concern purely with prediction.

With Jevons came at least one major change in the aim of economic science. The explanation of production and distribution became at best secondary to that of allocation. I hope that this particularly major change in aim is already clear from my previous discussion of economic equilibrium.

Yet even with this change, the understanding of the early marginalists of explanation as nomological seemed not to change greatly. Clark, for example, continued to speak very explicitly of the "natural laws" governing "the creation and use of wealth."

Clearly the most significant change in what economic theorists took as the central aim of their scientific work came with the Chicago economists. On the one hand, we see the expansion of the scope of economic science, starting in one phase of Knight's work, to bring within its ambit "all practically real problems," his view that all problems of human behavior are really, in one aspect, economic problems.

A second novel element in the Chicago tradition's views on the aims of economic science was the replacement of causal explanation by prediction as the chief aim of science. Knight's work lacks talk of natural laws. Moreover, what he does say about the aims of science suggests that natural laws are simply no longer of interest to the scientist. One has the clear impression in Knight's work, and even more clearly in that of Friedman, that if the predictions turn out right, nomological structure is of absolutely no interest, much as Friedman claims very explicitly that the truth of the assumptions by which the predictions are generated is of absolutely no interest.[12]

In addition to these major shifts in aim, there have also been shifts in some of the subsidiary aims of economic theorizing. I noted above and in Chapter 2 that scientists sometimes give up a certain type of explanation as one of their aims. For most of its life the economic tradition has taken it as a very fundamental aim to explain the behavior of economic aggregates as functions of the behavior of the individuals that compose those aggregates. As I noted, this is clearly an aim that economic theorists inherited from the general intellectual agenda of the classical modern period. The theory of Keynes, of course, abandoned this aim to some extent. Yet it is abundantly clear that at least a large part of the economic profession at present continues to hold atomistic, individualistic explanation as a central aim of scientific theorizing in economics.

Finally, I would note the extent to which mathematization of economic theory became an important theoretical aim in economics from the time of Jevons and Walras. I noted in the last chapter Jevons's claim that "economy, if it is to be a science at all, must be a mathematical science." This constituted not simply a new development in the area of method, but a modification in the economic theorist's notion of what economic science was about, thus a change in the aim of their work.

Method. In talking about changes in the aims of economic science I have already noted some changes in method. This should hardly be surprising. As should now be abundantly clear, it frequently happens in science that the pursuit of a particular set of methods comes to be elevated to the status of a fundamental aim of science, simply as science. Thus, we have already seen the mathematization of economic theory that came with the rise of marginal analysis. Similarly, we have already seen the methodological move to theory assessment solely in terms of predictive power. Also we have noted the Keynesian softening of methodological individualism.

There is, however, one other important change in economic theorists' views on method that I shall identify. This change seems to originate in the work of Mill and achieves perhaps its culminating expression with Jevons. Among those who did significant work in the development of economic theory, Mill and Jevons also wrote extensively on issues of scientific method in general. Mill, like most of the classical modern theorists before him, thought that scientific method was fundamentally inductivist. In his *System of Logic*[13] Mill tried, among other things, to lay down definitively the principles of inductive reasoning that he thought underlie science. To this day most introductory logic texts give some exposition of "Mill's method." Jevons, by contrast, was a critic of Mill's inductivism, advocating instead a hypothetico-deductive view of scientific method. Jevons claimed that science started out with hypotheses from which it then proceeded to deduce consequences. These consequences, then, were subject to either confirmation or refutation.[14]

Mill and Jevons both, however, saw political economy, or economics, as operating by a different method from the physical sciences. They both claimed that the method of their science was fundamentally deductive. For Mill this arises from his understanding of political economy as a "moral or mental science." Perhaps his clearest exposition of his views on the method of political economy is given in his 1836 essay, "On the Definition of Political Economy and on the Method of Investigation Proper to It."[15] In that essay Mill gives the following characterization of political economy:

The laws of the production of the objects which constitute wealth, are the subject-matter both of Political Economy and of almost all the physical sciences. Such, however, of those laws as are purely laws of matter, belong to physical science, and to that exclusively. Such of them as are laws of the human mind, and no others, belong to Political Economy, which finally sums up the result of both combined.[16]

These laws of the human mind are deducible from the most fundamental law of mind, "that man desires to possess subsistence, and consequently wills the necessary means of procuring it."[17] For this reason, then, Mill concludes that "we have characterized [the science of political economy] as essentially an *abstract* science, and its method as the method *a priori*" (Mill's emphases).[18]

In the introduction to *The Theory of Political Economy* Jevons gives a strong general endorsement of Mill's view of method in political economy:

The science of Economics, however, is in some degree peculiar, owing to the fact, pointed out by J. S. Mill and Cairnes, that its ultimate laws are known to us immediately by intuition, or, at any rate, they are furnished to us ready made by other mental or physical sciences.... From these axioms we can deduce the laws of supply and demand, the laws of that difficult conception, value, and all the intricate results of commerce, so far as data are available. The final agreement of our inferences with *a posteriori* observations ratifies our method. But unfortunately this verification is often the least satisfactory part of the process.[19]

This view of the science of economics is reflected neatly in the opening lines of Jevons's *Theory:*

The science of Political Economy rests upon a few notions of an apparently simple character. Utility, value, labour, land, capital, are the elements of the subject; and whoever has a thorough comprehension of their nature, must possess or be soon able to acquire a knowledge of the whole science.[20]

It is, of course, worth noting that among the "inferences" that follow from the comprehension of those concepts will be a collection of predictions about economic behavior. In this sense, Jevons's introduction of a deductive methodology into economic science may be viewed as a step toward the instrumentalism of Friedman. Yet I would hasten to point out that Jevons's position does not imply Friedman's. Jevons's "inferences" clearly include Friedman's predictions, but the predictions of a theory form only a fairly small subset of the total set of consequences. Moreover, as Jevons notes, he views the agreement of those inferences with our experience as "often the least satisfactory part of the process." Thus it would be quite illegitimate for some methodological follower of Friedman, for example, to claim that his or her position was simply following in the tradition of Jevons.

Theoretical ontology. I trust that the fact that there has been a significant change in economic theory at this level since the publication of *The Wealth of Nations* was made adequately clear in Chapter 1. Clearly at the purely formal level, methodological individualism has been one of the constants in mainline economic theory. Purely at the level of formal structure, economic theory has only included one type of entity, the individual. As should be clear from the last chapter, Keynes and those economists who follow in his tradition constitute the only significant departure from this position within the main stream of development. (I am, of course, identifying the institutionalist tradition here as outside that main stream of development.)

Yet as I argued at some length in Chapter 1, the continuity of a single-sorted or single-type economic theory, a theory whose formal structure draws no distinctions among different types of entities about which predication may be made within the theory, really only tends to hide a discontinuity of great proportions. Once we move to look at the interpretation of the formal theory we see that the development of the modern theory of the firm generated a change in the domain of the theory. Originally the domain of the theory was composed of flesh-and-blood human economic agents. This theoretical domain remained constant from the time of Smith throughout the nineteenth century. As I noted in the last chapter, Marshall and even Clark generally maintained a theoretical ontology of human individuals, although Clark departs from this to some extent in his analysis of "factoral" distribution and Marshall in his talk of "the representative firm." Clark did recognize that the managerial corporation seemed to constitute something entirely different from genuine biological individuals, and that recognition posed to him a threat to all of economic theory, "vitiating the action of economic laws."

By the time we find Robinson writing in 1933, however, the domain has been expanded to include firms. Knight speaks of firms, individuals, and families. At present we find economic theory having a domain that includes idealized biological individuals, families, households, and firms. Together they comprise the domain of individual entities about which economic theory makes its various claims. While we may be able to recognize firms, households, families, and individual humans as different kinds or types of entities, economic theory has no mechanism within its formal structure that allows for distinguishing different types. They are all simply "individuals."

Obviously there is debate over whether this lack of differentiation constitutes a problem, either in the theory of the firm or in any other area of economic theory. That debate, however, must be postponed for later chapters. At present what I am concerned to have shown is that there has been a genuine and significant change in the domain of economic theory, and that, as a result, we cannot accept the claim that economists are really dealing with the *same* theory that has been with us since *The Wealth of Nations*.

Conclusion

There have been profound and fundamental changes in economic science at virtually every level since Adam Smith wrote *The Wealth of Nations*. Yet there has also been some significant continuity within the main stream of economic thought, which I have argued has tended to be both overstated and misunderstood. There has been a pervasive tendency among a number of economists to view particularly their earlier predecessors through mid-to-late-twentieth-century-colored glasses. Yet to understand correctly the sense of tradition within the community of economists, it is important to identify both what the continuities have been and what they have not been.

While Gordon's "maximizing individual in a relatively free market" was not, as I have argued, Smith's postulate, it surely does have an ancestry in Smith's work. Moreover, that maximizing individual is clearly a central postulate in much of present-day economic theory, in particular in the marginalist theory of the firm. In that theoretical context there are interesting questions to be raised about whether we can reasonably speak both about maximizing activity and about the firm as an individual. In the next chapters I shall explore some of these questions. In the present chapter I hope to have cleared some of the ground necessary for that exploration by showing that the marginalist's current understanding of the firm does not have the kind of eternal, or even traditional, aura that economists often see it as having.

CHAPTER 5

Theories of the firm

One of the classic, and at the same time most modest, defenses of the reigning economic theory of the firm was Fritz Machlup's 1966 presidential address to the American Economic Association bearing the title "Theories of the Firm: Marginalist, Behavioral, Managerial." While any classification of theories of the firm into a few basic types will have some tendency toward artificiality, Machlup's division into these categories does succeed in drawing important distinctions. Moreover, that division seems to have come to be quite widely followed in subsequent discussion.

The reigning economic theory of the firm that Machlup defended in his address is, of course, a marginalist theory, which, of course, can be modified to give other variants. Behavioral theories of the firm are those that reject the maximization assumptions of marginal analysis and, as Machlup states it, "*observe* [Machlup's emphasis] how businessmen really act and by what processes they reach decisions."[1] Managerial theories, by contrast, take as their point of departure the separation of stock ownership and corporate control in the modern managerial corporation. These theories take very seriously the differences between the interests of stockholders and managers within a corporation. Moreover, the managerial theories recognize that modern managerial corporations frequently operate in imperfectly competitive markets, markets in which they have some substantial degree of control over prices. Because of these factors, they see the corporation as aiming at essentially managerial, rather than entrepreneurial goals, while nevertheless analyzing managerial activity on what are substantially marginalist behavioral assumptions.

In this chapter I shall follow Machlup's division of the three types of theories of the firm. My major concern will be to get clear on the core of the marginalist approach to a theory of the firm, particularly the narrowest, most traditional form of that theory that Machlup defends in his address. I shall also be concerned to lay out the basic directions in which behavioral and managerial theories proceed. Theory assessment is, by its nature, a process of comparison. Whatever strengths and weaknesses the marginalist approach to the firm has, both are best understood in the context of the comparisons among the marginalist approach and its chief theoretical competitors, which at this point in history are behavioral and managerial approaches. I shall not, at least explicitly, pursue such an assessment in this chapter. That task will be left for the remaining three chapters.

Marginalist theories

In the last chapter I argued that Gordon's claim that the "postulate of the maximizing individual in a relatively free market" has not been central to economic theory since Adam Smith. It has, however, constituted the most fundamental core of marginalist economic theory. As I noted in Chapter 3, one of the major developments within the marginalist tradition was the decision, which apparently by the mid-1930s had achieved the status of consensus, to treat the firm, whatever kind of firm it may happen to be, simply as an individual. If we take the firm to be an individual and then ask what it maximizes, profit would seem at least to be a reasonable first answer. The firm is a producer only, not a consumer. Thus it would seem inappropriate to speak of it as maximizing satisfaction in the manner in which consumers are supposed to maximize satisfaction. Since profit is the benefit the firm receives in return for its product once the expenses of production are subtracted, it would appear that the natural way of applying the fundamental economic assumption of self-interest to the firm would be to view it as a maximizer of profit.

The view of the firm as an individual that maximizes money profits is the form of marginalist theory that Machlup defends. I shall henceforth refer to that form as the "neoclassical" theory of the firm. It is surely important to note in passing that there have been marginalist theories of the firm that have seen the firm as maximizing things other than profits. In "Some Basic Problems in the Theory of the Firm" Andreas Papandreou, for example, suggests that profit maximization be replaced in the marginalist theory of the firm by "general preference-function maximization."[2] Machlup rejects this as well as a host of other possible "maximanda" as vehicles for altering the neoclassical theory.[3] Likewise, another version of marginalist theory of the firm, one about which I shall have more to say in Chapter 6, is the "set-of-contracts" view of the firm, according to which the corporation itself is seen as reducible to a set of contracts among the various parties that jointly make it up. While it is thus clearly possible, and perhaps sometimes desirable for the analysis of particular problems,[4] to develop varieties of extended marginalist analysis of the firm, the neoclassical version of marginalist theory continues to reign in the field of economics. For this reason I shall attend to it, and not any of its various extensions, in this exposition.

The neoclassical theory of the firm starts out with the claim that all firms are created and owned by individuals. While it is surely an obvious truth that all firms are created by individuals, with the help of a legal structure that makes incorporation possible, it is, as we shall see later, much more controversial to claim that all firms are owned by individuals. It is, in fact, controversial to claim that corporations are owned at all. Nevertheless, it is precisely this claim that corporations are owned by individuals, whether one individual, as in the case of the small owner-operated firm, or a vast number of individuals, as the theory claims to be the case with large managerial corporations of highly dispersed stock ownership, that allows for the assimilation of the notion of the firm to the notion of the entrepreneur, as noted by Papandreou, cited in Chapter 1. This assimilation, along with the assumption that individuals maximize their subjective utility, give the neoclassical theory of the firm its central assumption: Firms act in such a manner as to maximize money profits over some given period of time.

In fact, of course, relatively few economists would claim that firms actually attempt to maximize profits. The claim that they do so is simply a "partial truth" or an analytical claim that serves as a useful approximation to actual firm behavior. Nevertheless, the neoclassical theory of the firm is committed to the claim that the profit-maximization assumption provides a very powerful explanatory concept. Therefore, the "firm" of the theory comes to be an idealization, a producer or supplier of goods or services that engages in its economic activity in such a way as to maximize money profits. This goal of profit maximization will enter into every decision made by the firm.

The first interesting result that follows from the assumption of profit maximization is that the firm (the analytical firm of the theory, of course) will carry out its production up to that point at which marginal revenue equals marginal costs, that is, up to the point where the additional cost of inputs into the process of production will be greater than the additional revenue that it generates. The levels of production of all the firms producing a given commodity taken together constitute the total supply of that commodity.

The consumer counterpart to the profit-maximizing firm, of course, is the utility-maximizing individual. For any given commodity, each consumer has a level of demand relative to the price of that commodity. We see here two interesting facts. For every consumer there is a level of demand relative to price, and for every firm there is a level of production relative to price. If we take the total demand and the total supply for any given commodity, the neoclassical theory will give us a unique price at which supply and demand are equal. This is the equilibrium point. It will turn out that in a fully competitive industry, the total production of that industry will reach exactly the point of equilibrium, and that industry will automatically produce at the lowest possible total cost. Perhaps the crowning achievement of the neoclassical theory of the firm, given by a general equilibrium analysis, is that even given the mutual effects that various markets have on each other, a competitive equilibrium market structure generates a Pareto-optimal allocation of goods and services in society.

The neoclassical theory of the firm, of course, produces a considerable variety of more particular results. Yet I trust that the foregoing paragraphs will give the reader a fair taste of the general thrust of the theory.

The neoclassical theory of the firm, then, takes as its starting assumption the claim that the firm maximizes its profits in an effectively competitive market. At first blush this sounds simple enough, and my experience in teaching tells me that sophomores around the country really believe that this is what firms do. Yet of course, if we look at the actual behavior of firms of all shapes and sizes we see that the neoclassical starting assumption is patently absurd. In small firms, such as the traditional "corner grocery," we clearly see the firm sacrificing profits that might accrue to it for the sake of being a good neighbor, improving the appearance of the community, helping out the local Little League baseball program, and so on. The corner grocer doesn't sit down with his or her calculator and figure out whether such behavior will contribute to short- or long-range profits. Rather, the grocer simply sees such behavior as a part of membership in a broader community. Large firms seem likewise to engage in such "neighborly" behavior not infrequently, again apparently without questioning carefully whether it will contribute to short- or long-range profits. Yet we also, by contrast, frequently see in large firms managers giving themselves huge bonuses. In the vast majority of cases these bonuses could not be justified as leading to long-range maximum profits, while they clearly reduce short-range profits. Rather, they simply reflect the power of the managers within the firm to advance their own private interests at the expense of other interests within the firm.

Moreover, one of the most pervasive phenomena facing firms in the real world is uncertainty. We might well suppose that given our limited knowledge in the face of uncertainty, firms might well *try* to maximize profits, but surely they should seldom actually succeed in doing so. Or perhaps the uncertainty places firms in a position where they cannot even identify a position of maximum profits, given all the various foreseen and unforeseen possibilities facing them, and so they don't even *try* to maximize profits, but instead set for themselves more modest goals. Finally, everyone who has telephone or electric service knows that a number of real-world markets are not effectively competitive.

Clearly the economic defenders of the neoclassical theory are not blind to all these facts, as my sophomores sometimes appear to be. The firm of neoclassical theory is not supposed to be a portrayal of actual business firms in the world in which we all live. Machlup is very explicit on this point:

The model of the firm in that theory is not, as so many writers believe, designed to serve to explain and predict the behavior of real firms; instead it is designed to explain and predict changes in observed prices (quoted, paid, received) as effects of particular changes in conditions (wage rates, interest rates, import duties, excise taxes, technology, etc.). In this causal connection the firm is only a theoretical link, a mental construct helping to explain how one gets from the cause to the effect. This is altogether different from explaining the behavior of a firm.[5]

Given this understanding of what the firm is in the neoclassical theory of the firm, the matter is not nearly so simple as it sounded initially, nor is it obviously falsified by what we all observe of businesses in the real world.

Three things are, I think, important to be clear on if we are to understand the neoclassical theory of the firm: (1) What is it supposed to explain? (2) What is it taken to explain that it is not intended to explain? (3) What does it take to count either for or against its own acceptability?

As Machlup tells us, the neoclassical theory is supposed to "predict changes in observed prices . . . as effects of particular changes in conditions." It is, of course, a theory about microeconomic phenomena. Alexander Rosenberg has argued: "There is reason *not* to suppose that [micro]economic general statements are all, covertly or overtly, statements about average individuals and/or whole aggregates of individuals. Rather, it seems patent that they are about what they appear to be about: individuals."[6] If Rosenberg is right, then it would appear that the neoclassical theory should predict that if the minimum wage is increased and if my local supermarket pays its stock personnel at the minimum wage, then I should pay more for my groceries.

Yet again Machlup claims that this kind of prediction is not forth-coming from the neoclassical theory:

Let us again pose four typical questions and see which of them we might expect to answer with the aid of "price theory." (1) What will be the price of cotton textiles? (2) What prices will the X Corporation charge? (3) How will the prices of cotton textiles be affected by an increase in wage rates? (4) How will the X Corporation change its prices when wage rates are increased?

Conventional price theory is not equipped to answer any but the third question; it may perhaps also suggest a rebuttable answer to the fourth question.[7]

Thus, the neoclassical theory should lead me to suspect that my local supermarket might increase its prices if the minimum wage is increased, but the only thing that I could actually predict with any confidence on the basis of that theory would be that grocery prices should go up in the aggregate, but not the amount of that aggregate increase. Machlup notes that the price theory that is built up from the neoclassical theory of the firm is concerned with only the direction, not the magnitude of change.[8]

We see, then, that the neoclassical theory of the firm sets for itself a very modest explanatory agenda. It is designed to predict how certain kinds of changes in the economic environment will affect aggregate or average prices in a given industry. It is, if we are to take Machlup's defense seriously, not designed to offer advice to business people on how to operate firms in the real economic world. It is also not designed to give us a prescriptive view of the "proper" role of business in society. After listing ten different concepts of the firm, Machlup concludes that

this exercise should have succeeded in showing how ludicrous the efforts of some writers are to attempt *one* definition of *the* firm as used in economic analysis, or to make statements supposedly true of "the" firm, or of "its" behavior, or what not. Scholars ought to be aware of equivocations and should not be snared by them.[9]

It seems fairly general that theories are defended in their most modest forms – narrowly circumscribed to protect them from the pitfalls that beset broad application – yet in less defended moments they go on to receive such broad application while their pitfalls, which defenders took such pains to avoid, are blithely ignored. The neoclassical theory of the firm is surely not the only theory of which this is true. Machlup's is a typical *defense* of the neoclassical theory. He delineates the range of the theory's applicability very carefully to avoid extensions that will lead it into absurdity. Others less careful than

Machlup have one moment given precisely the kind of defense of the theory given by Machlup, and the next moment boldly gone where their defense claimed the theory should not have gone.

Machlup's careful denial of any resemblance between the "firm" of the neoclassical theory and firms of the real world is seldom explicitly and forcefully noted in the introductory economic textbooks where students of business administration learn the modest bits of economic theory that are required for degrees in business administration. The more common portrayal of the relation between the theory's firm and the world's firms is like that of Joan Robinson, cited in Chapter 3: "A *firm* is a concern very similar to the firms in the real world." If Machlup is right about the explanatory purposes of the neoclassical theory of the firm and the purely theoretical character of its central concept, then such a presentation is surely likely to mislead prospective managers by giving them a wholly inappropriate picture of the ways in which real firms operate.

One of the most flagrant examples of this common tendency to see the relationship between the firm of the neoclassical theory and firms in the real world as more than it really is lies in the area of business ethics, and in particular in the position of Milton Friedman. In *Capitalism and Freedom* Friedman makes the following claim:

The view has been gaining widespread acceptance that corporate officials and labor leaders have a "social responsibility" that goes beyond serving the interests of their stockholders or their members. This view shows a fundamental misconception of the character and nature of a free economy. In such an economy, there is one and only one social responsibility of business – to use its resources and engage in activities designed to increase its profits so long as it stays within the rules of the game, which is to say, engages in open and free competition, without deception or fraud.[10]

Friedman goes on to cite Adam Smith's famous "invisible hand" passage and argues that if society permits the firm to become something other than a profits maximizer, it will constitute a strike against the kind of freedom that Friedman sees as essential to a market economy. In short he is maintaining that the view of the firm as a profit maximizer should serve as a guide for public policy and social attitudes toward corporate governance, as well as a guide for individual firm decision making. This goes a very large step beyond Machlup's claim that such an understanding of the firm is useful only for making predictions about aggregate pricing trends.

If Friedman has shown that there is a "fundamental misconception," it seems that he has best shown that he, himself, has it and that it is a "fundamental misconception of the character and nature of" the neoclassical theory of the firm. He has taken a notion of the firm that, when it is carefully defended, is simply a heuristic construct within a tightly limited predictive construct and turned it into a normative ideal for firms and for society generally in the real world.

Whatever one may want to say in the end about the legitimacy of the neoclassical theory of the firm, one unfortunate fact is abundantly clear. The notion of the firm that forms the core of the neoclassical theory has shown a remarkable capacity to escape the constraints that careful defenders of the neoclassical theory, like Machlup, have set for it. The neoclassical theory must, as an absolute precondition for its scientific acceptability, either answer the criticisms that are leveled at its core notion of the firm when it is used as a model for real-world firm behavior, or else do a much better job of protecting society, especially businesspeople and students of business, from the misunderstandings created by those admittedly inappropriate extensions.

The final point I want to raise concerning the neoclassical theory of the firm is about justification, what is to count either for or against the rational acceptability of that theory. As I have already noted, Machlup and a host of others have gone to considerable lengths to make it clear that the actual behavior of business firms in the real world has very little to do with the neoclassical theory. Thus, empirical investigation of firm behavior in the real world cannot, according to the defenders of the neoclassical theory, falsify the theory or in any other way count against it. Evidence that firms do not behave in a profit-maximizing manner might lead one to say that the neoclassical theory fails to explain something that one would like to see explained; but, since the theory isn't (supposed to be) addressed to that set of problems, its failure to explain them surely cannot lead us to conclude that it explains badly what it is intended to explain.

What does count for or against the neoclassical theory of the firm, in the eyes of its defenders, is the aggregate behavior of prices. It is perhaps something of a misnomer to speak of the neoclassical theory of the firm as a theory *of the firm*. It is really not a theory of the firm, but a theory of prices. Machlup does, of course, specifically refer to it at points of his defense as a "price theory." Yet whether the neoclassical theory is well named or not is, in the end, of relatively little consequence. The key issue is whether it is good theory. Its defenders would have the entire issue of justification turn on its capacity to predict aggregate directional trends in pricing. As I shall argue in the next chapter, this is an inappropriately narrow placement of the justificatory issue, which should take a wider set of concerns into account, if for no other reason, because in fact a wider set of concerns actually does come into play within the standard applications of neoclassical theory. Because of this, in my assessment of the neoclassical theory of the firm in Chapter 6, I shall look at some of these broader issues while at the same time attending to the theory's predictive record.

Behavioral theories

Behavioral theories of the firm are strikingly different from marginalist theories of the firm, so different, in fact, that it seems strange that they should both be called theories of the firm. As I previously noted, marginalist theories of the firm are basically price theories. They purport to enable the theorist to predict aggregate directional pricing trends. Behavioral theories of the firm, by contrast, are theories of corporate decision making, although because of that they also generate an analysis of price as well. It is frankly surprising that behavioral theories of the firm and marginalist theories of the firm are usually regarded as competing theories, since they clearly do not purport to explain the same set of phenomena. They simply are not theories *about* the same thing. Yet as Machlup's title illustrates, and as is quite clear from the general discussion, these two types of theory are generally viewed as competing theories.

The first major difference between marginalist and behavioral theories of the firm lies in the area of method, the marginalist approach being deductive, the behavioral approach being inductive. The neoclassical theory of the firm is, or course, simply one of the phases of the more general marginalist program of economic analysis. It posits the firm as an individual maximizing economic agent and then looks to see what consequences follow from that assumption. Yet restricting its methodological scope even more, it goes on to stipulate that not all of the consequences of the assumption of the firm as an individual maximizing agent are to count as a part of the theory, rather only those that predict aggregate directional changes in price. To be a bit crude, one might say that the marginalist approach is to insert the firm-as-profit-maximizer assumption into the theory grinder, turn the handle, and then trim the rough edges off whatever comes out so that it will fit (ignore those predictions that go beyond aggregate directional changes in price).

By contrast, the behavioral approach starts by attempting, as I quoted Machlup at the beginning of the chapter, "to *observe* how businessmen really act and by what processes they reach decisions." The idea is that by observing a wide variety of instances of business decision-making behavior, the researcher may be able to detect certain basic patterns or processes of decision making. By understanding the basic processes at work, we may presumably be better equipped to develop public policy affecting corporate governance and may help business people and students of business to see what kinds of decision-making strategies work to what ends in the business world. Yet as we might expect, an unabashed inductivism tends to give very little clear direction to the process of theory formation. Again to be a bit crude, the behavioral approach is a bit like asking a medical researcher to look into some human bodies and tell us "what's going on in there."

An obvious corollary to this difference in view of method is a difference in what the behavioral theorist takes to count for or against a behavioral theory of the firm. In the first place, the behavioral theorist will be concerned with a broader range of predictions. Since a behavioral theory of the firm is not simply a price theory, it follows that predictions other than those about aggregate directional changes in price will serve as tests for the theory. The behavioral theorist, then, is also concerned about the theory's ability to account for the actual decisions made by decision makers in real-world business corporations. Yet because the behavioral theorist is concerned not simply with the outcome of the decision process, but with the process as well, it is important to the behavioral theorist that interviewed businesspersons see their decision-making processes along much the same lines as the theory views them. Behavioral theories, unlike their marginalist counterparts, are concerned with the accuracy of their "picture" of the managerial process.

When we move beyond the level of method and justification, the central difference in substantive theory between marginalists and behavioral theorists seems to concern the relationship between the firm and its economic environment. A central premise of the marginalist theory of the firm is what Spiro Latsis calls "situational determinism,"[11] the view that the behavior of the firm is determined by the objective constraints of its economic environment (competition, demand, etc.), rather than by any conscious set of internal decisions. By contrast, the behavioral theorist holds a distinctly different position, best summed up in Cyert and March's *A Behavioral Theory of the Firm:*

The modern "representative firm" is a large, complex organization. Its major functions are performed by different divisions more or less coordinated by a set of control procedures. It ordinarily produces many products, buys and sells in many different markets. Within the firm, information is generated and processed, decisions are made, results are evaluated, and procedures are changed. The external environment of the firm consists, in part, of other firms with comparable characteristics. If the market completely determined the firm's economic behavior [as it is taken to by the marginalist], these internal attributes would be little more than irrelevant artifacts [as the marginalist takes them to be]. But the market is neither so pervasive nor so straightforward. The modern firm has some control over the market; it has discretion within the market; it sees the market through an organizational filter.[12]

For the behavioral theorist, these various processes that go on and are coordinated within the firm are among the fundamental determinants of firm behavior, including its pricing behavior. Thus, a behavioral theory of the firm is committed to analyzing these processes and their coordination. Because of this, theories of decision making drawn from both psychology and sociology have a relevance for the behavioral theorist that they clearly do not have for the marginalist. Not only is the process of individual goal formation important, but so is the process of group goal formation. Coalition formation, bargaining, subgroup identification, and so on are all parts of this process of forming goals at the organizational level, and hence are of interest in behavioral theories of the firm. If it may be more appropriate to call the neoclassical theory of the firm a "price theory," it may equally be more appropriate to call the behavioral approach to the firm "organizational analysis."

With this far more fluid and organizational view of the firm, profit maximization is the first thing to go. Because of the fluid situation of the firm – taking seriously the context of uncertainties within which firms operate in the real world – profit maximizing ceases to be a possible goal. Herbert Simon in particular has noted that the context of corporate decision making is characterized by a limited or "bounded rationality"[13] and by major lacunae in the corporation's knowledge of the relevant factors in its economic environment, rather than by the marginalist's assumptions of perfect rationality and complete knowledge. The firm in such a condition of uncertainty may well not know what course would produce maximum profits. Even if that course should be hit upon, the firm could never *know* that some alternative course might not have produced even higher profits.

Moreover, because of the institutional and collective character of the corporation, profit maximizing ceases to be a motivated goal for the firm. Corporate goals are, by the nature of the corporation, collective goals. Given the often conflicting variety of concerns that motivate the various people and groups that make up the corporation, it is clearly implausible to think that profits, perhaps the primary goal of the shareholders (one of the least powerful groups within the corporation), should prove a dominating goal in the determination of corporate behavior. Even if the stockholders were the only, or at least the decisive, determinants of corporate goals, differences among the time frames over which the stockholders are concerned to generate returns would make talk of profit maximization inappropriate. The stockholder whose interest is short-term return in the context of a corporate takeover threat will have very different interests than the stockholder whose investment concern is to finance his ten-year-old daughter's college education.

What is left in place of profit maximization is the need to mediate the various goals that are involved within the organization in such a way as to keep the various people and groups within the corporation generally satisfied. Profits are not maximized. Rather, to use a term brought into currency by Simon, they are "satisficed,"[14] kept at a level that will keep current and prospective stockholders satisfied.

While the notion of satisficing is not amenable to the kind of neat mathematical analysis that has helped to make maximization such a popular goal, the behavioral theorists have not purchased their increased contact with the firms of the real world at the expense of mathematical rigor and sophistication. In particular, the immense developments in the field of artificial intelligence have made it possible for behavioral theorists to develop a wide variety of computer simulations of various decision-making strategies. If indeed rigor can be identified with the use of formalism, the behavior theorists of the firm have been quite as rigorous as the marginalists.

To date the behavioral theorists have produced very interesting managerial models and have had a significant impact in the teaching of business management. What remains to be seen, I think, is whether the very heavy reliance on an inductivist methodology will prevent those who work with these managerial models from ever advancing to the level of full-fledged theory.

Managerial theories

Managerial theories of the firm are at the same time significantly similar to and significantly different from behavioral theories. They are alike in two particularly important ways. First, managerial theories and behavioral theories of the firm share a common rejection of situational determinism. Both of them take it as an importantly given fact that firms operate in an environment that places constraints upon their behavior, but that still leaves room for what Cyert and March spoke of as "discretion within the market." As a second point, both managerial and behavioral theories of the firm take as a central part of their task the explanation of the behavior of business firms, not simply the behavior of aggregate prices. Thus, managerial and behavioral theories are at least *about the same thing* in the sense that both of them set for themselves a broader explanatory project than that set by marginalist theories.

The differences between managerial and behavioral theories of the firm are likewise twofold. At the level of aim, managerial theories are not concerned to picture the actual process by which firms reach decisions. They are vitally concerned with the conflicts of interests and aims that beset corporate decision making, but their main point of focus is not on the process by which such conflicts get resolved, but rather on the character of the conflicting goals and interests themselves, what Oliver Williamson calls a "realism in motivation" rather than a "realism in process."[15] This leads to the second point of difference, one that appears at the level of method. Managerial theories of the firm are not as rigidly inductivist as are the behavioral. They start out not with a massive observation of selected business decisions, but with an examination of the "respects [in which] managers may be motivated to attend to other-than-profit goals."[16]

The managerial approach to the firm is far closer to the marginalist analysis than is the behavioral approach. Managerialism, as I noted above, avoids the kind of naive inductivism that dominates the behavioral program. Managerialism, unlike the behavioral approach, is at least arguably a more faithful extension of the kinds of observations made by both Mill and Marshall about the managerial corporation than is the present-day marginalist approach to the firm. Managerialism starts out with one of the basic assumptions that has remained constant within the economic tradition since Smith, the claim that economic agents are generally self-interested. The managerialist then goes on in a very traditional manner to see what follows from this postulate of self-interest. The central difference between the managerial and the marginalist theories of the firm lies in the managerialist's treatment of the firm as an organizational collective under the control of a distinctive managerial group with a distinctive managerial interest, by contrast with the marginalist's treatment of the firm as a simple economic individual with a simple entrepreneurial self-interest (profit).

Again I think it is important to point out that the claim that economic agents are generally self-interested does not imply the additional claim that a number of contemporary economist would add to it, namely, that all human behavior is basically economic, and hence that all human behavior is egoistically motivated. Rather, the claim that economic agents are generally self-interested is one that has had wide acceptance even beyond the economic tradition. In Plato's discussion, in *The Republic,* of the living conditions of the rulers of his ideal state, he shows a strong concern to insulate those rulers from the economic life of the community. They are not to own property or to deal in trade. Plato's arguments for these restrictions seem to hinge on the assumption that economic activity is generally self-interested. Thus, one important means of ensuring that rulers will rule for the best interest of the community, and not in their own self-interest, is to insulate them from individual economic activity.[17]

In the initial chapter of *The Economics of Discretionary Behavior,* Williamson tells his reader that his "analysis centers attention on the discretionary behavior of managers in their operation of the business firm."[18] In this Williamson identifies both of the major points at which his managerial theory of the firm differs from the neoclassical theory of the firm. The first point of departure, as I noted, lies in the managerialist's rejection, in common with the behavioral approach, of situational determinism. While the neoclassical theorist argues that such situational imperfections as uncertainty, monopoly and oligopoly, and so on are predictively insignificant for the economic theorist, the managerial theorist sees them as significant and *theoretically important* facts about the economic world. They are theoretically important because they make room for discretionary behavior on the part of the firm, which, in the areas of pricing and otherwise, is not determined exclusively by situational constraints of the market. Rather, those constraints are sufficiently loose that firms must make decisions about how they will behave, and those decisions must invariably involve discretionary responses in anticipation of the behavior of significant competitors in the market, as well as a host of other uncertain factors.

The second point of the managerialist's departure from the neoclassical theory of the firm lies in the recognition that firms are operated by salaried managers. In Chapter 1 I noted that the conflicts of interest generated by the separation of stock ownership from business control within the managerial firm were quite clearly recognized in the history of economic theory from Smith to Marshall and Clark. The basic shape of the problem was fairly well recognized well before Berle and Means rediscovered it in the early 1930s.[19] Yet if the problem puzzled people like Marshall or enraged people like Clark, it was all neatly dissolved as the modern marginalist theory of the firm developed, also in the early 1930s, under the influence of the kind of analysis of the firm (as individual) supplied by Robinson and others.

As long as firms are controlled by owner-managers, it is at least plausible to identify the self-interest of that owner-manager with profits. With the rise of the managerial corporation and the consequent separation of stock ownership from business control, a theoretical problem arises. Either theory must recognize that the corporation is a social institution in which a variety of individual interests meet, or theory must find some form of heuristic device that will allow it to speak of a single kind of "firm-interest." Marginalist theories of the firm, as we have seen, adopt the latter approach. Managerial theories of the firm, by contrast, take the first option, treating the firm as a social institution and acknowledging that effective control is exercised by salaried managers with interests that are in significant measure distinct from the interests of the stock owners.

Starting from this point, the approach of a managerial theory of the firm is:

(1) to indicate in what respects managers may be motivated to attend to other-than-profit goals, (2) to translate the motivation of managers to an analysis of operations context, (3) to identify the necessary conditions for discretionary behavior to be of quantitative importance, (4) to develop the implications, direct and indirect, of a theory based on this position, and (5) to examine the evidence of such behavior.[20]

Managerial theories of the firm, then, basically involve an analysis of the managerial role within the corporate organization, on the assumption that managers are self-interested economic agents. The theory then attempts to draw out the deductive consequences of such an analysis and to test those consequences against the actual behavior of managers within firms and the behavior of firms both inside and outside of the market. Clearly, the view of method here is deductive, not inductive as it was with the behavioral theorists.

Following the line of development already indicated, it is clear that profit maximization is also the first casualty of the managerial approach, as it was with the behavioral approach. In a situation of discretion and managerial control, it is obvious that there are a number of respects in which managers may and presumably will be motivated to attend to goals other than profits. Most obviously this will be the case in the area of managerial compensation. It will also tend to be the case in the area of earnings retention, sometimes in responses to takeover attempts and in a variety of other business contexts. Simple profit maximization "ignores that the allocation of resources within the firm by those who control the decision-making machinery can be done in ways that selectively promote the decision makers' interests at the possible expense of profit."[21] Note that the crucial difference here from the marginalist theory of the firm concerns talk about the significance of allocation *within* the firm, and the acknowledgment that control of the firm's "decision-making machinery," the firm's political structure, is important for understanding the behavior of the managerial corporation.

Once profit maximization is gone, however, managerial theories cannot rest simply with a mélange of managerial interests. The project of replacing profit maximization with some adequately clear set of corporate behavioral goals requires the placement of managerial discretionary control within the context of corporate organization. It requires an analysis of the kinds of constraints, both from within and without the corporation, that place some limits on managerial discretion. Clearly, there is some minimum level below which profits cannot fall without creating a significant adverse reaction among stockholders, either in the form of a reduction of invested capital or of an attempt to vote management out of office. Equally there may be certain kinds of business decisions that have at best debatable impact on profits yet may create an undesirable political or economic backlash among either the stockholders or the consuming public. These and a wide variety of other factors – including, very significantly, corporate organizational structure – set up the constraints within which managerial discretionary behavior occurs.

Williamson's work, in particular, has distinguished among different broad types of corporate organizational structure. The central thrust of his *Corporate Control and Business Behavior,* for example, is to distinguish between U-form corporate organization (the older form of *unitary* organizational structure composed of a number of functional divisions) and the M-form corporate organization (an organizational innovation giving rise to a *multidivision* organizational structure composed of semiautonomous divisions).[22] Williamson subsequently goes on to distinguish the H-form corporate organization (a *holding* company form of organization) as yet a distinct variation on the M-form organization. Perhaps Williamson's most central contention is that the advent of the M-form corporate organization has tended to rationalize business decision making by placing top executives in a position less involved with the particular functioning units, and hence better able and better motivated to regard the viability (profits) of the firm as a whole. "The M-form organization thereby attenuates managerial discretion in what had previously been U-form firms."[23]

Lest one get the impression, however, that the M-form organization returns us to marginalist profit maximization, Williamson follows this up with a caveat: "The attenuation of managerial discretion does not, however, imply its elimination. Rather, the argument is comparative. Albeit in reduced degree, continuing managerial discretion can be expected to survive those direct effects."[24] The particular group interests of top administrative staff, both in the firm as a whole and within its several divisions, can still be expected to work to some degree, although a lesser degree than in U-form organizations, against the overall interests of corporate profit. This kind of analysis of the constraints on discretionary behavior and on the organizational context may be of particular value as either society (through the government) or various constituencies within the corporation wish to modify those constraints in various directions.

The managerial theorist must then go on to identify those areas wherein discretionary behavior is economically significant, generates consequences (including predictions based on the analysis given of managerial discretionary behavior), and tests out those predictions in the observable world of business operation. It is important to note, by the way, that the predictions that will be significant to a managerial theory of the firm will not be limited to predictions about aggregate directional changes in price. Rather, a wide variety of predictions – ranging from those about management stances in labor negotiations, managerial compensation, and responses to takeover bids, as well as to changes in price – will be relevant to the assessment of a managerial theory. It is equally important to note that, by implication, there will be areas of firm decision and behavior in which discretionary behavior will not be of economic significance. What is most crucial to note, however, is that the assessment of theories of the firm for the managerialist, as it is in principle, if not in reality, for the marginalist, is carried out by testing the theory's logical implications against our experience of the world.

Given the managerial theorist's retention of the neoclassical assumption of self-interest on the part of managers, it may be claimed that managerial theories are simply extensions of the more traditional marginalist program in economics. To do so, I would suggest, probably depends largely on how broadly we take the notion of "extension." If managerialism is an extension of marginal analysis, it surely is not a simple one. As Williamson notes, managerial theory is "unlike neoclassical analysis [in that] internal organization is specifically held to be important."[25] In particular, the managerial approach to the firm abandons methodological individualism, as I characterized that view in the last chapter. According to advocates of managerial theories of the firm, there are certain actions, most conspicuously managerial ones, that are basic constituents of the institution of the managerial corporation such that an agent's performing those actions is crucially a matter of his or her standing in social-political relations to other agents. The language I have used here is drawn from Sensat's characterization of the "asocialism" constraint of methodological individualism as explained in the last chapter. This difference is fundamental and, as I shall argue, carries an important part of the key to any useful advance in economic theory.

Conclusion

In this chapter we have looked at three different theories of the firm: marginalist (in particular its neoclassical form), behavioral, and managerial. The marginalist theory continues to reign in the textbooks and within the economics profession generally. The other theories tend to get more attention from students of business administration. One of the reasons for this is that the marginalist theory of the firm is basically a price theory, not a theory of general firm behavior. There are other reasons as well, as will become more apparent in Chapter 6.

It is clear that the behavioral and managerial theories have rather broader aims than the marginalist theories. They are theories not only about price, but about a broad range of firm behavior. They both depart from the marginalist central assumption of situational determinism, seeing discretionary behavior as a crucially important fact about the economic life of the contemporary firm. Equally, they both take the corporation to be an institutional collective in theory as well as in reality, while the marginalist approach is to treat the firm as a single-interest individual at least in theory.

At the same time, managerial theories and marginalist theories stand together, as opposed to behavior theories, in rejecting an inductivist view of scientific method. They start out with a common general view of motivation, differing mainly on how that applies within the corporation, and deduce consequences. At least in the ideal these consequences are then tested in order to assess the theory. (Of course marginalism has very frequently been criticized for paying no more than lip service to the actual testing of its predictions against experience.) Behavioral theories, by contrast, are explicitly inductivist. They purport to start with observation, with the hope of generating theory out of the collections of observations that researchers compile.

It is clearly the case that each of the approaches has produced interesting and valuable insights in our attempt to understand the firm as it works in the general economy. Yet it would be a mistake to move from this recognition to the kind of polyglot position advocated by Brian Loasby, wherein each of the approaches is taken for what it wants to be, with little or no attempt to reach any kind of evaluative conclusions about their relative merits.[26] As I shall argue over the course of the next three chapters, that process of relative evaluation is important not only because we wish to come to a clearer understanding of the managerial firm; it also forms a useful step in the process of understanding the present state of general economic theory.

CHAPTER 6

Confusions and problems with the marginalist view

I remember many years ago, in the closing and very unpopular phase of U.S. involvement in Vietnam, that people would occasionally joke about that involvement, saying, "It's a crummy little war, but we should be thankful for it since it's the only war we've got." At times one senses a similar attitude toward the marginalist theory of the firm, even among its most resolute defenders. One simply does not see the marginalist theory of the firm proclaimed as one of the glowing centerpieces of marginalist economic analysis. Rather, that theory has been the subject of serious criticism, examination and reexamination, and careful defense almost from its earliest days (at least if we are to agree with Machlup in finding the theory's infancy in the early work of Chamberlin and Robinson). The first serious criticism in England came in 1939 with Hall and Hitch's "Price Theory and Business Behavior."[1] On this side of the Atlantic a spirited battle over the value of the marginalist theory of the firm, a battle that seems to have continued with only periodic lulls since its inception, started in the pages of the *American Economic Review* in 1946 and 1947.[2]

Machlup concludes his famous defense of marginalist theories of the firm very modestly: "I conclude that the choice of the theory has to depend on the problem we have to solve....Deficiencies in marginal analysis have been shown and recognized."[3] The customary defense of the marginalist theory of the firm is twofold. According to the first, that theory succeeds well in explaining the very limited set of problems to which it wishes to address itself. According to the second defense, it has a higher level of predictive value than its behavioral and managerial alternatives. The crucial difference between the two lines of defense is that the second is comparative while the first is not.

The first defense is of very limited value. Consider the following parallel. It seems to be generally conceded that the Ptolemaic theory of astronomy did a good job of predicting observed celestial motion, at least as good a job as the marginalist theory of the firm does of predicting aggregate directional changes in price. We might imagine someone advocating a Ptolemaic theory of celestial motion, claiming

110

that it is entitled to be regarded as justified because it does a good job of predicting what its advocates intend it to predict. I take it that those of us who are tolerant would probably say something like "Well, of course you can do that, and you can claim your 'theory' as a neat forecasting device." But even the most tolerant among us would be disinclined to regard the rejuvenated Ptolemaic theory as good *science*. Few universities would rush to include the "new" theory in their science curricula. Work on the theory would not be widely supported as a worthy recipient of grant money from the National Science Foundation. Yet the first kind of defense, just noted, which is often put forward on behalf of the marginalist theory of the firm could equally well be put forward in the above manner on behalf of the resurrected Ptolemaic theory, as well as for the "theory" of water witching. It may well warrant the use of the model for certain purposes, but it can never warrant the level of respectability that marginalists wish to claim for their theory of the firm.

Thus, it is on the second line of defense that the marginalist theory of the firm must survive or fall, the claim that it has a better predictive capacity than its theoretical rivals. The crucial claim for the defender of the marginalist theory is that for all the problems facing the marginalist theory, it is still preferable to anything else available. In the remainder of this chapter I shall look at some of the chief confusions and problems that beset the marginalist theory of the firm and lead its defenders and detractors alike to view it as one of the more troubled components of the general marginalist economic program. Also I shall put forward an explanation for the continued dominance of the marginalist theory of the firm and claim that given the present state of the study of economics, that dominance is basically reasonable.

Confusions

As one examines both the criticisms and the defenses of the marginalist theory of the firm, two confusions about the theory emerge: What exactly is the theory about, and how crucial is the assumption of profit maximization to the basic program of the theory?

When I speak of confusion as to what exactly the marginalist theory of the firm is about, I have in mind two aspects of that problem. One is confusion about microeconomic theory generally: Are the laws of general microeconomic theory about real individuals in the world or about aggregates of individuals or "average" individuals? The general view of economic theorists seems to be that microeconomic predictions are about general trends within the larger economy. This would imply

that microeconomic laws are about aggregates of individuals or average individuals. In the realm of the theory of the firm, Machlup is
extremely clear on this point. The marginalist theory of the firm does
not give predictions about how particular firms will adjust their pricing
policy in response to a change in the economic environment. It may,
he says, give us "a rebuttable answer" to that question. By this I take
it that Machlup means to say that if a particular change in the economic
environment will drive up the price of U.S.-made automobiles, then
there is reason to think that I may well have to pay more for a new
Ford. Yet the reason to think this is that Ford Motor Company may
very well be an average automobile manufacturer and my local Ford
dealer may be an average automobile retailer. Yet the reason the
neoclassical theory gives no more than a rebuttable answer is that
there may well be factors at play that will lead either Ford Motor
Company or my local Ford dealer to deviate from that average. Thus,
Machlup is very clear in claiming that the laws of the marginalist
theory of the firm are about aggregates of individuals or about average
individuals.

Yet for all the clarity of Machlup and others on this point, many
people seem to continue to claim that microeconomic laws are about
individuals, and hence that the theory of the firm ought to give me
something more than a rebuttable answer to the question of how
corporation X will respond to an increase in the legal minimum wage.
It is surely striking that Rosenberg, writing ten years after Machlup's
famous defense, could claim, as I noted in the last chapter, that "it is
patent [my emphasis] that [microeconomic laws] are about what they
appear to be about: individuals." Rosenberg acknowledges, of course,
that some microeconomic statements are about average individuals,
but the cases he raises for this are very explicit claims about averages.
Many of the general statements produced by the marginalist theory
of the firm are not explicitly about average firms, and would thus
seem to fall into the class of general propositions that Rosenberg takes
to be about individual firms.

I take it that chief among the reasons why Rosenberg and a good
many other people take it as "patent" that the general statements of
microeconomic theory are about individuals is that the domain of
microeconomic theory is composed of individual economic agents. If
a theory starts out by assuming a domain of individuals, then the
various predications made by the theory are necessarily about those
same individuals. Accordingly, the universally quantified (general)
statements in which the theory results will also have to be about those
and only those things that inhabit the domain of the theory. Since

the domain of the marginalist microeconomic theory is a domain of individuals (granted, individuals of a wide variety of different types), it must follow that the general statements of microeconomic theory must be about these same individuals. This much would seem to be a simple consequence of methodological individualism as I have already characterized that view.

The logic of this argument is flawless. The problem is in what we tend to understand by that initial claim that economic theory operates with a domain of individuals. In Chapter 1 I argued that economic theory since the time of Adam Smith has undergone a highly significant change in that its domain has been expanded from simple flesh-and-blood individuals to include firms, families, and households, things that in the normal run of things, we regard as groups. Actually, the situation is rather more complicated than my analysis of Chapter 1 suggested. Perhaps, in fact, Alan Nelson is correct in his claim "that we do not yet understand how social scientific facts about markets or more highly aggregated structures can actually be explained by theories of individual behavior."[4]

While Nelson may well be right in this claim, I do think that the story of the emergence of modern equilibrium economics from classical political economy affords us the beginning of an understanding of the problem. There was a time, in the first century of modern economic theory, when the domain of economic theory was composed of flesh-and-blood individuals. As I noted in Chapter 4, Mill claimed that political economy was a "moral," or perhaps more informatively a "mental," science. Its general results are implications of what he spoke of as "the law of the mind." Knowledge of this law is available to each of us by introspection. Yet with the rise of marginal analysis the blood was slowly drained from economic agents. Jevons, of course, insisted that political economy, if it be a science at all, must be a mathematical science. While Jevons spoke of the "ultimate laws [of political economy being] known to us immediately by intuition," it is certainly clear that intuition does not yield the kind of precise mathematical laws that Jevons thought were required for scientific political economy. The mathematical tools that came to be applied in economic theory by the marginalists required a modification in the economic agents that constituted the domain of economic theory.

Older economic theory required self-interested individuals. Flesh-and-blood people, without saying that they are pure egoists, clearly do have a strong element of self-interest in their motivational structure. Moreover, that element of self-interest certainly tends to dominate what might be fairly narrowly defined as economic activity. The marginalist agent, however, is not merely self-interested, but rather a maximizer. Not only is the maximizing agent further removed from what we see of human behavior than is the merely self-interested agent, but work in the other social sciences has made it increasingly clear that flesh-and-blood individuals are less rational then even the earlier economists assumed. Given what everyone, even economic theorists, knows about the motivational structure of genuine human individuals, the marginalist program of mathematical analysis clearly has led to a wedge being driven between the individuals of economic theory and flesh-and-blood people.

I take it that this wedge is one of the most fundamental issues at stake in the controversy over the "realism of assumptions" that has been going on since even before the publication of Friedman's "Methodology of Positive Economics." Mainstream economists are not bothered – and it is not clear, at least in principle, that they should be bothered – by the fact that real people are not perfect economizers. The use of idealizations in theory is both legitimate and necessary. The question should not be whether it is legitimate for economic theorists to use an idealized economic agent. Rather, it should be whether the particular type of idealized economic agent that is used in theory contributes to the development of good theory.

In any case, the fact that the domain of economic theory is not populated by flesh-and-blood people or by actual business firms, but rather by rational economic persons and by the heuristic firms of marginalist theory must substantially modify our understanding of our previous line of argument which concluded that the general statements of microeconomics must be about individuals. Surely at one level those claims are about individuals, but the individuals they are about are not natural individuals, but rather analytical individuals, rational economic persons and heuristic firms, perhaps what Nelson calls "representative individuals."[5] Any move from those kinds of claims about individuals to those about the real economic world must be mediated by the claim that theoretical individuals reflect certain general tendencies in actual individuals, and hence that the claims about theoretical individuals can serve to ground claims about "averages" of real individuals or about the aggregate behavior of real individuals far better than they can serve to ground those about concrete flesh-and-blood individuals.

It is, of course, open to the critic of marginalist economics to say that he or she would like a theory that could generate predictions about concrete human individuals much like the predictions that physicists are able to give about concrete physical objects. Yet it clearly does involve a confusion about marginalist economics if the critic argues that its claims are *about* concrete individuals and are falsified by the fact that many concrete individuals don't act that way.

The second aspect of confusion as to what exactly the marginalist theory of the firm is about concerns the explanatory scope of the theory. Because I dealt with this confusion in the previous chapter, there is little need for me to say much about it here. Machlup is again very clear on this point. The marginalist theory of the firm is intended to predict aggregate directional changes in price, nothing more. Machlup gives a strong impression that he might advocate some other theory for the purpose of solving a different economic problem. If economists and their business and political followers were consistent in only using the marginalist theory of the firm for the purpose of predicting such changes in price, there would be no confusion on this point. The defenders and opponents of that theory could settle into a reasonable dispute about whether the marginalist theory of the firm or one of its rivals did a better job of predicting price changes. Unfortunately that has not been the case.

In the last chapter I cited Milton Friedman's argument that the real-world firm has a "social responsibility" to maximize profits. He is not isolated in this kind of position. It has become almost a commonplace, at least within certain ideological circles, that "the business of business is business" – that profit maximization is either an inviolable natural tendency or a moral purpose of the real-world business firm. When students of business administration are introduced to the theory of the firm in their "Introduction to Economics" classes, the restrictions of Machlup are seldom made so forcefully as when the theory is being defended against the criticism that firms don't really maximize profits. Many of these students leave the classroom thinking not that profit maximization is the core element in a heuristic device for predicting price changes, but that it is the entire point of business activity in the real world.

I am not suggesting that the marginalist theory of the firm lacks clarity as to its explanatory scope, but rather that two factors combine to generate a natural and understandable confusion among at least students of business administration and the general public about the explanatory scope of the marginalist theory. The first of those factors is a common lack of careful delimitation of the theory in its classroom presentation. The second is a tendency to play on the ambiguity of the term 'firm' – between its reference to a kind of entity in the real world of economic activity and its reference to a heuristic construct in economic theory – in an attempt to bolster a particular brand of social ideology. The lack of clear delineation of the theory in classroom presentation is, I am convinced, quite innocent in its motivation. The play on ambiguity to support a social agenda is, I think, less so. The marginalist theory of the firm is not intended to explain either the intrafirm allocation of corporate resources or the internal decision-making process of the firm; nor is it intended to provide a moral model for the place of the business firm in society. To present it, even by suggestion, as doing any of these things is to promote significant confusion about the scope of the marginalist theory.

The second confusion about the marginalist theory of the firm is about the significance of the assumption that firms are maximizers of profits. On the one hand, the profit-maximizing firm is surely the heart of the marginalist theory of the firm. The self-interested economic agents of the classical political economists became, at the mathematizing hands of the marginalists, maximizers. When the firm was introduced into marginalist economic theory as another kind of individual economic agent, with its utility being profit, it could scarcely have been viewed as anything but a *profit* maximizer. On the other hand, from the time of Smith it has been recognized that under perfect competition in a free market, the natural tendency of profits is toward a minimum. If profits are high, some competitors will reduce prices in an attempt to gain a larger share of the market. This will cause all producers in the market to reduce prices to this lower price. The natural force of competition will operate in this manner to force prices ever lower until they reach a point at which they can no longer be reduced without falling below the cost of production. Thus, again under perfect competition in a free market, the maximum attainable profit is also the minimum profit required in order to avoid bankruptcy. It follows that under the conditions assumed by the marginalist theory of the firm, the following assumptions are effectively equivalent, that is, they will lead to precisely the same consequences:

   A1.   Firms act in such a manner as to make as much profit as possible.
   A2.   Firms act in such a manner as to avoid bankruptcy.

As Latsis has noted:

At equilibrium then each seller is faced with the following choice: either to sell *q* or go bankrupt. Whether he maximises profits or is content simply with satisfactory profits, whether he is an optimist or a pessimist, a risky or a cautious personality will make no difference to his decision. There is only one policy he can adopt if he wants to remain in business.... There seems to be a persistent failure to notice that the behavior of the seller under perfect competition is over-determined and that a weaker assumption could do the same job: namely, the assumption that the firm avoids bankruptcy.[6]

Latsis's point here is that according to the marginalist theory, it is the forces of the market that determine prices, and hence the pricing behavior of the seller. The market determines these prices, as I have pointed out, at the minimum level at which the seller can operate. Prices above that level will be forced downward by the competitive force of the market mechanism. Thus, the behavior of the seller is overdetermined in the sense that the seller has no real choice about profit levels if he or she wishes to remain in business. Maximum profits are the same as minimum bankruptcy-avoiding profits. This is the profit level that will dictate the firm's behavior.

What is perhaps more than a bit ironic is that the following assumption,

A3.   Firms act in such a manner as to make at least a satisfactory level of profit;

is not equivalent to (A1) and (A2), since (A3) alone is inconsistent with the equilibrium condition that profits be zero. Yet clearly faced with a choice between (A1), where equilibrium profits are zero, and (A3), there is little doubt about which assumption any businessperson would choose. Needless to say, it sounds very strange to say that satisfactory profits would be preferable to maximum profits. This surely should suggest that the claim involves some strange equivocation on the term 'profit'. Yet that in itself should simply serve to reinforce my claim that the profit-maximization assumption for the marginalist theory of the firm is of somewhat confusing significance.

Along similar lines, Loasby also notes that profit maximization only becomes a necessary assumption once elements of monopoly are introduced into the economic environment.[7] Latsis and Loasby both note that once the assumption of perfect competition is withdrawn, economists equally tend to back away from the assumption of profit maximization.

Perhaps it is unfair to say that there is a confusion about the marginalist theory of the firm on this point. It is not the case that marginalists have argued that profit maximization is the only assumption that will do or that it will give different results than a bankruptcy-avoidance assumption would. Yet if Latsis is not correct in claiming that there is "a persistent failure to notice that the behavior of the seller under perfect competition is over-determined," there is surely a persistent failure to acknowledge that the profit-maximization assumption could be replaced by any of a number of weaker-sounding, but effectively equivalent assumptions.

The assumption of profit maximization clearly does have one advantage over any of its effective equivalents. In a marginalist economic theory in which other economic agents are assumed to be utility maximizers, it surely adds to the systematicity of the overall theory if the theory of the firm that it includes treats firms also as maximizers. Certainly, some forms of managerial theory, as I noted in Chapter 5, speak of utility-maximizing mangerial decision makers. Yet when we move to talk of the firm itself as an individual economic agent, the most natural way to speak of the utility of the corporation is in terms of profits. Moreover, systematic neatness is surely a legitimate consideration. If several assumptions do indeed perform the same job, the scientist will generally be well advised to adopt the one that fits in most naturally with the other assumptions of his or her theory. Thus, I think it would be silly to suggest that the marginalist theory of the firm should replace its assumption of profit maximization by a weaker-sounding equivalent. What I would suggest, however, is that microeconomic theorists might well serve the community of theory users if they would explain more clearly that under the situational constraints of the marginalist theory of the firm, the assumption of profit maximization is a great deal less ambitious than it at first sounds, and that it is in the situational assumptions that the real action lies.

Problems

The major alleged problems of the marginalist theory of the firm fall also into two areas: problems of predictive failure and of theoretical fit. The alleged problems of predictive failure are of particular significance since, as I noted at the beginning of this chapter, the most crucial of the customary defenses of that theory hinges on its predictive superiority over its rivals. Problems of prediction likewise take two forms: failure to make predictions at all about things that the critic thinks should be the subject of predictions, and the making of incorrect predictions where the theory does make predictions.

By now it should be painfully obvious that the marginalist theory of the firm is supposed to make predictions about aggregate directional changes in price and is not supposed to tell us much of anything about business behavior. We have seen that advocates of the marginalist theory have frequently tried to stretch it to apply to actual business behavior, and that within the confines set by the theory itself, such stretching is quite illegitimate. We have also noted that critics of the theory have complained that it lacks contact with the conduct of business people in the real world. One thing, then, that seems patent is that a good many economists, both advocates and critics of the marginalist theory of the firm, would like to have a theory that would be of value to business decision making, not just to public policy decision making. Writing as early as 1952, Kenneth Boulding expresses such a hope:

It is quite obvious that the marginal analysis, useful as it is as a tool of general static equilibrium economics, is not particularly useful as an instrument of analysis of actual business behavior. . . . it seems not unreasonable to hope that . . . economists might even be of some use to businessmen, and their modest triumphs at the level of national accounting might be matched in the next generation, in the realm of business practice.[8]

We are, of course, now well into that next generation. There has been progress in the project of understanding business practice. That progress has not, however, come through the marginalist theory of the firm, but rather, from the behavioral and managerial approaches. There are two reasons why the marginalist theory of the firm has been of no help in our attempt to understand business practice. The first is the theory's commitment to methodological individualism. Given marginalist economics's commitment to the "asocialism" constraint identified in Chapter 4, the marginalist theory of the firm cannot explain firm behavior as constituted out of the actions of those individuals who comprise the firm. That would require taking account of corporate institutional structure, the individuals' "standing in social relations to other agents." The marginalist theory's alternative is to take the firm, itself, as a basic individual agent. As a result the theory can take no account of the collective character of the firm, which is absolutely essential to understanding its practice. As Cyert and Hedrick point out, within the marginalist theory of the firm, "there are no organizational problems nor is there any room for analysis of the internal decision-making process."[9]

The second reason is equally based at the heart of the economic tradition. In Chapter 4 I claimed that one of the central points of continuity within the economic tradition since Smith has been a commitment to the preferability of nonintentional over intentional coordination of economic activity. Generally speaking, the whole tradition has been built around the attempt to comprehend a variety of forms of nonintentional coordination in "free" markets. The basic difficulty in dealing with corporate practice within such a theoretical framework has been long recognized. Writing in 1953, Andreas Papandreou claims:

The adequacy of the economist's frame of reference in dealing with the wide variety of behavior problems which do not involve conscious interdependence among the acting agents cannot be seriously subjected to question. As soon as we leave the realm of unconscious interdependence, however, and attempt to deal with problems of deliberate cooperation we find ourselves increasingly falling back on concepts and generalizations whose relationship with the main body of thought is more or less tenuous.[10]

Thus, both the methodological individualism and the commitment to nonintentional coordination (Papandreou's "unconscious interdependence") stand as significant obstacles to the marginalist theory of the firm's ever coming to be of much help in understanding business practice. It is an open question, I take it, how much we ought to be critical of the marginalist theory on this count. Surely a theory need not be able to explain *everything* that some people would like it to explain. Yet in this case it is at least a major point of contention. As Cyert and Hedrick note, there "has been the lack of agreement on the crucial questions to which the theory of the firm should address itself."[11] Generally speaking, the broader the set of phenomena that a theory is able to explain, the better. Whether the failure of the marginalist theory of the firm to explain much of business behavior is an extremely serious problem or not, it seems clear that even the theory's advocates find some dissatisfaction in its failure to explain more broadly.

It is surely far worse for a theory to make predictions about some set of phenomena and have those predictions turn out faulty than it is simply not to make predictions abut that set of phenomena. This is especially true of the marginalist theory of the firm, since it rests its major theoretical defense on its predictive record. In his *Methodology of Economics: Or How Economists Explain*, Blaug identifies three significant areas of alleged predictive failure for the marginalist theory of the firm:

1. The theory predicts unequivocally that a profit maximizing firm in a perfectly competitive market will not advertise: it has no incentive to do so because additional output can only be produced at rising marginal costs.[12]

Clearly, of course, advertising exists. Now at first blush, this looks like it is simply a prediction about business behavior, and hence not a prediction that would be relevant to the self-proclaimed scope of the marginalist theory. Yet there is a very clear claim about price here as well, the claim that there should be no price at which a seller of advertising services should be able to make any profit. The fact, then, that advertising is a highly profitable industry would seem to constitute evidence against the marginalist theory.

2. Traditional theory of the firm predicts that a proportionate tax on business income, such as the corporate income tax, is not shifted by the firm to its customers in the short-run, because the tax reduces the level of profits but not the volume of output at which profits are maximized.[13]

Yet Blaug notes that the best empirical evidence available indicates that the incidence of such a tax is in fact frequently shifted to the consumer.

3. The prediction of traditional theory that a rise in money wages will lead to a fall in the volume of employment offered by firms is not borne out by evidence on short-run employment functions, which seem to exhibit remarkable stability in the face of wage inflation.[14]

All of these predictions are simple consequences of traditional price theory, hence they are within the scope of the marginalist theory's self-adopted explanatory agenda. Each of them provides an instance of presumed predictive failure.

An additional point of the theory's predictive failure that is worthy of mention is its failure to give a plausible account of the price of business-managerial labor. The fact that virtually every economist, from Samuelson in his introductory text on, will agree that the control of business executives over their own salaries regularly leads those salaries (the price of a certain variety of labor) to be significantly higher than would serve the end of profit maximization constitutes an acknowledgment of yet another area of predictive failure.

The fact that a theory does at points, even at significant points, produce incorrect predictions, should not lead to its immediate abandonment. Theories are never perfect, finished products. In defense of the marginalist theory one could respond that Blaug's examples point out anomalies that require further attention from the marginalist theorist. Also, like any scientific investigator, the marginalist may be able to identify other factors in the economic environment that lead to the apparently anomalous results. Even the most elementary exploration of the philosophy of science shows that there are a number of perfectly legitimate ways of saving a good theory from a few empirically bad test results. Yet of course, those same theory-saving devices may also be brought to the rescue of bad theory as well.

In connection with the area of predictive failure that I noted regarding managerial salaries, it is important to recognize that there is one variant of marginalist analysis of the firm, the so-called set-of-contracts theory of the firm, that in some of its presentations continues to maintain that managerial salaries are set at profit-maximizing levels. This set-of-contracts theory essentially eliminates the heuristic notion of the firm, seeing the corporation instead as simply a set of contracts among the various parties that jointly compose the corporation. Armen Alchian and Harold Demsetz, and Michael Jensen and William Meckling maintain that through the function of capital markets, corporate risk bearers (stockholders and other lenders of equity capital) exercise effective control over managerial behavior.[15]

Eugene Fama, however, likewise an advocate of a set-of-contracts view of the firm, points out that

when management and risk bearing are viewed as naturally separate factors of production, looking at the market for risk bearing from the viewpoint of portfolio theory tells us that risk bearers are likely to spread their wealth across many firms and so not be very interested in directly controlling the management of any individual firm. Thus, models of the firm, like those of Alchian–Demsetz and Jensen–Meckling, in which the control of management falls primarily on the risk bearers, are not likely to allay the fears of those concerned with the apparent incentive problems created by the separation of security ownership and control.[16]

Fama himself argues that the managerial labor market provides generally effective control over managerial salaries, and hence an effective solution to that problem of incentives. Fama claims that the separation of security ownership and control "can be an efficient form of economic organization."[17] Fama does not, however, make the more ambitious claim that profit maximization on the part of the particular firm can adequately explain the price of managerial labor. Risk bearers, after all, are concerned with their aggregate portfolio, not with the operation of each particular firm:

No claim is made that the wage revision process always results in a full ex post settling up on the part of the manager. There are certainly situations where the weight of anticipated future wage changes is insufficient to counterbalance the gains to be had from ex post shirking, or perhaps outright theft, in excess of what was agreed ex ante in a manager's contract....

The extent to which the wage revision process imposes ex post settling up in any particular situation is, of course, an empirical issue. But it is probably safe to say that the general phenomenon is at least one of the ingredients in the survival of the modern large corporation, characterized by diffuse security ownership and a separation of security ownership and control, as a viable form of economic organization.[18]

Fama's argument, then, cannot be taken to show that the profit-maximizing firm leads to prices for managerial labor roughly as we find them in actuality. Rather, his position is that a contract view of firms, characterized by risk bearers who are concerned to maximize their portfolio return and by managers who are concerned to maximize their expected career returns, can, at least in part, explain the economic viability of the large managerial corporation in an economic world of partial, but imperfect competition. That claim, unlike the more ambitious (but also more implausible) claims of Alchian–Demsetz and Jensen–Meckling, does not contradict my claim that managerial salaries constitute another area of predictive failure for marginalist theory.

The impact of these examples of Blaug's and mine should, I think, reinforce the claim that I put forward at the beginning of this chapter to the effect that the neoclassical theory of the firm is far from a robust piece of theory. It may well be defensible, but is clearly somewhat troubled. If it is preferable to its competitors on the basis of its predictive success, it may be more due to the poverty of its competitors than to the richness of its own resources. Yet of course, it is not at all obvious that the marginalist theory of the firm is preferable in prediction to its behavioral and managerial competitors. Quite the contrary, at very least we can say that those competitors predict considerably more broadly and probably just as successfully as the marginalist theory.

The final problem I shall identify for the marginalist theory of the firm is that of theoretical fit, by which I mean that the large managerial corporation is simply not the kind of thing that can fit very naturally into a theory the domain of which includes only individuals. If we take the basic body of economic theory as it existed, say, around the time of Marshall and Clark, there is strong reason to see the large managerial corporation as a type of entity that should not fit into the theory, to use Clark's wonderfully poignant phrase, "vitiating the action of economic laws."

There are three things about the large managerial corporation that lead one to suspect a lack of natural compatibility with pre-1930 marginalist economic theory. The large managerial corporation is large, it is corporate, and it is not naturally mortal. As I have already noted in Chapter 1, Clark's very strong condemnation of the large managerial firm hinged on the first two of these points. In the first place, the fact that such a corporation is large means that it has power far beyond that which traditional economic theory had foreseen for any economic agent other than the government. Indeed, it is well known that a number of present-day corporations are larger, in terms of their economic operations, than a number of sovereign governments in the world. This kind of power quite naturally skews the balance of power that is so essential to the theoretical operation of the "economic laws."

It is important to note that Clark did not regard this largeness as the problem in itself. Governments are large, but Clark was no anarchist. Rather, Clark saw the problem as arising in the fact that the large managerial corporation was large *and* was still treated in the law as if it were simply an individual. Thus, the law failed to take account of the disparity in power created by the rise of the large managerial firm. Yet all this is exacerbated by the fact that such a firm was corporate. In bringing a large number of different individuals together under a common decision-making process with no *one* person responsible, the firm created what Clark rightly called "a semi-public power." The firm created an authority structure with the capacity to levy what amounted to heavy fines on those within its control who violated the authority of the firm. Clark recognized these firms as having a kind of power similar to government, in consciously directing and organizing the affairs of many men and women, but as these firms were not recognized as constituting a public power they were not subject to the same kinds of constraints and public responsibilities as normal *public* powers. The fact that, by the time of Clark, "economics" had emerged from "political economy" as a discipline that took its task as investigating economic phenomena independently of political processes made the recognition that the economic institution of the managerial corporation had an ineradicable political character a theoretical problem of major proportions for Clark.

The fact that corporations do not naturally die constitutes an additional problem. The fact that individual entrepreneurs do eventually die and that they frequently have a number of offspring, leads, at least in theory, to a periodic dispersal of the controlling assets of owner-managed businesses. This is not the case with the large managerial firm. The structure of such a firm makes it, again, more like a country. It can go on from generation to generation with an increasing concentration of both economic and political power.

It is important to make clear that I do not think that these are undesirable features of the corporation. To suggest that bigness is badness and that the economy should revert to "those golden days of yesteryear" before the rise of the managerial corporation would be both naive and foolish. The point I want to make is that these features of the large managerial corporation make it fit poorly into traditional economic theory. Moreover, it should be clear from Chapters 1 and 3 that virtually all of the great economic theorists prior to the development of the modern theory of the firm agreed with this judgment about the corporation. There was very clearly in the minds of Smith, Mill, Marshall, and Clark a significant tension between the laws of classical economic theory and the existence of the large managerial corporation. It seems patent that all of these thinkers would have rejected the notion that the economic tradition could provide a natural home for a theory of the large managerial firm.

Nevertheless, the modern marginalist theory of the firm did emerge and did so, as I noted in Chapter 1, through the very simple device of expanding the domain of the theory. Just as the law of Clark's time took the large corporation as an individual, so did the theory by the time of Robinson take the large corporation as a simple individual. The theory simply added corporations to the domain, speaking indiscriminately of "firms" whether they be corner groceries or multinational corporations. It went on to make substantially the same assertions about all firms that it had initially made about private entrepreneurs. A producer is a producer is a producer.

Now that the marginalist theory of the firm has been with us a while, we see economists speak as though General Motors were as natural a part of the economic world as any of its workers or individual consumers. In Chapter 3 I quoted comments of Milton Friedman on complex enterprise economies. If we look again at part of what Friedman had to say, we should, I think, find it remarkably peculiar:

As in that simple [exchange] model, so in the complex enterprise and monetary exchange economy, co-operation is strictly individual and voluntary provided: (a) that enterprises are private, so that the ultimate contracting parties are individuals and (b) that individuals are effectively free to enter or not to enter into any particular exchange, so that every transaction is strictly voluntary.[19]

We might well ask whether very much individual and voluntary exchange can occur, according to Friedman's characterization, in an economy in which large managerial corporations play a major role. Clark recognized, as Friedman seems not to, that corporations are not genuinely *private* enterprises. They are semipublic. The only sense in which the ultimate contracting parties can be viewed as individuals in such an economy is if we simply stipulatively define corporations to be individuals. Of course, the various people, the stockholders, laborers, managers, consumers, and so on, involved with the corporation are individuals, but collectively the stockholders, managers, laborers, and so on comprise a creature called the corporation. That collective is a party to each of the various contractual relationships that bind all those individuals together as well as to both suppliers and consumers.

Similarly, in many cases of exchange the individual is hardly *effectively* free to enter or not enter into the exchange. There is, of course, a technical sense of freedom in which I am free not to enter into an exchange relationship with my local electric company, but it is awfully hard, even for Friedman I should think, to regard that technical freedom as effective.

What I would hope to have shown thus far in this chapter is fairly modest. I would not suggest that the problems I have identified with the marginalist theory of the firm should lead to its abandonment. I do, however, think it should now be apparent that the marginalist theory is susceptible to some quite natural, yet serious confusions and that it has some significant shortcomings as a predictive instrument. I shall argue in the remainder of this chapter that the central reason for the marginalist theory's continuing strength among economic theorists is the fact that it has developed as a part of the general marginalist program in economics. While this is so, I think it should also be apparent at this point that it is nevertheless a rather peculiar and unnatural part of that tradition.

Why the dominance of the marginalist view?

In the final part of this chapter I shall argue that the continuing dominance of the marginalist theory of the firm is not a function of its predictive superiority over its rival theories of the firm. It seems in fact that simply as theories of the firm, the major theoretical alternatives to the marginalist theory are superior to it. The marginalist theory of the firm has, however, the immense advantage of being embedded within a broader economic theory. To date, no alternative theory of the firm has been developed as a part of a comprehensive and well-developed theory of economics.

This assessment leads me to two conclusions. First, barring the development of an alternative comprehensive economic theory that might provide a home for a preferable theory of the firm, marginalist economic theorists are justified in maintaining their commitment to the marginalist theory of the firm. Second, given the clear inadequacy of the marginalist theory of the firm, in my view, as well as the fact that the marginalist program has other significant shortcomings, there is a strong need for alternative developments of economic theory that might be generated as extensions of current theories of the firm into theories of the economy as a whole.

As I already noted, the marginalist theory of the firm is customarily defended on the basis of the claim that it is a superior predictive instrument to its various theoretical rivals. Yet we have seen that it predicts a much narrower range of phenomena than its chief theoretical rivals, and that it has significant shortcomings as a predictive instrument in its own restricted area of concern. Indeed, one cannot leave the discussions of the theory of the firm without the impression that marginalist theorists of the firm talk a great deal about the predictive superiority of their theory, but that they make that claim more or less as an a priori article of faith. One simply does not see any careful development of the predictions made by the rival theories and comparative evaluation of the relative success of the predictions made by these theories.[20] The marginalist's claim to predictive superiority, at least in the restricted area of the theory of the firm, appears to be primarily an unsupported expression of commitment to that theory, wrapped in the rhetoric of the conventional marginalist methodological position.

The real justification for the marginalist theory of the firm, as well as the real explanation of its continuing dominance among economic theorists, does not come from below, but from above.[21] It is not justified, nor is it generally held, because of its predictive relation to facts of the economy. To the extent that it is justified and that it is generally held, it is simply because it is a component of the broader marginalist economic program.

As a result, it is illegitimate to assess simply the theory of the firm in isolation. It is something of an unnatural extension of the marginalist theory of economics that existed prior to the development of the theory of the firm. Yet it is, I think, the only way in which marginalist economic theory could possibly have dealt with the modern firm. Given the whole economic tradition's commitment to methodological individualism, to the "asocialism" constraint in particular, the only way marginalism could treat the firm would be as simply another individual. Thus, while there is an inherent tension between the social and institutional character of the modern firm and the individualism of traditional economics, it would have, as I shall argue more fully in the last chapter of this book, required a more radical revision of the economic tradition than was possible within the limits of the marginalist program to deal with the firm as a genuine collective.

In any case, the response of the marginalist economic theorists to the need to develop a theory of the firm was, as I noted in Chapter 1, to assimilate the notion of the firm into that of the entrepreneur. Thus, the large managerial corporation is treated as if it were just another individual businessperson. The marginalist commitment to methodological individualism remains intact. The marginalist theory can continue to assert the same propositions as it could before the large managerial corporation came to be viewed as a significant factor in the economy. In short, marginalist economic theory is able to maintain both an apparent ontological and a propositional continuity with the simple heuristic trick of declaring all firms to be theoretical individuals.

The continuing dominance of the marginalist theory of the firm, at least among economic theorists, is a simple corollary of the continuing dominance of the general marginalist economic theory. While it is easy to argue that the marginalist theory of the firm has strong theoretical rivals, one cannot make the same claim for the general marginalist economic theory. This is not to say, of course, that there are no economists who oppose the marginalist theory. Particularly since the economic difficulties of the 1970s, there has been a proliferation of economics journals publishing work from various nonmarginalist perspectives.

The Marxian economic tradition goes back even longer than the marginalist tradition. The institutionalists trace themselves back to the work of Thorstein Veblen, one of the earliest explicit critics of marginal analysis.[22] Both traditions have a long history of theoretical opposition to the marginalist program. There are also now the post-Keynesians, who see themselves as offering new directions for theoretical development in economics. Given this level of opposition, it may seem surprising to juxtapose the claim that marginalist economic theory is seriously unsatisfactory with the claim that it has no strong theoretical rivals. Yet that is precisely what I wish to do.

The problem is basically this: While each of the major theoretical rivals to marginalist economics rests on a valuable and in some cases brilliant insight, the fact of the matter is that none of them has yet given rise to an adequately articulated comprehensive theory capable of posing a serious challenge to the, perhaps problematic, yet surely brilliantly articulated and systematic monolith of marginalist economic theory. Certainly in any of its more orthodox forms, Marxian economics has been faced with immense empirical problems. Either as Marx developed it or as revised by Lenin, Marxian economic theory has not withstood the test of human experience. By contrast, the variety of more flexible adaptations of Marxian economics simply don't offer any widely agreed-upon, well-articulated comprehensive economic theory. Along the same lines, the American institutionalist tradition has been so wedded to a radically inductivist methodology that it likewise has not yet been able to develop any well-articulated and systematic economic theory, its advocates instead being content with piecemeal bits of economic generalization. Similarly, the so-called post-Keynesians offer a collection of interesting and sometimes useful bits of theory, yet they have not brought these into anything resembling a systematic comprehensive theory. What these various approaches to economics have done is offer us an interesting set of directions in which economic theory might be developed, but as yet none of them has been given the development that would be needed to pose a serious challenge to marginalist economic theory. Such a challenge can only come when one of these, or perhaps some other rival approach, offers a comprehensive theory of substantial systematicity and clear articulation rivaling what we find in marginalism.

We have seen that the marginalist theory of the firm is beset by a number of problems. Most marginalist economists, in fact, acknowledge quite openly that the theory of the firm is one of the weaker elements within the marginalist program. To use Hempel's very useful distinction between "support from below" (empirical support) and "support from above" (theoretical support), it is clear that the marginalist theory of the firm receives relatively little support from below. Yet what it lacks in support from below it more than makes up for in support from above. As part of marginalist economic theory, it enjoys the support given to that whole broader theoretical enterprise.

Yet at the same time, the marginalist theory of the firm is a weak part of general marginalism. If marginalist economic theory spawns a weak and troubled theory of the firm, we should be led to ask, how might general economic theory be improved to give us a better theory of the firm?

At present, however, marginalism and the marginalist theory of the firm constitute the only viable general and comprehensive economic theory. Those alternative approaches to the study of economic phenomena that appear to have some hope of significant viability have yet to develop comprehensive theory. And the sole alternative comprehensive economic theory, classical Marxism, is simply not viable. The result is that marginalism must continue to dominate at the present time. Marginalist economists are surely right to continue to develop and refine their comprehensive theory in order to see how far and in what directions it can be pushed. Yet at the same time, the opponents of marginalist theory must be encouraged to try to develop their economic insights into comprehensive theory. Neither marginalism nor science nor the people whose lives are profoundly influenced by economic policy benefit if marginalism is allowed to carry the day by default.

In the final two chapters of my analysis of the managerial firm as an anomaly for marginalist economic theory, I shall note what I see as the most salient features of the large managerial firm that prove anomalous for marginal analysis, and then examine the issue of how much departure from the general economic tradition and from marginalist economic theory in particular would be required in order to generate a better theory of the firm. Such a theory would be desirable, and a search for it might well serve as a guide to the development of an alternative general economic theory.

CHAPTER 7

The shape of the large
managerial corporation

In Chapter 8 I shall examine the theoretical impact of a better theory of the firm. I have suggested, thus far, that both managerial and behavioral theories of the firm offer significant improvements over the reigning marginalist theory. What I have not done, however, is give a clear identification of those characteristics of the large managerial firm that most significantly call for a change in theoretical structure. In the present chapter I shall take the first steps in supplying such an identification.

There are three areas in particular in which the marginalist theory of the firm is unsatisfactory: its understanding of the notion of firm profit (which it takes to be identical in both the managerial firm and the entrepreneurial firm); its general failure to note that the managerial firm is not simply an instrument of its owner-stockholders, but instead involves the interaction of a number of different constituent groups; and, finally, its failure to note the importance of corporate organizational structure. These last two points, of course, require that the analysis of the managerial corporation attend to its character as a polity, a corporate body, not just as an economic agent.

The corporation and profits

As already noted, the traditional marginalist theory of the firm takes the firm as simply a maximizer of profits. The firm is, of course, also a producer, but it produces purely for the sake of profits. Because of the centrality of profits to the marginalist understanding of the firm, it is, I think, appropriate to start the present examination by looking at what the actual behavior of firms in the real world would indicate about the role of profits for the firm.[1]

It is important at the outset to note that this examination is not concerned with the heuristic "firm" of the marginalist theory. That theoretical entity, assumed to maximize profits, is also assumed to produce only one product, to be a price taker (i.e., to have no impact on the price level of the single commodity it produces) and so on. Quite apart from any relationship between the theoretical entity called "the firm" and any actual business enterprises in the real world, the marginalist theorist is committed to the belief that a theory constructed on the basis of this kind of entity will accurately predict aggregate directional changes in prices. At present, I am concerned instead with whether actual business enterprises are maximizers of profit.

As far as I can see, the position that they are is most commonly held on the basis of the "natural selection" argument. In its briefest form, the argument is that since competition will drive non-profit-maximizing firms out of the market, firms that remain in the market must be profit maximizers. The argument may be opposed on either empirical or theoretical grounds. Empirically, it may be claimed that firms that engage in behavior that is clearly not profit maximizing do survive in the market. Theoretically, it can be argued that the market mechanism does not in all circumstances select in favor of profit-maximizing behavior.

The natural selection argument is not an argument for profit maximization as a (or the) motive of firm decision making, but rather as a mode of *behavior*. The conclusion of the argument is not that business decision makers sit in their offices thinking about how to maximize profits, come to a conclusion about how that is to be done, and then frame the behavior of their firms accordingly. Motive, presumably, has at best a rough correlation with outcome, and it is outcome that determines survival. What the natural selection argument concludes is that whatever may be the actual motives involved in business decision making, if they lead to behavior that succeeds in maximizing profits the firm will survive. If they lead to behavior that fails to maximize profits, the firm loses out in the battle for survival to its profit-maximizing competitors. As Friedman states the argument:

Let the apparent immediate determinant of business be anything at all – habitual reaction, random choice, or what not. Whenever this determinant happens to lead to behavior consistent with rational and informed maximization of returns, the business will prosper and acquire resources with which to expand; whenever it does not, the business will tend to lose resources and can be kept in existence only by the addition of resources from outside.[2]

It may well be apparent at this point that the natural selection argument entails a denial of any significant managerial discretion. According to the scenario envisioned by the natural selection argument, the choice facing the decision maker in a firm is not whether to maximize profit or to pursue some other goal. Rather it is, effectively, whether to maximize profit or go bankrupt. Thus, the argument returns us to at least some form of counterpart to the marginalist theory of the firm. It takes as a portrait of corporate reality what the marginalist theory of the firm takes simply as a theoretical construct. The natural selection argument genuinely takes the situation of the firm to be so determinate as to render the firm's choice one of maximum profits or bankruptcy.

In Chapter 6 I noted that within the marginalist theory's assumption of perfect competition, the assumption of profit maximization is effectively equivalent to the assumption of bankruptcy avoidance, and assumes a lower level of profit than would be assumed by profit satisficing. Given that the natural selection argument is committed to the claim that the real-world economic environment is as determinate as the theoretical world of the marginalist theory, it follows that the argument's conclusion could equally be stated as bankruptcy avoidance, which, as envisaged by the argument's situation of determinacy, would amount to the same thing. Profit satisficing, in fact, would have better survival value than would profit maximization at competitive equilibrium. The natural selection argument, then, does not support profit maximization in the strong sense in which it might be viewed as a genuine alternative to satisficing or various other positive profit alternatives.

Since the situational determinism that is assumed in the natural selection argument is dependent upon an economy that is sufficiently competitive to drive non-profit-maximizing firms into bankruptcy, the argument's advocates are also committed to denying that there is any significant impact of monopoly in capitalistic economies. This may initially seem bizarre, but in fact Friedman argues very explicitly that monopolies, other than those fostered by government action, do not form a significant element in the total U.S. economy.[3] Note, however, that in noncompetitive segments of the economy, the natural selection process will not be operative. In a noncompetitive market the price at which profit will be maximized will be substantially higher than it would be in a competitive market. Thus, in a noncompetitive market a firm could presumably charge less than the profit-maximizing price for its goods and still remain in business. So it would appear that the strongest conclusion that could be forthcoming from the natural selection argument would be that firms which operate in competitive markets would be profit maximizers.

Yet even this conclusion may well not be justifiable on the basis of natural selection considerations. There are a number of considerations which suggest that, given the corporate character of the corporation, firm decision makers may well, and in fact successfully do, pursue goals other than maximizing corporate profits. Moreover, the empirical study of the firm seems to support the conclusion that firm decisions, at least in areas where executive interests are at variance with profit considerations, regularly do sacrifice profit to other considerations.

The first thing that follows upon a recognition of the corporate character of the modern managerial firm is its composite nature. Different groups carry out different functions in the overall operation of the firm. In particular, corporate decisions are made by management. Since the primary economic benefits that accrue to managers come in the form of executive salaries and benefits, with dividends and increases in stock prices constituting only a subsidiary source of benefit, there is, initially, strong reason to believe that as economically self-interested agents, executives may be more strongly motivated to maximize executive compensation, subject to the constraint of satisfactory profit levels, than they will be to maximize profits.

It may, of course, be objected, as some of the set-of-contracts theorists noted in Chapter 6 have stated, that corporate managers are responsible to boards or directors who are elected by stockholders who therefore have the final decision-making power in the managerial corporation. Yet this would be much like arguing that the former Soviet Union was a democracy even prior to its late political reforms simply because it held elections. In the vast majority of cases, corporate elections are like old Soviet elections. Each year when I receive the ballot to which I am entitled by the small number of shares in IBM that I own, I am presented with a slate of nominees for open directorships. There is one candidate for each vacancy. My choice is to vote yes or no for the slate with which I am presented. This, of course, is precisely like the old Soviet elections, not like those that we would normally recognize as democratic. Moreover, I have not chosen stock in IBM over stock in other companies that have genuinely democratic election of directors. I do not know of such companies. I, as a potential investor, am given a choice simply among a group of firms all of which have essentially self-selected management and directorates.

This lack of power on the part of stockholders, widely recognized by commentators from Alfred Marshall to Carl Icahn, is well explained by John Palmer:

When stockholders are numerous and widespread, with no single stockholder owning very much of the stock, their control of the corporation is likely to be weak and its managers will have de facto control of the corporation. The likelihood of this situation arises from the difficulty the multifarious stockholders have in meeting and agreeing on some course of action alternative to the one proposed by the corporation's managers. Furthermore, because the incumbent management controls the dissemination of information about the corporation and has relatively easy access to the proxy mechanism, disaffected stockholders find themselves at a disadvantage in terms of cost, time, and information if they try to unseat the incumbents.[4]

Moreover, as I noted in Chapter 6, Eugene Fama has shown convincingly that even large stockholders regularly lack the incentive to pursue that level of control which they might, in principle, assert.

Additional reason to believe that corporate decision makers frequently make corporate decisions that further their own interests, sometimes at the expense of the profit interests of the firm, is provided by ordinary observation of firm decisions. In the mid-1980s when the U.S. automobile industry rebounded, largely because the U.S. government was able to persuade Japan to adopt voluntary restrictions on auto exports to the United States, two of the "big three" auto manufacturers responded by giving huge bonuses to top executives, bonuses that surely appeared to constitute a corporate expense that showed no promise of contributing to increased profits in the future. Similarly, in the recent wave of corporate takeover attempts, executives have appeared willing to make great sacrifices in corporate profits, sometimes even potential sacrifices of corporate survival, in order to protect their own continued power within the organization. These particular lines of behavior, and a general pattern of executive behavior of which such cases constitute but the extreme examples, seem clearly to belie the view that the real-world firm is a profit maximizer in a real world in which firm behavior is in fact controlled by salaried managers. Non-profit-maximizing firms do seem to survive.

Beyond all of this, however, there are strong theoretical reasons for the claim that the process of economic natural selection does not invariably favor profit-maximizing strategies. The first of these deals with the cost of information. It may well be that information can be assumed to be costless for the theoretical firm of the marginalist theory, but if we are talking about real-world business enterprises it should be abundantly clear that information costs.

Herbert Simon has long argued that because of both the uncertainty involved in business decision making and the cost of information, the criteria involved in actual business decision must be quite different from profit maximization. The actual process, as Simon argues, involves the business decision maker's setting a goal or "aspiration level." If there is a course of action A known and available to the decision maker that can be expected to achieve his or her aspiration level, then the decision maker chooses A. If there is no such course of action known and available, then he or she must undertake a search process for some previously unknown course of action that can be expected to achieve the aspiration level.[5] Because searching for new information is costly, it is more reasonable for the decision maker to start with some given level of aspiration (presumably some positive level of profit), rather than undertaking the initial search process that would be necessary to determine how profits would be maximized (if it is even possible to make such a determination).

Sidney Winter brings this issue of information costs explicitly to bear on the natural selection argument.[6] He develops a set of formal models of firm decision making on the basis of which he argues that natural selection considerations support profit maximization at most only in those situations in which the economic environment is substantially stable. In those environments in which there is significant novelty, selection considerations support quite different strategies, such as minimizing average total costs.[7] This result is somewhat ironic, since the kind of context in which natural selection considerations are normally thought to be most applicable is that in which environmental factors change and survival is based on ability to adapt to that change.

Winter also argues that natural selection considerations may equally militate in favor of non-profit-maximizing policies in environments characterized by what he calls "common subjective constraints":

The profit maximizing response may be ruled out by the constraints that decision makers believe to exist or choose to recognize. For example, it may well be that bribery of judges, civil servants and the employees of other firms is indulged in to a lesser extent than, objectively speaking, the pursuit of maximum profits would dictate. Observance of ethical constraints may nevertheless be viable behavior, provided the rewards of nonobservance are not too great and the moral force of the constraints generally recognized.[8]

Winter's point is that if such things as ethical constraints (and other forms of purely subjective constraints) are shared by all or almost all of the economic competitors in a given environment, their observance by a particular firm will not place that firm at a competitive disadvantage relative to other firms in the environment.

A striking example of a failure to note this fact is Friedman's treatment of discrimination in *Capitalism and Freedom*. Friedman argues that: "The man who objects to buying from or working alongside a Negro, for example, thereby limits his range of choice. He will generally have to pay a higher price for what he buys or receive a lower return for his work."[9] Friedman's claim is that the need to maximize profits will drive discrimination from the market, because the employer who will not hire minorities will have to pay a higher price for labor because he or she buys in a restricted labor market. The vendor who will not sell to minorities must, he tells us, sell at a lower price because he or she sells in a restricted market. Thus, the employer or vendor will be forced by his or her nondiscriminating competitors to either stop discriminating or go out of business.

We have here a remarkable case of maintaining theory, the facts be damned. While it has not completely escaped Friedman's attention that in the hundred years following the legal elimination of slavery in the United States, market forces have failed to eliminate discrimination, his ad hoc explanations of that fact – government interference with the operation of the markets, lower productivity of women and nonwhite males, and so on – seriously strain one's credulity. Yet even aside from that issue, if Friedman's economic theory had allowed him to take account of the social environment in which economic transactions occur rather than focusing myopically on bilateral transactions in isolation from any social context, he might have noticed that Winter's point about "common subjective constraints" perfectly accounts for the historical fact of racial discrimination. In almost all communities in the United States, almost all employers and vendors shared the same set of subjective prejudices that prevented them from hiring minorities for any but the most menial and low-paying jobs. This fact meant that the discriminating employer or vendor did not have to worry about competition from a nondiscriminating competitor. There simply were virtually no significant nondiscriminating competitors. Moreover, minorities themselves, who might most plausibly have become nondiscriminating competitors, faced a major barrier to entry into the market because lending institutions as well shared the common "subjective constraint" (racial prejudice).

In a sense Friedman's argument against legislative elimination of racial discrimination, if we supplement it with a premise drawn from common observation, provides a wonderful argument against the view that firms are profit maximizers. The argument runs as follows:

1. If firms are profit maximizers, then market forces would eliminate racial discrimination in the United States. (Friedman's theoretical claim)
2. Market forces did not eliminate racial discrimination in the United States. (Observational premise, and the additional modest assumption that if market forces were going to eliminate discrimination, they would have done so within a time span of less than a century)

3.   Therefore, firms are not profit maximizers.

Since, *pace* Friedman, wage and employment discrimination may well be consistent with profit maximization,[10] I do not want to place too much weight on this argument. Nevertheless, Winter's claims about common subjective constraints provide both a theoretically and empirically persuasive response to Friedman's position on discrimination, as well as a strong rebuttal to the natural selection argument for profit maximization.

If managerial corporations are not profit maximizers, the question of what role profits do play in the managerial corporation must still be addressed. I have already noted Herbert Simon's long-standing contention that firms are not profit maximizers, but are instead profit satisficers. As Simon explains:

In most psychological theories the motive to act stems from *drives,* and action terminates when the drive is satisfied. Moreover, the conditions for satisfying a drive are not necessarily fixed, but may be specified by an aspiration level that itself adjusts upward or downward on the basis of experience.

If we seek to explain business behavior in the terms of this theory, we must expect the firm's goals to be not maximizing profit, but attaining a certain level or rate of profit, holding a certain share of the market or a certain level of sales. Firms would try to "satisfice" rather than to maximize.[11]

It is clear, I take it, that firms are satisficers. They set certain levels of profit, sales, and so on that they wish to attain. Their behavior is then regularly designed in order to attain these levels, which the firm regards as satisfactory. Yet Simon's theory does not tell us very much about what those levels are. As Winter points out:

The satisficing principle is not, of course, a theory of the firm. As a basic tool for theory construction, it is certainly no more effective than the profit maximization assumption as a device for ruling out possibilities. To the extent that selection considerations lend it support, it is largely because the explicit recognition that conceivable modes of behavior remain unconsidered provides an escape from the *reductio ad absurdum* of information costs. At some level, all goal seeking behavior is satisficing behavior.[12]

In the end I want to argue that a fundamental reason why even Simon's notion of satisficing proves problematic in our attempt to understand the behavior of large managerial corporations is that the very idea of profit, which maintains a certain clarity when we apply it to the business operation of a private entrepreneur, becomes almost completely artificial when we try to apply it to the business operation of a corporation. Certainly we do have a relatively clear stipulative characterization of corporate profits as that part of revenue which either is returned to stockholders or reinvested in the business enterprise, yet this stipulated notion of profit does not, I think, provide much help in understanding the corporation, even as a purely economic agent.

Once upon a time the idea of profit made clear sense in business. A person (a biological person) invested his or her money in a business. That meant purchasing or renting a physical location in which to operate the business, purchasing raw materials and machines, hiring laborers, perhaps borrowing some money from a lending institution, and so on. The businessperson sold his or her product or service in the market at some price. That portion of the income generated from sales – minus that which had to be paid for facilities, materials, machinery, labor, perhaps interest on the money borrowed, and so on – was his or her profit, which the businessperson could use for the support of his or her family, for personal luxuries, or perhaps for reinvestment in the business. That minimal level toward which profits tended in the view of the classical political economists was the level required for the businessperson's support of self and family. If a person could not make enough profit to support self and family, he or she would be forced to make a living in some other manner. Profit, in short, was that portion of the business's revenue that was left over for the purposes of the owner.

The problem with the idea of profit arises as a consequence of the problem with the idea of corporate ownership. If it were reasonable to regard the stockholders as genuine owners of the corporation, with power to make decisions about what portion of the leftover corporate return to take as dividends for the support of their families and habits and what portion to reinvest in the business operation, then it would make perfectly good sense to speak of a concern for profit as central to the business organization. That view of stockholders is, however, quite untenable. The stockholder's actual role in his or her relationship to the corporation is far more accurately viewed as lender rather than as owner.

If we compare the large managerial corporation to the small owner-managed business firm, it would seem that the role of the stockholder is somewhat closer to that of the banker who lends capital to the small business than it is to the business's owner who actually has control over that capital. The chief difference would seem to be that the bank receives a predetermined and constant rate of return on the capital that it has lent, whereas the stockholder receives a rate of return on the capital that he or she has invested that is variable and dependent on the profitability of the business. It is substantially this view that is the chief insight of the set-of-contracts theory of the firm. As expressed by Harold Demsetz in "Toward a Theory of Property Rights":

Shareholders are essentially lenders of equity capital and not owners, although they do participate in such infrequent decisions as those involving mergers. What shareholders really own are their shares and not the corporation. Ownership in the sense of control again becomes a largely individual affair. The shareholders own their shares, and the president of the corporation and possibly a few other top executives control the corporation.[13]

If Demsetz's view is essentially correct, then that portion of corporate revenue which is paid out to stockholders in the form of dividends is in principle not different from what governments, churches, families, and other organizations pay in the form of interest to those who lend them money. While hardly telling, it is at least worthy of note in passing that the U.S. Internal Revenue Service classifies dividends and interest together for income tax purposes.

It follows that if the corporation's return to stockholders is best viewed as being more or less a non-fixed-rate interest payment, the traditional notion of profit seems to have little role left to play. Corporate survival depends on satisfying the economic demands of all those parties who have economic demands to make against the corporation (herein lies the chief appeal of Simon's notion of satisficing) – to pay enough in wages to ensure an adequate work force, to pay enough return to stockholders to maintain their investment in the corporation, to pay enough in managerial salaries to ensure an adequate managerial force, and to pay bills to its other suppliers and creditors. Corporate expansion depends on having some revenue left over beyond this to reinvest in the business. Unlike the individual entrepreneur, the corporation has no family or private habits to support.

Once satisfactory stockholder dividends are recognized as a business expense – just like satisfactory wages and salaries, interest payment, and so on – rather than something to be paid after business expenses, the notion of profit as a defining mark of corporate business pretty well disappears. If satisfactory stockholder dividends are regarded as a business expense, then the existence of some excess return over business expenses is no longer a necessary condition for corporate survival. It is clearly necessary for expansion, which is, in general, a good thing for business.

My claim has not been that profits, as traditionally defined, are not important to the corporation, but rather that the notion of profit, as traditionally defined, is not a useful notion to apply to corporate business in the same way it is applied to individual entrepreneurial business. The notion of profit needs to be either expanded or virtually eliminated. What is and must be genuinely of interest to the firm, taken simply as an agent in the market, is the size of that part of its revenue that is available to be distributed among its stockholder, management, and labor constituencies. Obviously, how that part of its revenue actually gets distributed among those constituencies will also be an important economic concern of the corporation, but that concern takes one inside the corporation as an institution.

I want to emphasize that I am not simply talking about gross revenue. Surely, all other things being equal, corporations will want to increase their gross revenue. This will be so because normally such an increase will also translate into an increase in that part of the gross revenue that is available for distribution among stockholders, management, and labor, as well as reinvestment in the operation. Yet that part of the corporation's gross revenue that is thus available is arrived at by taking gross revenue, and subtracting the cost of machinery, the nonlabor costs of plant maintenance, interest, supplies, and various goods and services that are purchased from outside sources. For lack of a better name let us call it the corporation's *extended profits*. I should perhaps add that what is reinvested in the business operation should be taken as a part of a corporation's extended profits because that reinvestment is normally undertaken for the purpose of increasing future extended profits. Thus, it is substantially akin to savings for families. It affects not only the future return to those presently involved in the corporation, but also the return to those individuals who will constitute the corporation in the future as well.

The corporate constituencies

I have claimed that the corporation is composed of a number of different groups or constituencies, and that it is simply untenable to view stockholders as functioning, in any meaningful sense, as the owners of the managerial corporation. It is, therefore, equally untenable to view the modern corporation as simply "an instrument of the stockholders." In actual fact it is far more plausible that a corporation more commonly functions as an instrument of its management. Similarly, viewed as legal fictions created by public charter, corporations can also legitimately be viewed as instruments of the society at large. One thing that seems to be perfectly clear about the corporation, speaking generally, is that any claim that it is the exclusive instrument of a single person or group is extremely likely to be wrong. This, of course, should hardly be surprising if we are prepared to take the corporate character of the corporation seriously.

In traditional theory stockholders and management seem to be thought of as somehow "inside" the corporation, while society at large is "outside." Society at large and the particular community in which the firm operates have traditionally been viewed simply as parts of the environment within which the firm carries out its economic transactions. I have already suggested that the chartered character of the corporation makes the society at large far less external to the corporation than the traditional view of the firm would suggest. Similarly, in certain circumstances at least, the community or communities within which the corporation operates may equally be less external than has generally been supposed. In a major city, say New York or Chicago, it may be reasonable to regard a particular corporation that has a facility there as simply an employer, and it may be reasonable for the corporation to regard the city as simply the environment within which it is located. In a small community, however, the situation is significantly different. In Columbus, Indiana, for example, it is not reasonable to regard Cummins Engine as simply an employer, nor can Phillips Petroleum be so regarded in Bartlesville, Oklahoma. These cities are not simply parts of the environment in which these companies do business. Rather they are the companies' "towns."

The relationship between New York City and any of the many firms that operate there is very different from the relationship between Bartlesville, Oklahoma, and Phillips Petroleum. The company town and its company exist in a kind of symbiotic relationship in which the town has, over the years, provided the company with a unique environment in which to grow, and the company, in turn, has provided the town with a financial base. The fact that the firm has not seriously had to compete for workers in the local labor market, nor has it had to compete with other significant business interests in its various expansion plans, has placed the company in the company town in a noncompetitive situation that renders the traditional analysis of the relationship between firm and environment largely inapplicable.

Finally, the traditional view that the relationships between firms and their consumers, on the one hand, and firms and those who comprise their labor force, on the other hand, can be adequately regarded as simple market relationships is also unsatisfactory. In those markets that are genuinely competitive or in markets for goods with perfectly elastic demand, it may be reasonable to view the relationship between firm and consumer as free and reciprocal. Yet in significantly monopolized or oligopolized markets for commodities with inelastic demand, consumers are not able to exercise the kind of market control over firms that traditional theory posits.

Similarly, the high level of specialization involved in many varieties of labor (a person cannot be a bricklayer today and a cabinetmaker tomorrow), the limited geographic mobility that characterizes the situation of a large number of laborers, and the fact that most communities do not have a number of firms competing for all of the various segments of the labor market together imply that market forces frequently do not give labor the kind of market control over firm abuses that traditional theory posits.

I have identified six groups, or constituencies, of the firm: stockholders, managers, labor, consumers, local communities, and society at large. Each of these has a legitimate stake in the behavior of the firm. The stockholder wants return on his or her investment. Management and labor each want stable and reasonably remunerative employment, opportunity for advancement, and so on. Consumers want reasonably priced goods and services of reasonably high quality. Local communities want an economic base. Society at large presumably wants a collection of things. For reasons that I have alluded to, none of these stakes are handled with general adequacy by the traditional view of the firm that regards stockholders and managers as somehow comprising a unified enterprise while the labor, consumers, local communities, and society at large are simply parts of its outside economic environment. An adequate institutional view of the firm requires that each of the groups identified be taken, as I have suggested, as a *constituency* of the firm. The particular relationships between the firm and each of its various constituencies constitute an important part of the overall institutional context of the firm.

This notion of constituency is in some ways similar to the notion of corporate "stakeholder" developed in R. Edward Freeman's *Strategic Management: A Stakeholder Approach*.[14] There are however significant differences. Freeman's work is primarily an attempt to develop a theory of sound management strategy. As a result, Freeman treats management, the present decision makers of the corporation, as "internal" to the corporation, while all the other corporate "stakeholders" are "external."[15] Moreover, Freeman's characterization of a stakeholder as "any group or individual who can affect or is affected by the achievement of the firm's objectives"[16] is too broad for my purposes. As Freeman's concern is with management, it is surely reasonable to attend to all those groups "who can affect or [are] affected by" the firm. Some of those groups, however – competitors and the media, for example – do not exist in the kind of symbiotic relationship with the firm that would qualify them for my notion of constituencies. Constituencies, as I identify them, are groups that are essential to the very existence of the firm. Without any one of the constituencies that I identify, the business corporation, in its present form, would cease to exist. My notion of constituency is far closer to the initial notion of stakeholder developed at the Stanford Research Institute in 1963 ("those groups without whose support the organization would cease to exist")[17] than it is to Freeman's notion.

Nevertheless, the position that I maintain shares a common basic perspective with Freeman's view on the nature of the corporation. While Freeman speaks at a number of points about the stockholders as "owners" of the corporation, he appears to use the term 'owners' in a purely conventional sense. His notion of stockholder "ownership" does not carry with it any special right to have the corporation run in the interest of the stockholders. Instead, Freeman's approach "dictates a conception of the role of the executive as one who serves a set of stakeholders of the firm and as one who is the guardian of the direction and values of the enterprise."[18] On the final page of his book Freeman urges the development of a notion of "the manager as fiduciary to stakeholder" as a replacement for the more traditional notion of the manager as a fiduciary to stockholder.[19] In this plea, Freeman shows that his view of the corporation, like my own, would basically replace an ownership analysis of the corporation with what is basically a constituency analysis.

Similarly, the understanding I wish to advance regarding corporate constituencies appears to be very similar to that put forward in the chapter on corporate governance in Williamson's *The Economic Institutions of Capitalism*.[20] There, Williamson identifies as corporate constituencies labor, owners, suppliers, customers, the community, and management. More carefully guarded than Freeman's use of the term, Williamson's use of 'owners', largely as a nod to traditional usage, includes all suppliers of finance for the firm, stockholders and other lenders as well.[21] Williamson's central contention in his discussion of managerial corporations as they relate to these constituencies, a contention that I would fully endorse, is that "since imperfect markets afford very unsatisfactory relief against corporate malfunctions, all constituencies require direct access to corporate governance lest their legitimate interests be ignored or abused."[22]

The one distinct constituency that I identify, and that neither Freeman nor Williamson do, is the broadest of the corporation's several constituencies, the general public. For some of the country's largest corporations – IBM, General Motors, and so on – perhaps the general public might be viewed as the community in which the corporation operates. Yet the general public must be viewed as a constituency of even the smallest of corporations, initially because of the fact that corporations are publicly chartered. The corporate form of business is a creation of the general public.

A glance at the historical roots of the modern corporation helps us to better understand the relationship between it and the general public. Richard Eells and Clarence Walton identify two strands in what they call the "genealogy of the modern corporation":

> The present-day business corporation has two genealogical lines. One line derives from the crown-chartered companies created by the medieval Church and the sovereign states of western Europe. These were the creatures, clearly and directly, of the Church and of the political sovereigns from the 12th century on....
> But the other line of descent is the more important.... Men formed [business organizations] without the sanction of a sovereign as far back as we can trace business activity under modern conditions. They obviously drew on the traditional right to form churches, guilds, local towns or boroughs, libraries, and clubs of all sorts without reference to the political state.[23]

One cannot understand the modern corporation without attending to both lines of this genealogy. Clearly, the modern corporation is quite different in its relation to the state from the royal companies of the colonial period, such as the Hudson's Bay Company, the British East India Company, and the like. Yet while Eells and Walton may be correct in claiming that the more important line of corporate genealogy is that which derives from free associations, that line by itself cannot account for the corporation in its modern form.

Abram Chayes explains the coming together of the two genealogical strands to give birth to the very earliest business corporations:

> In the sixteenth and seventeenth centuries, this idea of the legal unity of a group fused with the financial device of joint stock trading to bring to birth the business corporation. At first it too is an organ for accomplishing things the [British] monarchy, newly energetic, wants done...the development of foreign trade, colonization, privateering, the development of native sources of munitions.
> The charter of incorporation continues to include such incidents as monopoly of trade to particular parts or in particular goods, or exemptions from certain burdens and extractions.... The corporation is necessary because the objects pursued are beyond the reach of the members as individuals. The needed amounts of capital are too great, the risk is too high, the duration of the enterprise too long. The corporation is a legal institution which can hold the aggregated capital of many over a period of time unaffected by the death or withdrawal of individuals.[24]

Chayes might also have noted that those purposes which lie "beyond the reach of the members as individuals" also lie beyond the reach of the members as private co-partners. In particular the issues of risk and organizational duration would lead to significant problems if business enterprise were limited to individuals and purely private partnerships. In that case it would be extremely difficult to generate the capital needed for large business ventures. The legal limitation of liability that is a central feature of the modern corporation is crucial to the important public purpose of generating large concentrations of capital. Similarly, those same public purposes require that there be an entity capable of surviving the death or withdrawal of particular partners. Thus, the public charter of the corporation, carrying with it a certain set of privileges and exemptions, was initially developed to serve certain purposes of the king and continues to exist because it serves certain purposes of the public.

Because of the fact that the corporate form of business is a creature of public creation and exists to serve certain public purposes, the public is surely one of its significant constituencies. I have already noted that one of the chief purposes that has led the public to charter corporations has been modern society's need to generate large accumulations of capital. Undoubtedly this is the chief purpose for which the corporation was developed. Yet once developed, the corporate relationship with the public is surely not limited to that purpose of capital accumulation. The corporation remains a public creature, a socially created institution. Its relationship with the public is as complex as that of any other social institution. I shall not go into any greater detail about the character of that relationship or about any of the obligations in either direction that follow from it. Rather, I am simply concerned to establish that the general public is in fact appropriately regarded as a significant corporate constituency. The fact that corporations are publicly chartered, and that this chartering process exists for public purposes, should leave little doubt about the existence of such a relationship with the public.

In viewing the corporation as composed of these several different constituencies, it follows that the relationship between each of these groups and the corporation as a whole cannot adequately be treated simply as a market relationship between independent economic agents. Given this, our understanding of the corporation must go beyond its multiplicity of bilateral financial transfer relationships and look at both internal and external social relationships. I shall look only at those internal relationships over the remaining part of this chapter.

Corporate institutional structure

What distinguishes between a mere collection of individuals or interest groups and an organization is structure. A mere collection of individuals – a mob or a crowd, for example – has no formal structure. As anyone who has witnessed a mob must surely recognize, it can give rise to particular modes of behavior but cannot make a decision. This, I take it, is because a mob cannot deliberate. The moment a mob begins to deliberate it acquires some element of formal structure and ceases to be a mob. An organization, by contrast, has a clear formal structure. By means of this structure it can carry on deliberation and reach decisions. As a result, an organization can act, whereas a mob can merely behave.

In like manner a mere collection of interest groups or constituencies, lacking a stable and unifying decision-making structure, can be no more than a short-term coalition. It can manifest short-term patterns of more or less coherent behavior around those issues on which the interests of the different groups remain sufficiently convergent. Divergent interests, however, usually tend to dissolve the coalition. Like a mob, a mere coalition is incapable of the kind of long-term collectively deliberate behavior that characterizes the activity of an organization.

A satisfactory understanding of the managerial corporation must come from a theory of conscious coordination of economic activity, a theory of collective activity. It must, therefore, deal with the organizational structures that transform and coordinate the various bits of individual activity that are put into the collective into a more or less unified and coherent output of activity. The structure of the corporation, to take the particular type of collective that is the concern of this book, is what takes the individual behaviors of the various constituents of the corporation and transforms them into the activity of "the corporate entity." This "corporate entity" that is thus created can, because of the unity of action that springs from its organizational structure, be taken by the law as a legal person. The actions of the corporation are not simply reducible to the individual actions of those who make corporate decisions.

It is, I take it, incontrovertible that the exact same group of people, composing the exact same set of group constituencies, can come to very different sorts of collective decisions when placed under different forms of group organization. Even apart from the broad view of corporate constituencies that I outlined previously, the corporation must be viewed as an organization composed of individuals with at least partially diverging interests. All other things being equal, the stockholders will be primarily concerned with returns on investment, the managers with managerial salaries and benefits, and labor with wages and labor benefits. A corporate interest cannot simply arise of its own accord from the individual interests of those who make up the corporation. Apart from the constituency differences just noted, there will surely be additional differences within each group about more particular objectives and the preferred means of accomplishing them. Additionally, the broader society may choose to constrain the behavior of the corporation in various ways through the use of governmental action. As a result, the interests that come to shape the behavior of the corporation will be in large measure determined by the structure that dictates who makes what decisions and whose interests are even voiced in the decision-making process.

The most common arrangement of structure in U.S. business corporations has been to take the interests of a particular individual or, more often, a group of individuals, subject to governmentally imposed constraints, as automatically constituting the interests of the corporation, regardless of the interests of others who are also included within the corporation's various constituencies. In most cases this group has been the top management, although in particular decisions (wage and benefit packages, e.g.) it may be expanded to include union leadership, key major stockholders, or perhaps others. This structural arrangement has of late come in for a good deal of criticism as being one of the causes of the poor performance of U.S. business in the face of foreign competition.[25] Perhaps partially in response to this growing criticism, an increasing number of business corporations are taking account of a wider variety of interests in the corporate decision-making process.

In any event, the particular kind of function that moves from the individual interests of corporate constituents to corporate decision will be determined by the internal structure of the corporation combined with its external structural constraints. These will determine which decisions by which individuals in which cases will dictate for the corporation. To remind the reader of the variety of possible functions that enter into corporate decision making, one function that might be operative in the case of a particular governmentally imposed decision could be of the general form: Given any set of preferences of managers, stockholders, and laborers, corporation X will *not* sell goods to country Y. It should be clear then that what a corporation does depends only in part on what individuals and groups constitute the corporation. It also depends in part on the internal structure of the corporation and on the external structure of the corporation, the position that society has given the corporation within the broader set of institutions that make up the society.

The key to understanding the corporation as a locus of collective action, at the same time composed of and yet not reducible to its various constituencies, is the notion of "corporate internal decision [CID] structure" so well developed by Peter French:

Every Corporation has an internal decision structure. CID Structures have two elements of interest to us here: (1) an organizational or responsibility flowchart that delineates stations and levels within the corporate power structure and (2) corporate-decision recognition rule(s) (usually embedded in something called corporation policy). The CID Structure is the personnel organization for the exercise of the corporation's power with respect to its ventures, and as such its primary function is to draw experience from various levels of the corporation into a decision-making and ratification process. When operative and properly activated, the CID Structure accomplishes a subordination and synthesis of the intentions and acts of various biological persons into a corporate decision. When viewed in another way, as already suggested, the CID Structure licenses the descriptive transformation of events, seen under another aspect as the acts of biological persons (those who occupy various stations on the organizational chart), to corporate acts by exposing the corporate character of those events. A CID Structure *incorporates* [French's emphasis] acts of biological persons.[26]

The notion of a CID structure allows us to distinguish, for example, between two communications from a plant manager to a quality control engineer, one a corporate order, the other a personal request. The personal request may well be backed up by personal *power* within the corporate group, but it lacks corporate *authority*. It lacks legitimacy. Every organization, I take it, has some such internal decision procedure. The procedure may either be highly formalized and explicit or may be substantially informal, perhaps customary, and implicit. In either case, however, the procedure stipulates what particular individuals (identified by organization position) are entitled to make what decisions through what processes and have those decisions regarded as decisions of the organization. Even the chief executive officer of a corporation is limited as to which of his or her personal desires can be transformed into aims of the corporation. Providing lavish gifts for a spouse or lover may well be a CEO's private desire, but it would be quite remarkable to find a corporation in which the CEO could, without limitation, transform such a desire into a goal of the corporation.

As should be clear from this, the CID structure performs two absolutely essential functions, corresponding to the two elements that

French identifies. First, in providing "corporate-decision recognition rule(s)," the CID structure provides a means of identifying certain acts as genuinely corporate acts. Corporations frequently adopt explicit statements of policy to the effect that the corporation will pursue certain goals and follow certain procedures, and not others. Some of these policy statements, for example, may be incorporated into a corporate "code of ethics." Others may deal with issues that have little or nothing to do with ethics. Even those corporations that have relatively little in the way of explicit statements of corporate policy will have certain tacit principles roughly delineating the general aims of the corporation. To requote French, the "organizational or responsibility flowchart that delineates stations and levels within the corporate power structure" also forms a part of the corporate-decision recognition rule by indicating which individuals within the corporation are authorized to make certain kinds of decisions for the corporation and under what kinds of circumstances.

Some form of corporate-decision recognition rule is clearly crucial to the corporation's ability to function as a legal entity. If there is some kind of legal wrongdoing within the corporation, say fraud or sexual harassment, the question must invariably arise whether the corporation or some individual within the corporation should bear legal liability for the act. Presumably, it is not reasonable for the corporation to bear legal liability for every bit of wrongdoing that is committed by any corporate employee within the context of his or her employment. Yet equally it would seem clear that if a corporate employee commits some form of legal wrongdoing that is either encouraged or mandated by that employee's corporate superiors in accordance with corporate policy, the corporation itself should at the very least share legal liability for the wrongdoing. From a legal point of view, then, the corporate-decision recognition rule(s) are necessary in order to allocate legal liability.

The organizational flowchart of the CID structure is equally important, making it possible for the corporation to behave in a more or less consistent manner. To take a trivial example, if there were not at least some element of hierarchical organization in an automobile production plant there would be no guarantee that those who made the wheels and those who made the hubs would make those parts with the same number and spacing of holes for the lug nuts that attach the wheels to the hubs. More generally, in a corporation that involves more people than the members of a single family it is virtually impossible that any consensus about the aims and activities to be carried on within the corporation should arise without some structure of authority to generate and enforce such a consensus.

In making the claim that a "CID Structure *incorporates* acts of biological persons," French may be taken to bring together both of these functions of the CID structure: on the one hand, by bringing the acts of different biological persons together into one more or less coherent pattern of behavior, forming one behavioral "body" out of many biological bodies; on the other hand, by specifying certain of the acts of those biological persons as acts of the larger corporate person.

As I have already noted, CID structures will be highly explicit in some corporations, whereas they may be largely implicit and a matter more of custom in others. Even beyond that, some corporations may effectively have two CID structures. There will be the explicit and formal policies of the corporation and the official lines of authority through which corporate decisions are supposed to be reached. Yet on top of that there may be another power structure, one that is composed of unwritten customary practices of the corporation and of unofficial chains of personal power. A person who does not rank high on the formal chain of command may well exercise considerable power within this unofficial structure, either because of longevity within the corporation, because his or her judgment is held in high esteem by those higher up on the official structure, or because he or she is a particularly vicious and effective political infighter and is generally feared by others within the corporation. Note that power within the unofficial structure may be possessed because of either desirable or undesirable personal characteristics. Moreover, it may often be the case that the unofficial chain of command and the implicit principles of corporate practice will play a larger role than the formal authority structure and the explicit corporate policies in determining actual corporate behavior.

I want to argue that it is generally undesirable for a corporation of any significant size either to lack a formal and explicit CID structure or to have that structure easily circumvented by informal principles of operation or channels of control. Initially I want to argue this not on ethical grounds, but on grounds relating simply to corporate efficiency. There is no questioning the fact that an informal and unofficial chain of command may function quite as efficiently as formal and official chains of command for the purpose of coordinating the activity of the biological persons that make up the corporation. All that is required to fulfill that function of the CID structure is that there be some structure of power that is acknowledged by the biological persons whose activities are to be coordinated.

A first area in which a clear and explicit CID structure benefits the corporation is in curbing the tendency of the official chain of command to promote ends that may very well not be legitimately taken as corporate ends. A smooth functioning unofficial decision structure is at least as likely to serve the private ends of those who hold power within that structure as it is to serve the ends of the corporation. Given what I have said already in this chapter, this notion of corporate ends may still seem obscure. I think, however, that an example should serve to clarify my point. Suppose that Jones is a salesperson for the X Corporation. He has been with the X Corporation for twenty years and over that time has acquired a reputation as being a dangerous enemy in intradepartmental politics. Suppose that he is in the practice of extorting kickbacks from the clients to whom he sells X Corporation products. Moreover, in order not to be priced out of competition, Jones must sell X Corporation products at a price well below what he could get for them if the clients didn't need to pay the kickbacks. Finally, suppose that Jones justifies selling at relatively low prices to those higher up in the X Corporation as necessary in order to maintain a high volume of sales. Clearly, I take it, the ends served by Jones's activity serve his private interests. He takes in not only the ordinary salary and sales commissions, but a good bit on kickbacks as well. Just as clearly, his activity does not serve the interests of the corporation. As I have constructed the case, the corporation gets a smaller return than it would if Jones did not extort the kickbacks. Similarly, the corporation may well be the recipient of a certain amount of hostility from its clients because of Jones's behavior. Finally, his practice of extorting kickbacks surely tends to promote a general business climate unlike one in which X Corporation wants to buy and sell.

I take it that a CID structure which would make likely the discovery and censure of behavior like that ascribed to Jones in my example would generally serve the interests of the corporation. In general the more a corporate decision structure allows for the informal negotiation of the interests to be served and protects the unofficial exercise of power (not to be confused here with initiative), the more likely it will be that some biological persons within the corporation will use corporate resources to further their own private ends at the expense of the goals of the corporation.

A second area wherein a clear and highly explicit CID structure tends to promote corporate efficiency is in its tendency to encourage individual initiative within the corporation. One of the well-known problems of loose lines of authority is that they tend to assign credit and blame according to political power rather than accomplishment. Business ethics texts are filled with cases in which costly mistakes were covered up within the corporate structure, often to the point where they became even more costly, simply because the person responsible for the mistake was politically well placed. Accordingly, lower-level employees will be less likely to be innovative and to show initiative if they are confident that their superiors will claim credit for any success that follows from the innovation or initiative.

Again, generally speaking, corporate efficiency is enhanced by a CID structure in which people can be held accountable for both their good and their bad decisions. Obviously, initiative will be discouraged if such clear channels of command and responsibility are combined with a top management that will swiftly punish the author of any failed innovation, but it is equally true that innovation and initiative can only thrive in a corporate environment in which people are encouraged to be creative and are at the same time given both the credit and *appropriate* blame for the results of their creativity.

Finally, a third area in which clarity and explicitness in a CID structure is helpful is in adopting corporate goals. As already noted, once the notion of the corporation as a profit maximizer is abandoned the notions of corporate interests and goals start to become fairly obscure. What we see is a collection of different constituencies with partially overlapping and partially diverging interests vying with each other to have their own group goals incorporated into the aims of the corporation. If the corporation has little in the way of an explicit statement of policy and principle, then the de facto corporate goals are likely to be substantially the private or group interest goals of those who happen to hold the dominant power within the corporation. The determination of corporate goals will be left to a sub-rosa process of behind-the-scenes negotiation and political intrigue. By contrast, in the process of developing, modifying, and maintaining an explicit CID structure the formation and maintenance of corporate goals is carried on in an environment that is far more open. It becomes clear what interests are being served and what goals the corporation has adopted for itself. If some among the constituencies of the corporation take issue with these goals, they can at least be clear about what they are opposing, and they are likely to have a far better idea about how and with whom they should negotiate in an attempt to modify those goals.

All of this, of course, should imply that corporate goals are to a significant degree subject to negotiation (within certain constraints placed by the need to generate adequate financial return), the need to obey the law, and so on. My claim is that the process by which corporate goals can best be negotiated is one in which clear corporate policy is determined through clear channels of corporate authority, which, however, will not guarantee good policy or satisfactory attention to all the claims of the various corporate constituencies. But it should make it easier both to recognize inadequate policy and to focus attention on any failures to attend adequately to various constituent interests. To the extent, then, that a corporation is not to be identified with any one or two of its constituencies, but involves the coming together of all of them, clarity and explicitness of its CID structure not only help the corporation to protect itself against those of its members who would use corporate resources to advance their own private interests at the expense of the interests of the corporation and help the corporation by assigning clear responsibility to the biological persons who make up the corporation, but also help the corporation to constitute itself as a person distinct from its various constituencies, a person with genuinely corporate goals and activity.

Conclusion

In this chapter not only have I argued that corporations in the real world of business are not profit maximizers and should not be regarded as such, but I have argued the far stronger claim that the traditional notion of profits, drawn from its natural home in individual-entrepreneurial business, is not even a very helpful analytical tool in the project of understanding corporate business. It should follow from this that any attempt at a theoretical understanding of the managerial corporation that takes the notion of profits as somehow centrally definitive of the firm must prove severely limited.

What lies at the heart of the managerial corporation is that it is corporate, it is a whole composed of parts that are, moreover, not simply indiscriminate individuals. Rather, the individuals who compose the corporation find themselves naturally aligned in a number of distinct constituent groups.

Equally important, what distinguishes a corporation as corporate, rather than merely aggregative, is the fact that it must have a particular form of institutional structure. Structure, as any of a number of writers on management have pointed out to the business community and to the general reading public as well, makes all the difference in the world to a business's ability to function. There are, of course, a number of different ways in which institutions, business or otherwise, can be structured. If we are to study seriously the reasons why some institutions flourish, while others flounder, in substantially similar external environments, one of the chief things we will need to consider is the differences in structure manifested in those institutions.

The lesson should be clear as it applies to any hope that as Boulding, noted in Chapter 6, expressed it now over a generation ago, "economists might even be of some use to businessmen, and their modest triumphs at the level of national accounting might be matched in the next generation, in the realm of business practice." That lesson is that a satisfactory economic understanding of the managerial corporation must attend to the institutional-corporate character of the corporation. It must move the focus of analysis away from profit and place it instead on issues of constituent interests and institutional structure.

CHAPTER 8

The theoretical impact of a better theory of the firm

Over the course of the past seven chapters we have looked at the development of the marginalist theory of the firm as a part of what now stands as traditional economics and at key characteristic features of the modern large managerial corporation. I have argued, first, that the rise of the marginalist theory of the firm constituted a major change of near revolutionary proportions in the fabric of the tradition in economic theory going back to Smith. Yet I have also suggested, second, that something very much like the present marginalist theory of the firm was the only way of developing a theory of the firm and, at the same time, maintaining a commitment to the methodological individualism that has dominated economic theory since the time of Smith. As a third point, I have argued that while the marginalist theory of the firm is a significantly troubled aspect of economic theory, it nevertheless retains its dominance, at least among economic theorists, by virtue of its status as a part of the more general marginalist theory. Finally, I have argued that those features of the large managerial firm that are most characteristic of that institution are precisely those that are most at odds with the core commitments of traditional marginalist economic theory as I have identified them in Chapter 4.

Undoubtedly many questions remain, but surely one of the most important ones as well as the one that will provide the focus for this final chapter, is this: How significant must be the changes in general economic theory in order for such a general theory to accommodate a more fruitful theory of the firm? We see two quite different answers given to that question. On the one hand, Mark Blaug claims:

The basic problem is that we simply cannot evaluate the traditional theory of the firm without evaluating the whole of neoclassical price theory: the theory of the firm is only a single strand in what is in fact a more comprehensive scientific research program in microeconomics. In praising or condemning the conventional theory of the firm, we necessarily pass judgment on the power of the larger research program of which it forms an integral part.[1]

In short, Blaug sees any revision in the marginalist theory of the firm as striking at the very heart of the economic tradition.

By contrast, Boulding claims:

The essential conceptual framework behind the classical economics is that of supply and demand analysis – the assumption that an improper relationship between production and consumption would have an impact on prices. The theory of maximizing behavior and the marginal analysis comes into economics at a second level of analysis – that of explaining the character of the supply and demand functions. As such it is not essential to economic analysis. It is a sort of porch to the main edifice, which may be remodeled without much affecting the central structure. . . .
This extension of theory [to include a preferable theory of the firm] will not, however, overthrow the existing structure of analysis, which emerges clearly as an important special case. It is not likely to make any spectacular changes in a static theory; it may reasonably be expected to throw new light on economic dynamics.[2]

Boulding, in other words, thinks that a preferable theory of the firm can be constructed neatly within the bounds set by the economic tradition.

At least a major part of the disparate analyses of Blaug and Boulding stems from the fact that they differ in what they identify as "the tradition." Note that Blaug talks of the "neoclassical" tradition. I take it that when "neo" is placed in front of "classical" in talking about the history of economic theory, we are talking about the tradition as it has descended from Jevons and Walras. Clearly, maximizing behavior and marginal analysis are very much at the heart of this tradition. These features are what distinguish "neoclassical" from "classical" economics. Boulding, by contrast, is talking about the classical tradition going back to Smith. He sees maximizing behavior and marginal analysis, quite rightly as I argued in Chapter 4, as something that was a later accretion to the tradition. Yet Boulding also sees maximizing behavior and marginal analysis, and it is not so clear that he is correct on this point, as elements that can now be stripped away from the economic tradition nearly as easily as they were added on in the 1870s. I think that there should be serious doubt as to whether the process of scientific change is quite as reversible as Boulding seems to suggest.[3]

Yet there still seems to be a significant disagreement between Blaug and Boulding on the theoretical impact of a better theory of the firm. Blaug does not believe that the marginalist theory of the firm can be supplanted without a wholesale and radical change in the structure of economic theory. Boulding, by contrast, thinks that the theory of the firm can be modified with minimal effect on the larger economic structure.

Boulding is wrong in this disagreement because he fails to identify correctly the source of the basic problem with the marginalist theory of the firm. This is particularly frustrating because his article, "Implications for General Economics of More Realistic Theories of the Firm," contains an analysis that should have led to a correct identification of the problem. Like so many other writers on the theory of the firm, Boulding focuses on the assumption of profit-maximizing behavior on the part of the firm. He notes, quite correctly as I have argued in the last chapter, that firms do not in fact act that way, and that they should not be expected to act that way. Among the reasons Boulding cites in support of his claim is that firms are organizations that involve a "control mechanism" that "always involves a number of parts."[4] This recognition of the control mechanism involved in firm behavior should have led Boulding to realize that profit maximization is not the real issue here.

In Chapter 6 I argued that the assumption of profit maximization is not central to the marginalist theory of the firm. Given the situational constraints that the theory places on the firm, the profit-maximization assumption is effectively equivalent to a number of other, more modest, assumptions, for example, the assumption that firms avoid bankruptcy. Clearly no one would regard the assumption that firms are bankruptcy avoiders as "unrealistic." The reason that the marginalist theory assumes profit maximization instead of bankruptcy avoidance has to do with systematicity rather than with the particular results that follow from the assumption. Other economic agents are utility maximizers. The most reasonable way to treat the firm on a par with other agents in the economy is to view it also as a maximizer.

This equivalence of more realistic assumptions about profit motivation with less realistic ones, under a situational determinism, should lead to a recognition that the more serious culprit in the marginalist theory of the firm is not the assumption of profit maximization, but rather the situational determinism itself, the construction of a set of situational constraints such that firm behavior is determined by those constraints rather than by the firm's own decision-making mechanism. When those constraints are relaxed – for example, in imperfect or monopolistic competition models – the assumption of profit maximization does come to imply different results from the assumption of bankruptcy avoidance. Yet in the case of such a relaxation of constraints, the theory has little other than considerations of systematic neatness to guide it in the selection of assumptions. There is simply not any alternative assumption that has both sufficient precision to advance the marginalist project vis-à-vis the firm and unambiguously superior empirical support over that given to profit maximization.

Yet behind all this, the most central feature of the marginalist theory of the firm that leads to its unsatisfactoriness is its commitment to methodological individualism. It is marginalism's commitment to methodological individualism that leads it to treat the firm as an indiscriminate individual, and hence as an entity that must be viewed as a maximizer of some sort if it is to fit in systematically with the various other individuals in the theoretical ontology. Methodological individualism allows no room for any kind of analysis of intracorporate decision processes or control mechanisms. Boulding's recognition of this problem of the control mechanism should have led him to see that methodological individualism, not the assumption of profit maximization, constitutes the central defect of the marginalist theory of the firm. Such a recognition, however, would have forced Boulding to modify his conclusion about the depth of the impact of "more realistic theories of the firm." While Boulding is surely correct in noting that marginal analysis is not an essential part of the economic tradition going back to Adam Smith (although marginalism clearly is *the* living heir to that tradition), methodological individualism clearly is an essential part of that whole tradition, as I have already argued in Chapter 4. All of the better theories of the firm require a setting aside of the asocialism constraint required by a strict methodological individualism. Given the centrality of methodological individualism to the tradition, Boulding is clearly wrong in suggesting that relatively minor adjustments in traditional economic theory will suffice for grounding a better theory of the firm.

I am not sure what Boulding means by "the existing structure of analysis." It may well, for all that I have said so far, be possible to extend economic theory beyond the constraints of methodological individualism while retaining a good deal of the present structure of economic theory if we don't understand its "structure" to include its commitment to analysis of all economic activity as a function of the behavior of theoretically basic discrete individuals unaffected by a context of social-political relationships. Similarly, while Blaug is right in saying that in assessing the marginalist theory of the firm, "we necessarily pass judgment on the power of the larger research program of which it forms an integral part," it still does not follow that the replacement of one of the central commitments of that research program would leave us with a type of economic theory totally unlike the present program. The "implications for general economics" of preferable theories of the firm are undoubtedly highly significant. The changes required would significantly alter at least the theoretical perspective that we bring to the study of economic phenomena. Yet it is not clear, at least at the outset, that those implications would have to be of a radically revolutionary sort.

The change in the economic world

There is, I take it, little question of the fact that changes in the world sometimes require changes in theory. A new phenomenon may occur. A new bit of scientific instrumentation is developed that allows us to discover new ranges of data. Such changes in the world give the scientist new problems to explain or may force the conclusion that old phenomena need to be explained in new ways.

It should be perfectly well established by this point that the modern managerial corporation is a relatively new phenomenon in the economic world. Managerial corporations of limited liability, as Mill noted, were not even legal in England until 1855, seven years after the publication of the first edition of his *Principles of Political Economy*.[5] At least as a significant agent in economic affairs, it clearly comes after the rise of the economic tradition based in part on methodological individualism. Economists of virtually every theoretical stripe have recognized this change in the structure of economic society. In Chapter 1 I noted Clark's recognition (in horror) that there was a new type of entity in economic society. From quite another tradition, the U.S. institutionalist John R. Commons observed that "collective action... did not begin generally, for America, until the decade of the 1850's."[6] Perhaps no one put it more poignantly than Papandreou, borrowing on the analysis given in Joseph Schumpeter's *Capitalism, Socialism, and Democracy*:

To the...question...whether or not the changes that have taken place in the structure of our economy amount to a new society, the answer given by most seems to be, "Yes."...Social revolution is taking or has taken place. The "battleground" is the enterprise itself. The "revolutionary" is the capitalist-entrepreneur, himself the victim of his own "revolution." The heir apparent is the "manager," the "planner," the "bureaucrat."[7]

Finally, as I noted in Chapter 3, even Milton Friedman notes that the development of what he calls "enterprises" introduced a new element into our economic society, although, in Friedman's case, he sees no need for any new analytical device in response to that development.

The analysis that Papandreou borrows from Schumpeter is particularly penetrating. It reveals both the evolutionary and the revolutionary character of the rise of the firm. On the one hand, it recognizes the firm as a product of the success of entrepreneurial capitalism. A kind of efficient routinization is introduced not only into the physically productive labor of the capitalist enterprise, but also into innovation and the organizational activity of enterprise as well. This routinization creates the modern manager as a kind of highly specialized laborer. Yet this analysis also recognizes the revolutionary element as well in observing that in this process of routinization, the individual entrepreneur of classical theory is supplanted by the bureaucratic manager as the central force driving the engine of production. Coordination of economic activity ceases to be unconscious, run by an invisible hand coordinating the independent activities of numerous entrepreneurs, as it is according to theories based on methodological individualism. Rather, such coordination becomes, within the firm, the labor union, and various other social collectives, very conscious, guided by the very visible hand of the manager or bureaucrat. The social world in which the manager reigns is quite significantly different from the world in which the classical entrepreneur reigned.

In traditional theory the entrepreneur is constrained by the need to remain solvent in a highly competitive market situation. Prices cannot fall below that level required for the entrepreneur to sustain his or her enterprise. Yet prices cannot rise above that level to which competitors can afford to reduce their prices and yet sustain their enterprises, since knowledgeable and self-interested consumers will invariably purchase products at the lowest available price. When some of those constraints are relaxed, traditional theory tells us that the entrepreneur, because of the general self-interestedness of economic agents assumed by the theory, will pursue greater profits. With the rise of the manager, traditional theory should tell us that the corporate concern with profit, where not determined fully by the mechanism of a perfectly competitive market, should extend only insofar as profit is in the interest of the manager. Under those circumstances, the firm might be expected to have a paramount concern with profit only to the extent that owners enjoy effective control over managers. Yet if we are to believe Alfred Marshall, even in 1890 that was not generally the case. Owners appear in general to have very little control over managers. This leaves managers effectively free to run corporations in the pursuit of the interests of the managers, subject to whatever constraints the situation imposes.

Recently, proposals have been raised on behalf of worker control of business.[8] In principle, worker control is no different from managerial control. Both involve the use of corporate assets in pursuit of the interests of one group (at the expense of other groups) within the corporation. The central difference between worker control and managerial control is that workers comprise a large group within the corporation, managers a very small group. At least in terms of the equity of distribution, this leaves worker control on more defensible ground than managerial control.

Both the economic and the broader social ramifications of the present arrangements are scathingly characterized by business manager-entrepreneur and sometimes corporate raider Carl Icahn:

When America built its economic leadership, managers were accountable to owners. If a company was in trouble, the Carnegies or Mellons or Morgans fired the president. But as stock ownership dispersed, management became accountable to no one. Boards became a travesty, made up of rubber-stampers. When it was time to choose a successor, directors would go after someone "likable."

All this makes a modern chief executive much like a feudal baron. He has a retinue, though the courtiers are more likely to be fawning MBAs than squires, and the symbols of power are jets and yachts instead of horses or castles. But make no mistake, a strongly knit corporate aristocracy exists in America.

The top man, what's more, usually finds expanding his power more important than rewarding owners.[9]

If Icahn is right, and the study of both managerial behavior and U.S. society strongly suggest that he is, then the rise of the modern managerial corporation has created an economic world quite different from that envisaged by traditional economic theory. The role of the manager appears to have a profound impact on what goes on in the economy, in terms of distribution, production, and allocation. Yet the role of manager is one that gets no explicit mention within the framework of traditional economic theory. Marginalist economic theory gives us firms and households. Moreover, as we have already seen, the firm is effectively treated as an entrepreneur. It would surely seem that the manager is too important a component of modern economies to be ignored by theory.

What becomes readily apparent from Icahn's reflections on the U.S. corporation, as well as from some of the pre-1930s discussions of the managerial organization of business, is that the major constraints on managerial behavior must come from the way the role of management is structured into the organization of business. The behavior of the modern manager, unlike that of the traditional entrepreneur, is not, as I argued in Chapter 6, tightly constrained by the forces of the market. Sufficiently high-level managers have made decisions that have left their companies bankrupt and still retired on extremely large pensions. To the extent, then, that business behavior is going to be rational from the point of view of the corporate entity, not just from the point of view of the private interests of the manager, managerial behavior must operate within sufficiently restrictive constraints set by corporate organizational relationships.

If the day of the entrepreneur is over, as Icahn, Papandreou, Schumpeter, and a host of others seem to suggest, the present period is best viewed not as the day of the manager-bureaucrat, but as the day of the organization. To accept the day of the managerial corporation as the day of the manager-bureaucrat would be, as Icahn implies, to accept merely a new kind of feudalism. If the traditionally alleged virtues of entrepreneurial capitalism are to survive (or revive) in these days of the corporation, the invisible hand of the market must not be succeeded by the iron hand of the manager, but by the visible hand of the organization. Even outside the corporation, a very large part of the economic behavior of individuals has its primary impact on economic society as it is mediated by some organization, whether that be corporation, labor union, or the like. The contemporary economic world is no longer simply a world of individuals, but instead a world of individuals within organizations.

The needed change in economic theory

As I argued in the last chapter, the key operative factors in the life of the managerial corporation are no longer owner-entrepreneur and profit. Rather, they are constituency and organization. From this it must surely follow that an economic theory that centers its analysis of the economic phenomenon of production on the notions of firm-entrepreneur and profits will, to that extent, prove unsatisfactory. Somewhere along the line, the key operative factors in the actual process of corporate life must find a place in economic theory.

It should be clear at this point that the group, the economic collective or organization, is not simply the sum of its parts. It is, in a sense, a function of its parts, but the precise character of the function is determined by the organizational structure of the group. Moreover, it should also be clear that economic institutions can be organized in different ways, just as political institutions can be organized in different ways. Icahn's reflections on the U.S. manager reflect the way business operates on a certain model of organizational structure, a structure wherein management has virtually unconstrained discretion to run the corporation. Yet it is equally possible to organize economic institutions in ways that will place certain clear constraints on managerial behavior. Surely one of the central lessons of Williamson's work, for example, is that the M-form corporate structure channels managerial motivation in a more efficient manner than does the U-form corporate structure.[10] Similarly, corporations sometimes will have ethical codes and statements of long-range policy, and I take it that it is even possible that there could be restrictions on corporate charters, all of which might constrain managerial behavior in the direction of the attainment of certain ends desired by various corporate constituencies.

Collective action, like all human action, is directed to the attainment of some end or ends. Yet there is a certain givenness to individual ends that is clearly not present in collective ends. We frequently can and do attempt to influence individual ends, by various means of persuasion. Yet we cannot actually *change* those ends without doing some sort of violence to the individual. All those means by which an individual's ends are changed, not simply influenced – brainwashing, controlled conditioning, surgical alteration of the brain, and so on – accomplish their objectives by leaving the individual under a more or less alien control. In this sense, then, normal individual ends are, whether right or wrong, given in the individual (I am not in any sense trying to discount the influence of a wide collection of environmental factors on the formation of those ends).

Institutional ends are not simply given once we know what individuals comprise the institution. This in itself should serve to demonstrate that the institution is not simply the sum of the individuals that comprise it. To have institutional ends we must also have an organization of the institution that will generate those ends from the ends of the various individuals influenced by the institution. The institution must, in other words, have a polity. The general direction in which I am arguing should, of course, now be transparent. I want to argue that in a modern organizational economy, economics cannot have the kind of independence from politics that has been assumed by neoclassical theory.

The position I am advocating is not, I think, as radical a departure as it appears from the basic aims of even marginalist economics. Let us return for a moment to Jevons's characterization of the central problem of economics. "Given, a certain population, with various needs and powers of production, in possession of certain lands and other sources of materials: required, the mode of employing their labor which will maximize the utility of the produce."[11] In the time of Jevons the needs of the various members of society were supposedly expressed in a decentralized market. Similarly, society's powers of production operated on a sufficiently small scale to produce most effectively in such a decentralized market. Now, however, a great many of those needs are expressed through highly centralized organizations. Moreover, organizations have now come to occupy the central role in society's powers of production, as the scale of production has expanded to a point requiring administrative coordination by professional managers. If the problem of economy at all concerns the efficient satisfaction of human needs, then economic theory must surely treat the mechanisms through which those needs are expressed as well as the agents of production that make possible the satisfaction of those needs. In a time when the mechanism for expressing needs is a decentralized market and when it is simply individuals who control the powers of production that produce the objects for satisfying them, it is reasonable for an economic theory to deal only with isolated individuals interacting in such a market. However, when that whole process involves a host of complex and interrelated institutions, then an adequate economic theory must be able to treat those institutions as well.

Similarly, the traditional theory of economic equilibrium is concerned with decentralized economies in which the behavioral decisions of economic individuals are made independently of each other. Clearly any economy, even a modern organizational one, has aspects of decentralization in it. As clearly, there are realms of economic activity in which individual decisions are made in relative independence. It is in these areas where the traditional marginalist theory has achieved its greatest triumphs. Yet it is important for a general theory of the economy to be comprehensive, to be able to deal with not only the areas of decentralized decision making in our society, but the areas of centralized, bureaucratic decision making as well.

If economic theory is to be comprehensive in this sense, it needs to provide an account of collective action, which requires a significant expansion of the scope of economic theory. We may study individual ends in the manner in which traditional economic theory has done by taking the ends as given and going on to investigate the most reasonable means of accomplishing those ends. Yet when we move to the study of collective ends, it becomes important to extend our investigation into the area of group decision making – that process whereby institutional ends are formed, as well as the process whereby means are determined for the pursuit of institutional ends.

Ironically, decision making is the one important component of collective action that is almost completely ignored in Mancur Olson's book bearing the very promising title *The Logic of Collective Action: Public Goods and the Theory of Groups*.[12] The term 'decision making' in fact never even appears in his index. Olson makes an important contribution in recognizing the distinctiveness of group behavior, in particular that "it is *not* [Olson's emphasis] in fact true that the idea that groups will act in their self-interest follows logically from the premise of rational and self-interested [individual] behavior."[13] Groups, at least large groups, often fail to optimize their collective self-interest.[14]

Olson is concerned with how such factors as the size and composition of groups affect their ability to achieve their goals. Most interestingly for my purposes, he identifies a kind of group that he calls "federal," "a group divided into a number of small groups, each of which has a reason to join with the others to form a federation representing the group as a whole."[15] This notion of federal group has considerable potential value in providing an analytical tool for the analysis of the managerial corporation. It is, for example, clearly a more general notion than Williamson's idea of the M-form organization, and hence may well provide the kind of analytical category in terms of which to treat different corporate constituencies coming together in a single corporation. Unfortunately, Olson does not go on to apply this tool of analysis to the corporation. His interest in the corporation seems instead to be limited to explaining why stockholders in corporations of diffuse stock ownership prove unable to exercise effective control over management.[16]

To the extent that Olson is concerned with decision making, it is limited to charismatic decision making, to the exclusion of bureaucratic decision making. Given the role of bureaucracy in most modern organizations, in the managerial corporation in particular, this is quite remarkable. His discussion of group decision making occurs at the very end of his 1971 appendix, where he deals with the incorporation of the concept of the entrepreneur into his analysis. "Imaginative entrepreneurs will be able to find or create selective incentives that can support a sizable and stable organization providing a collective good to a larger group."[17] While what Olson calls "entrepreneurial" decision making surely does play a role in the modern managerial corporation, decision making in the managerial corporation is far more frequently better understood as bureaucratic.

To date, much of the most impressive work in the analysis of decision-making processes has been done by behavioral theorists of the firm. There is surely a good deal of promise in the project of extending this work into a general theory of economics. Cyert and Pottinger give something of an outline of a part of that project:

> We believe that the most reasonable policy for economists is ... with the help of the psychologist and the organization theorist, to try to construct a microeconomic theory based on a theory of the firm which explains the decision processes involved in these facts. In order to do this the economist must understand more about the activities of the decision maker or decision making group. ... On our view the job of the economist is to demonstrate through the use of all knowledge available to him why the firm stops its search process when it does, to explain how the forces within the organization and the market have combined to make the level of investment in the plant what it is, and to show how the effects of the various competing groups within the firm and the market forces have worked to determine price changes and output in particular cases. This is a formidable task, but it is nowhere written that the doing of science must be easy.[18]

The crucial point that Cyert and Pottinger make is that economic decisions are made through a combination of forces within the organization and within the market.

The study of how the "various competing groups within the firm" have worked to determine firm aims is, at least in part, a study in politics. It involves the study of the organizational patterns through which individual aims are both shaped by and transformed into group aims.

It is important that an economic theory expanded to deal with the managerial corporation be able to examine a variety of different decision-making models, or models of social choice for social institutions generally, much as Williamson examines different models for social choice within present business management.[19] If it is through organizational decision-making processes that individuals express their various aims, it becomes important to examine the extent to which various modes of organization actually succeed at giving expression to the aims of the various individuals that are involved with them. In politics, few of us would say that medieval monarchies are as good as Swiss democracy at expressing the political priorities of large numbers of members of society. Similarly, it must be abundantly clear at this point that certain modes of organizing economic collectives prove to be more effective means of expressing the economic and other aims of those in society who are affected by those collectives.

What one would hope for from such an examination of different forms of institutional organization would be a determination of those forms of organization that do a reasonable versus a relatively poor job of expressing the interests of the institution's various constituencies. It does not appear, for example, that those models that allow relatively unrestrained managerial discretion would come out strong in this area. This kind of analysis of satisfactory and unsatisfactory organizational forms should prove of significant benefit in the design of governmental policy in the area of corporate chartering and subsequent regulation. It should also prove of great benefit to those within corporations who wish to implement more rational organizational forms within their corporations.

This is not the place and I am not the person to develop a comprehensive economic theory that would be adequate to ground a better theory of the firm. My purpose here is primarily to suggest what it seems to me must be included in such a theory. The single most fundamental modification of existing theory must be the development of a theory of conscious coordination.[20] Traditional economic theory has done quite an impressive job of constructing a theory of unconscious coordination, a theory of independent individual agents interacting in markets or market-like mechanisms. Yet if economic theory is to prove adequate to the modern world, a world in which there is at least as much conscious coordination of economic activity through economic organizations as there is unconscious coordination, then traditional theory must be supplemented by a theory of such conscious coordination, in short, a theory of collective action.

It is somewhat surprising that institutional economics, whose program starts out with a concern to understand collective action, has thus far done very little to develop such a theory of conscious coordination. There are two features of the institutionalist program that seem to me to have prevented institutional economists from developing the kind of comprehensive economic theory for which their program had such rich potential. The first problem is the institutionalists' inadequate view of method. The restriction of institutional analysis to the description and classification of existing institutional forms makes it impossible to generate the kinds of general hypotheses that will give rise to genuine and comprehensive theory.

The second problem is the assumption of all too many institutionalist economists that institutions are predominantly static. Wendell Gordon, for example, claims that institutionalist economics has traditionally held a view of institutions as: "(1) static, (2) inherited from the past, (3) past-glorifying, (4) psychologically defensible, (5) dictatorial, and (6) creatures of habit."[21] Simply by virtue of the fact that institutions are given a stable organization, are routinized, there is a sense in which they are static. Simply by virtue of the fact that or-

ganizations have authority, there is a sense in which they are dictatorial. However, it is important to realize that human institutions have
shown a remarkable plasticity, an ability to adapt to significant change.
They have routinized innovation in a wide variety of ways, showing
themselves to be remarkably resilient.

Unfortunately, what we might call the "methodological collectivism"
of most institutional economists has led them to fail – just as marginalist economists have failed – to recognize the dynamic interplay between human individuals and the institutions within which they live
and work. Marginalist theory, and traditional post-Smithian theory
more generally, have failed to account for the role of the collective
in economic society. Marginalist analysis has not taken account of the
ways in which individuals and their behavior are shaped by the institutions in which those individuals participate. All action is seen
simply as an arithmetic function of individual action. By contrast,
institutional theory has tended to regard institutions as static and
given, with individuals as little more than cogs within those institutions. As such, institutional analysis has taken little account of the ways
in which institutions are shaped and enlivened by the interests and
activities of the individuals who participate in them. All action is simply
a function of the interplay between the inertia of static institutions
and the dynamic impulse supplied by an ongoing development of
material technology. Human individuals get left out of institutional
analysis just as much as institutions get left out of marginal analysis.

The work of the behavioral theorists of the firm, by contrast, has
been much more fruitful in this area. The various models of decision
making developed by behavioral theorists in areas from chess playing
to the conduct of scientific research,[22] to business management, have
shown remarkable sensitivity to the interplay between individual and
group influences in decision making. Yet the behavioral theorists continue to be inhibited in the attempt to construct general theory by
their general inductivist methodology. As Cyert and Pottinger themselves have acknowledged, as long as the behavioral theorists work
primarily by developing computer simulations of various particular
decision-making processes they will make little headway in the direction of identifying the impact of different organizational models as
vehicles for expressing and realizing the aspirations of the individuals
that constitute the various organizational constituencies. While this
point is something that the behavioral theorists themselves acknowledge, it is also a serious methodological limitation in the potential
value of their program.

I am inclined to think that the most promising approach would involve something of an extension of the work of Williamson and others in developing managerial models of the firm. As I noted, Williamson has done some important work in examining the impact of various modes of organizing the managerial level of business. He now locates his "transaction cost economics" as "part of the New Institutionalist Economics research tradition."[23] The central concern of transaction cost economics involves "requiring the analyst to examine those microanalytic attributes of organization where the relevant comparative institutional action resides, by disclosing hitherto neglected transaction cost features, and by insisting that assessment be made not abstractly but in comparative institutional terms."[24]

Williamson's work does, as I noted in Chapter 5, retain much of the motivational structure of the marginalist tradition, but it also explicitly rejects the notion that rationality requires maximizing behavior.[25] With the rejection of maximizing rationality in favor of a more modest view of "bounded rationality," the situational determinism that I have all along argued is one of the chief problems of traditional analysis also falls. Similarly, as is by now apparent, Williamson's approach takes seriously the need to recognize an interplay between individual and institution. Obviously this approach needs to be extended, even within the analysis of business organizations. Very little, for example, has been done with what I have argued is the very fundamental notion of corporate constituencies. There needs, accordingly, to be more careful analyses – extending, for example, Williamson's preliminary discussions of constituencies in corporate governance[26] – of the likely impact of giving genuine voice in business decision making to constituencies of the corporation other than management.

What is now just a theory of the way in which management controls business corporations must be extended into a general theory of collective action. Nonmanagement groups clearly engage in collective action in a variety of areas but need to play a more important role in corporate governance if corporations are to serve well either the traditional economic concern with efficiency or the broader social concern with equity. The general kind of analysis carried on within a very restricted area by Williamson should be carried out within a wider variety of economic institutions. The key lies in providing an analysis of the ways in which the institutional relationships within which individuals produce and consume shape both individual and aggregate economic behavior. This general approach, I think, has considerable promise of providing a base for a general theory of collective action.

While some such modification of economic theory seems to be required simply by the normal demands of science, it is perhaps even more strongly required by the demands of public policy. Certainly one of the most significant economic problems to have befallen the United States since the great depression has been the savings and loan crisis of the late 1980s. That crisis was brought on largely by the development of the junk-bond market, which in turn was a product of the hostile takeover boom of that same decade. There is, I would submit, strong reason to believe that the development of these conditions was a direct result of the fact, noted three-quarters of a century earlier by Clark, that "the law still treats [the corporation] somewhat as though in its collective entirety each one were an individual." While the law has been struggling to develop principles to help guide decisions about the rights and responsibilities of corporate management and stockholders to each other and to various other corporate constituencies, it gets no theoretical help from economics. Surely society can reasonably expect more. Economic theory must provide us with more than, to use Boulding's words, "modest triumphs at the level of national accounting," more even than matching triumphs "in the realm of business practice." At present what society needs from economists at least as much is a guide for the framing of business policy.

The impact on the old theory

I noted at the beginning of this chapter Blaug's claim that "in praising or condemning the conventional theory of the firm, we necessarily pass judgment on the power of the larger research program of which it forms an integral part." Clearly the last several chapters have constituted something of a condemnation of the traditional theory of the firm. If Blaug is right, that also implies something of a condemnation of the general marginalist economic theory, or, to use Blaug's words, the marginalist "program." It is important at this point to see how much condemnation is implied by what I have said above. First, there may be some benefit to distinguishing the marginalist theory from the marginalist program. By "the marginalist program," I shall understand the commitment to giving marginalist-type explanations to all economic phenomena. Thus the marginalist *program* carries with it a firm commitment to methodological individualism. To this extent then, the foregoing chapters imply a strong condemnation of the marginalist program. The analysis that I have given claims that there are large areas of economic phenomena that will resist any analysis given on the basis of methodological individualism.

In contrast, by "the marginalist theory," I understand a particular type of analysis of individual economic activity. The claims that I have made for the superiority of nonmarginalist theories of the firm do not imply the incorrectness of the marginalist theory as an analysis of individual economic behavior. They merely imply that the marginalist theory has a range of applicability that is far more limited than most mainstream economists would claim for it.

I have already argued that a general economic theory needs an account of both individual action and collective action, an account of both unconscious and conscious coordination of economic activity. There is nothing in the arguments developed thus far that would preclude a general economic theory that included a theory of unconscious coordination that was substantially a counterpart to the present marginalist theory. Presumably the present marginalist theory would not remain in precisely its current form as a simple part of the larger more comprehensive theory, just as Newtonian physics does not remain simply as a part of relativistic physics. Yet just as most of the basic laws of Newtonian physics are affirmed, at least in the form of rough counterparts, by relativistic physics; so we might well anticipate that much of the structure and many of the results of marginalist economic theory could be affirmed, again at least in rough counterpart form, within the new economic theory that would be required for an adequate account of collective action and the impact of collective membership on individual action.

In this sense, then, the development of an economic theory that would be able to deal with genuine collective action would not require the wholesale abandonment of whatever gains have been made by marginalist economics. Perhaps, as I earlier suggested, such development might even follow substantially along Williamsonian lines. Nevertheless, such a development must occur. When confronted with the weakness of the marginalist theory of the firm, the marginalist economist most often responds with something like "Yes, but look at all the things marginalist theory does well." My response to this is that if economics wishes to maintain a genuinely scientific perspective, it must not rest content with a particular range of triumphs, but must push on to strengthen itself in those areas where it is presently weak. The ubiquitous character of collective action in the real economic world makes it quite unreasonable to rest content with an economic theory whose weakness lies in the area of explaining collective action.

Conclusion

Before closing this book, a review of the main argument of the work is in order. In the present time, one in which corporations carry on by far the largest portion of economic activity in our society and in which corporations are as common a feature of the economic landscape as flesh-and-blood persons, there has been a tendency to think of the corporation as a kind of thing that has always been with us, created by God "in the Beginning." There seems also to be, as a corollary to this first tendency, a tendency to view the marginalist theory of the firm as an integral part of a venerable tradition of economic theory going back virtually unchanged to the work of Adam Smith. The first phase in my argument, then, has been to establish that the development of the marginalist theory of the firm, a development that goes back only into the 1930s, actually constituted a major, perhaps revolutionary, modification in the development of traditional economic theory. I also argue, however, that the development of the marginalist theory of the firm was only one of a large number of changes that have taken place within the economic tradition, and that about the only things that have remained constant since the time of Smith have been a general commitment to methodological individualism, a belief that economic agents are self-interested, and a preference for nonintentional (or unconscious) over intentional (or conscious) coordination of economic activity.

My argument then moves on, after surveying the central current types of theories of the firm, to argue that the marginalist theory of the firm is beset by a number of confusions and problems, noting particularly the very narrow range of behavior that it succeeds in explaining and the pervasive tendency among economists and their political followers to try to use that theory to explain or advocate behavior that falls outside the legitimate scope of the marginalist theory. I then argue that despite the failings of the marginalist theory of the firm already noted, that theory continues to retain broad allegiance, particularly among economic theorists. I argue that this allegiance to the marginalist theory of the firm is rational for the economic theorist not because of any support that the theory receives from its ability to predict what goes on in the economic world (since its predictive scope is not at all broad nor its success at all impressive), but rather because of the immense support that the marginalist theory of the firm receives simply by being a part of the general marginalist program in economics. It seems to be the only way of theorizing about the corporation without abandoning methodological individualism.

There is a two-way relationship between the marginalist theory of the firm and the general marginalist theory of economics. Just as the successes of the general marginalist theory of economics lend support to the marginalist theory of the firm, so the shortcomings of the marginalist theory of the firm reveal a significant weakness in the general marginalist economic theory. That weakness is the inability of marginalist theory to deal with collective action and with conscious coordination of economic activity.

The ultimate conclusions of this book are, first, that an adequate analysis of the firm must attend to the character of the managerial corporation as a genuine collective and to the very conscious kind of coordination of economic activity that goes on within the firm (to the notions of constituency and organizational structure); and, second, that the need to have an adequate theory of the firm should spur efforts to develop a new general theory of economics that would also be adequate to deal with collective action and conscious coordination of economic activity.

In Chapter 1 I noted Clark's contention that the failure of the law to recognize the collective character of the corporation led to social consequences of an extremely undesirable sort, "vitiating the action of economic laws...[and] perverting governments." That failure to recognize the corporation as a collective has beset economic theory as well as law. I have accordingly argued that the recognition of the collective character of the modern managerial corporation requires changes in economic theory, changes in our understanding of what constitutes the laws by which the economic world operates.

Notes

Introduction

1 Alfred D. Chandler, Jr., *The Visible Hand: The Managerial Revolution in American Business* (Cambridge, MA: Harvard University Press, 1977), pp. 16, 497.
2 See John Bates Clark, *Essentials of Economic Theory* (New York: Macmillan, 1924), pp. 376–77 (copyright 1907).

1. The hidden change in economic theory

1 A. W. Coats, "Is There a 'Structure of Scientific Revolutions' in Economics?" *Kyklos*, Vol. 22 (1969), p. 292.
2 D. Gordon, "The Role of the History of Economic Thought in Understanding Modern Economic Theory," *American Economic Review: Papers and Proceedings*, Vol. 55 (1965), pp. 123, 124.
3 Adam Smith, *An Inquiry into the Nature and Causes of the Wealth of Nations*, Vol. 2 (Oxford University Press, 1976), p. 741.
4 Alfred Marshall, *Principles of Economics*, 8th ed. (London: Macmillan Press, 1920), p. 303 (1st ed., 1890).
5 Clark, *Essentials of Economic Theory*, pp. 376–77.
6 Marshall, *Principles*, p. 302.
7 John Stuart Mill, *Principles of Political Economy*, Vol. 1, 5th ed. (New York: Appleton, 1894), p. 187 (1st ed., 1848).
8 See R. Joseph Monsen, Jr., and Anthony Downs, "A Theory of Large Managerial Firms," *Journal of Political Economy*, Vol. 73, No. 3 (June 1965), pp. 221–36. See also, Eugene Fama, "Agency Problems and the Theory of the Firm," *Journal of Political Economy*, Vol. 88 (1980), pp. 288–307; and Oliver E. Williamson, *The Economics of Discretionary Behavior: Managerial Objectives in a Theory of the Firm* (Chicago: Markham, 1967); idem, *Corporate Control and Business Behavior* (Englewood Cliffs, NJ: Prentice-Hall, 1970); and idem, *The Economic Institutions of Capitalism* (New York: Macmillan, 1987).
9 Clark, *Essentials of Economic Theory*, p. 1.
10 Kenneth E. Boulding, "Implications for General Economics of More Realistic Theories of the Firm," *American Economic Review Proceedings*, Vol. 42 (May 1952), p. 42.

11 Paul A. Samuelson and William D. Nordhaus, *Economics*, 12th ed. (New York: McGraw-Hill, 1985), p. 444.

12 Frank H. Knight, *The Economic Organization* (New York: Augustus Kelly, 1951), pp. 29–30. (Privately printed in 1933)

13 Ibid., pp. 23–24.

14 James M. Buchanan, "The Economizing Element in Knight's Ethical Critique of Capitalist Order," *Ethics*, Vol. 98, No. 1 (October 1987), p. 61.

15 Andreas G. Papandreou, "Some Basic Problems in the Theory of the Firm," in Bernard F. Haley, ed., *A Survey of Contemporary Economics*, Vol. 2 (Homewood, IL: Irwin, 1953), p. 183.

16 See Mark Blaug, *Economic Theory in Retrospect* (Homewood, IL: Irwin, 1962), p. 283.

17 See Boulding, "Implications for General Economics of More Realistic Theories of the Firm," p. 35; and Fritz Machlup, "Theories of the Firm: Marginalist, Behavioral, Managerial," *American Economic Review*, Vol. 57, No. 1 (March 1967), p. 3.

18 Blaug, *Economic Theory in Retrospect*, p. 284.

19 Machlup, "Theories of the Firm," p. 3.

20 See Joan Robinson, *The Economics of Imperfect Competition* (London: Macmillan Press, 1938); and E. H. Chamberlin, *The Theory of Monopolistic Competition*, 6th ed. (Cambridge, MA: Harvard University Press, 1948).

21 Milton Friedman, "The Methodology of Positive Economics," in Friedman, *Essays in Positive Economics* (Chicago: University of Chicago Press, 1953), pp. 7–8.

2. Four views of scientific change

1 Mark Blaug, "Kuhn versus Lakatos *or* Paradigms versus Research Programmes in the History of Economics," in Spiro Latsis, ed., *Method and Appraisal in Economics* (Cambridge University Press, 1976), pp. 149–50.

2 See Larry Laudan, *Science and Values* (Berkeley & Los Angeles: University of California Press, 1984), especially chap. 3.

3 Karl R. Popper, *Objective Knowledge: An Evolutionary Approach* (Oxford University Press, 1972), pp. 191–92.

4 See Stanley Wong, "The F-Twist and the Methodology of Paul Samuelson," *American Economic Review*, Vol. 63 (June 1973), pp. 312–25.; Lawrence A. Boland, "A Critique of Friedman's Critics," *Journal of Economic Literature*, Vol. 17 (June 1979), pp. 503–22; and William J. Frazer, Jr., and Lawrence A. Boland, "An Essay on the Foundations of Friedman's Methodology," *American Economic Review*, Vol. 73 (March 1983), pp. 129–31.

5 See Karl Popper, *Conjectures and Refutations* (London: Routledge & Kegan Paul, 1963), pp. 107–14.

6 Ibid., p. 215.

7 Karl Popper, *The Logic of Scientific Discovery* (New York: Harper & Row, 1965), p. 276.
8 Popper, *Objective Knowledge*, p. 191.
9 Bruce J. Caldwell, "Clarifying Popper," *Journal of Economic Literature*, Vol. 29 (March 1991), p. 30.
10 Margaret Masterman, for example, has identified no less than twenty-one different definitions of the term 'paradigm' in *The Structure of Scientific Revolutions* in her article, "The Nature of a Paradigm," in Imre Lakatos and Alan Musgrave, *Criticism and the Growth of Knowledge* (Cambridge University Press, 1970), pp. 61–65.
11 Thomas Kuhn, *The Structure of Scientific Revolutions*, 2nd ed. (Chicago: University of Chicago Press, 1970), p. 109.
12 Criticisms along this line are developed in greater detail in Larry Laudan, *Progress and its Problems* (Berkeley & Los Angeles: University of California Press, 1977), pp. 74ff.
13 Blaug, "Kuhn versus Lakatos *or* Paradigms versus Research Programmes in the History of Economics," p. 149.
14 Kuhn, *The Structure of Scientific Revolutions*, pp. 157–58.
15 Imre Lakatos, "Falsification and the Methodology of Scientific Research Programmes," p. 132.
16 Ibid., p. 135.
17 Ibid., p. 118.
18 See Laudan, *Science and Values*, pp. 23–41.
19 Ibid., p. 63.
20 Ibid., pp. 60–61.
21 Ibid., pp. 58–59.
22 Ibid., p. 50.
23 Ibid., p. 52.
24 Ibid.
25 Ibid., p. 53.
26 Laudan, *Progress and Its Problems*, pp. 78–79.
27 See Axel Leijonhufvud, "Schools, 'Revolutions', and Research Programmes in Economic Theory," in Spiro Latsis, ed., *Method and Appraisal in Economics* (Cambridge University Press, 1976), esp. pp. 66–67.
28 See E. Roy Weintraub, *General Equilibrium Analysis: Studies in Appraisal* (Cambridge University Press, 1985), pp. 112ff.
29 Ibid., p. 150.

3. A glance at the history of economic theory

1 T. W. Hutchison, in *On Revolutions and Progress in Economic Knowledge* (Cambridge University Press, 1978), identifies Smith, Ricardo and James Mill, Jevons, and Keynes as leaders of revolutions. Dudley Dillard, in "Revolutions in Economic Theory," *Southern Economic Journal*, Vol. 44 (April 1978), pp. 705–24, identifies Smith, Ricardo, John Stuart Mill, Mar-

shall, and Keynes as revolutionaries. Finally, B. J. Loasby, in "Hypothesis and Paradigm in the Theory of the Firm," *Economic Journal*, Vol. 81 (December 1971), pp. 863–85, speaks of the development of theories of monopolistic competition (Chamberlin) and imperfect competition (Robinson) as a paradigm change, hence a revolution. While Loasby does argue that Chamberlin and Robinson put forward theories that are significantly different, he does not seem to want to identify their theories as separate revolutions.

2 See especially, Smith, *Wealth of Nations*, Vol. 1, pp. 455–56.
3 Ibid., p. 67.
4 Ibid., pp. 264–65.
5 Ibid., p. 266.
6 Ibid.
7 Ibid., p. 267.
8 Spiro J. Latsis, "A Research Programme in Economics," in Latsis, ed., *Method and Appraisal in Economics*, p. 24.
9 Smith, *Wealth of Nations*, Vol. 1, p. 267.
10 David Ricardo, *Principles of Political Economy and Taxation* (London: George Bell & Sons, 1891), p. 1. (Originally published in 1817)
11 Blaug, *Economic Theory in Retrospect*, p. 85.
12 Ricardo, *Principles of Political Economy and Taxation*, pp. 65–69.
13 Mill, *Principles of Political Economy*, Vol. 1, p. 42.
14 Ibid., pp. 41–42.
15 Smith, *Wealth of Nations*, Vol. 1, p. 138.
16 Mill, *Principles of Political Economy*, Vol., 1, p. 259.
17 Ibid., p. 516.
18 Ibid., pp. 496–97.
19 Ibid., p. 497.
20 W. Stanley Jevons, *Theory of Political Economy*, 4th ed. (London: Macmillan Press, 1911), p. 267.
21 Ibid., p. 21.
22 Ibid., p. 3.
23 Jevons, *Theory of Political Economy*, 1st ed. (London: Macmillan Press, 1871), p. 58. (This passage is deleted in later editions.)
24 Jevons, *Theory of Political Economy*, 4th ed., p. 13.
25 Alfred Marshall, *Principles of Economics*, 8th ed. (London: Macmillan Press, 1920), p. v.
26 Ibid., p. vi.
27 Ibid., p. 14.
28 Ibid., p. 40.
29 Ibid., p. 49.
30 Alfred Marshall, *Industry and Trade* (London: Macmillan Press, 1919).
31 Reprinted in A. C. Pigou, ed., *Memorials of Alfred Marshall* (New York: Kelley & Millman, 1956), p. 307.
32 Blaug, *Economic Theory in Retrospect*, p. 375.

33 See A. C. Pigou, "An Analysis of Supply," *The Economic Journal*, Vol. 38, No. 150 (June 1928), pp. 238–57; and Lionel Robbins, "The Representative Firm," *The Economic Journal*, Vol. 38, No. 151 (September 1928), pp. 387–404.

34 Clark, *The Distribution of Wealth*, p. v.

35 Clark, *Essentials of Economic Theory*, p. 1.

36 Ibid., pp. 60, 62.

37 Chamberlin maintained that the two are clearly different theories; see *The Theory of Monopolistic Competition*, 6th ed. (Cambridge, MA: Harvard University Press, 1948), pp. 191–218.

38 Latsis, "A Research Programme in Economics," p. 27.

39 See D. P. O'Brien, "The Evolution of the Theory of the Firm," in Frank H. Stephen, ed., *Firms, Organization and Labor: Approaches to the Economics of Work Organizations* (New York: St. Martin's, 1984), pp. 31–35.

40 Robinson, *The Economics of Imperfect Competition*, p. 15.

41 Ibid., p. 17.

42 John Maynard Keynes, *The General Theory of Employment, Interest, and Money* (New York: Harcourt, Brace & World, 1935), p. 245.

43 Ibid.

44 Blaug, "Kuhn versus Lakatos *or* Paradigms versus Research Programmes in the History of Economics," p. 161.

45 J. W. N. Watkins, "Ideal Types and Historical Explanation," *British Journal for the Philosophy of Science*, Vol. 3 (1952), pp. 22–43.

46 Keynes, *The General Theory*, p. 96, cited in Watkins, "Ideal Types and Historical Explanation," p. 33.

47 Watkins, "Ideal Types and Historical Explanation," p. 33.

48 Keynes, *The General Theory*, pp. 90–91.

49 Ibid., pp. 94–95.

50 Buchanan, "The Economizing Element in Knight's Ethical Critique of Capitalist Order," p. 61.

51 Frank H. Knight, " 'What Is Truth' in Economics?" *The Journal of Political Economy*, Vol. 47, No. 1 (February 1940), p. 6.

52 Ibid.

53 Ibid., p. 6.

54 Ibid., pp. 26–27.

55 Ibid., p. 27.

56 See ibid., p. 5; and Frank H. Knight, *Risk, Uncertainty, and Profit* (Boston: Houghton Mifflin, 1921), p. 3.

57 Frank H. Knight, *The Ethics of Competition and Other Essays* (London: Allen & Unwin, 1935), p. 282.

58 See Knight, " 'What Is Truth' in Economics?" p. 29.

59 Ibid., p. 148.

60 Knight, *The Economic Organization*, pp. 98–100 (1st ed. 1933).

61 Knight, *The Ethics of Competition and Other Essays*, p. 291.

62 Knight, *Risk, Uncertainty, and Profit*, p. 291.

63 Ibid., p. 307.
64 Knight, *The Economic Organization*, pp. 124–25.
65 Ibid., pp. 23–24.
66 In Friedman, *Essays in Positive Economics*, pp. 3–43.
67 Milton Friedman, *Capitalism and Freedom* (Chicago: University of Chicago Press, 1962), pp. 13–14.

4. Agreement and disagreement within the tradition

1 Frank H. Hahn, "General Equilibrium Theory," in Daniel Bell and Irving Kristol, eds., *The Crisis in Economic Theory* (New York: Basic, 1981), p. 125.
2 Ibid., p. 123.
3 See Paul A. Samuelson, "Out of the Closet: A Program for the Whig History of Economic Science," *History of Economics Society Bulletin*, Vol. 9, No. 1 (1987), pp. 51–60.
4 Frank H. Hahn, "The Winter of Our Discontent," *Economica*, Vol. 40, No. 159 (August 1973), p. 324.
5 See Samuelson, "Out of the Closet," p. 52.
6 Julius Sensat, "Methodological Individualism and Marxism," *Economics and Philosophy*, Vol. 4 (1988), p. 190.
7 Ibid., p. 197.
8 An insightful analysis of the extent to which such individualism is imbedded in the entire intellectual fabric of classical modern thought, as well as a criticism of some very central aspects of that individualism, is provided by Annette Baier in two essays, "Intention, Practical Knowledge, and Representation," and "Cartesian Persons," in Baier, *Postures of the Mind: Essays in Mind and Morals* (Minneapolis: University of Minnesota Press, 1985), pp. 34–50, and 74–92, respectively.
9 Albert Einstein, "Zur Elektrodynamik bewegter Körper," *Annalen der Physik*, Vol. 17 (1905), pp. 132–48; and "Ist die Tragheit eines Körpers von seinem Energieinhalt abhängig?" *Annalen der Physik*, Vol. 18 (1905), pp. 639–41.
10 Friedman, *Capitalism and Freedom*, p. 13.
11 Smith, *The Wealth of Nations*, Vol. 1, p. 456.
12 See Friedman, "The Methodology of Positive Economics."
13 Mill, *A System of Logic*, 2 vols., 8th ed. (London: Longmans, Green, and Co., 1974).
14 See Jevons, *The Principles of Science*, 2nd ed. (New York: Macmillan, 1924).
15 John Stuart Mill, "On the Definition of Political Economy and on the Method of Investigation Proper to It," in *Collected Works of John Stuart Mill*, Vol. 4 (Toronto: University of Toronto Press, 1967), pp. 309–39.
16 Ibid., pp. 317–18.
17 Ibid., p. 317.
18 Ibid., p. 325.

19 Jevons, *Theory of Political Economy*, 4th ed., p. 18.
20 Ibid., p. 1.

5. Theories of the firm

1 Machlup, "Theories of the Firm," p. 4.
2 Papandreou, "Some Basic Problems in the Theory of the Firm," p. 210.
3 See Machlup, "Theories of the Firm," pp. 19–23.
4 See Richard M. Cyert and Charles L. Hedrick, "Theory of the Firm: Past, Present, and Future: An Interpretation," *Journal of Economic Literature*, Vol. 10 (1972), pp. 401–402.
5 Machlup, "Theories of the Firm," p. 9.
6 Alexander Rosenberg, *Microeconomic Laws: A Philosophical Analysis* (Pittsburgh: University of Pittsburgh Press, 1976), p. 45.
7 Machlup, "Theories of the Firm," p. 8.
8 See ibid., p. 15.
9 Ibid., p. 28.
10 Friedman, *Capitalism and Freedom,* p. 133.
11 See Latsis, "A Research Programme in Economics," pp. 16ff.
12 Richard Cyert and James G. March, *A Behavioral Theory of the Firm* (Englewood Cliffs, NJ: Prentice-Hall, 1963), pp. 1–2.
13 Simon illustrates how central the notion of "bounded rationality" is to his general position when he uses it in the title of a two-volume collection of his major article-length writings. See Herbert A. Simon, *Models of Bounded Rationality*, 2 Vols. (Cambridge, MA: The MIT Press, 1982).
14 See Simon, *Administrative Behavior*, 2nd ed. (New York: Macmillan, 1957), pp. xxiv–xxvi.
15 See Oliver E. Williamson, *The Economics of Discretionary Behavior: Managerial Objectives in a Theory of the Firm* (Chicago: Markham Publishing, 1967), pp. 11–12.
16 Ibid., p. 6.
17 See Plato, *The Republic of Plato*, F. M. Cornford, trans. (Oxford University Press, 1945), pp. 108ff.
18 Williamson, *The Economics of Discretionary Behavior*, p. 6.
19 See Adolf A. Berle, Jr., and Gardiner Means, *The Modern Corporation and Private Property* (New York: Commerce Clearing House, 1932).
20 Williamson, *The Economics of Discretionary Behavior*, p. 6.
21 Ibid., p. 19.
22 Williamson, *Corporate Control and Business Behavior.*
23 Williamson, *The Economic Institutions of Capitalism*, p. 320.
24 Ibid.
25 Ibid., p. 295.
26 See Loasby, "Hypothesis and Paradigm in the Theory of the Firm," p. 885.

6. Confusions and problems with the marginalist view

1 R. L. Hall and C. J. Hitch, "Price Theory and Business Behavior," *Oxford Economic Papers*, Vol. 2 (May 1939), pp. 12–45.

2 See Richard A. Lester, "Shortcomings of Marginal Analysis for Wage-Employment Problems," *American Economic Review*, Vol. 36 (March 1946), pp. 63–82, and idem, "Marginalism, Minimum Wages, and Labor Markets," *American Economic Review*, Vol. 37 (March 1947), pp. 135–48; Fritz Machlup, "Marginal Analysis and Empirical Research," *American Economic Review*, Vol. 36 (September 1946), pp. 519–54, and idem, "Rejoinder to the Antimarginalist," *American Economic Review*, Vol. 37 (March 1947), pp. 148–54; and George J. Stigler, "The Economics of Minimum Wage Legislation," *American Economic Review*, Vol. 36 (June 1946), pp. 358–65, and idem, "Professor Lester and the Marginalists," *American Economic Review*, Vol. 37 (March 1947), pp. 154–57. Also see Philippe Mongin, "The Early Full-Cost Debate and the Problem of Empirically Testing Profit Maximization," *Journal of Post Keynesian Economics*, Vol. 13, No. 2 (Winter 1990–91), pp. 236–51, for a valuable discussion distinguishing different strains in the historical arguments over the marginalist theory of the firm.

3 Machlup, "Theories of the Firm," pp. 30–31.

4 Alan Nelson, "Average Explanations," *Erkenntnis*, Vol. 30 (1989), p. 38.

5 Ibid., p. 26.

6 Latsis, "A Research Programme in Economics," p. 24.

7 Loasby, "Hypothesis and Paradigm in the Theory of the Firm," p. 884.

8 Boulding, "Implications for General Economics of More Realistic Theories of the Firm," p. 41.

9 Cyert and Hedrick, "Theory of the Firm," p. 398.

10 Papandreou, "Some Basic Problems in the Theory of the Firm," p. 184.

11 Cyert and Hedrick, "Theory of the Firm," p. 408.

12 Blaug, *The Methodology of Economics*, p. 177.

13 Ibid.

14 Ibid.

15 See Armen A. Alchian and Harold Demsetz, "Production, Information Costs, and Economic Organization," *American Economic Review*, Vol. 62 (December 1972), pp. 777–95; and Michael C. Jensen and William H. Meckling, "Theory of the Firm: Managerial Behavior, Agency Costs and Ownership Structure," *Journal of Financial Economics*, Vol. 3 (October 1976), pp. 305–60.

16 Fama, "Agency Problems and the Theory of the Firm," p. 295.

17 Ibid., p. 288.

18 Ibid., p. 306.

19 Friedman, *Capitalism and Freedom*, p. 14.

20 The one exception of which I am aware is Cyert and Hedrick, "Theory of the Firm," which gives a survey of articles appearing in three prominent economics journals over a two-year period applying rival theories of the

firm to different concrete problems. Not surprisingly, since Cyert is one of the chief architects of the behavioral theory of the firm, their assessment shows a modest preference for behavioral theories, yet they do conclude by noting that one of the most central issues involved in making any comparative evaluation involves the question of what a theory of the firm ought to be expected to explain.

21 See Carl G. Hempel, *Philosophy of Natural Science* (Englewood Cliffs, NJ: Prentice-Hall, 1966), pp. 38–40, for a discussion of "support from above," or theoretical support for scientific hypotheses. Hempel notes in his discussion that "the principle here referred to must be applied with discretion and restraint, however. Otherwise, it could be used to protect any accepted theory against overthrow: Adverse findings could always be dismissed as conflicting with a well-established theory" (p. 40).

22 See, e.g., Veblen, "The Limitations of Marginal Utility," pp. 620–36.

7. The shape of the large managerial corporation

1 This section is largely a revision of David E. Schrader, "The Corporation and Profits," *Journal of Business Ethics,* Vol. 6 (1987), pp. 589–93, 596–97, and 598–600, © 1987 by D. Reidel Publishing Company. It is reprinted here with the permission of Kluwer Academic Publishers.

2 Friedman, "The Methodology of Positive Economics," p. 22.

3 See Friedman, *Capitalism and Freedom,* pp. 121–32.

4 John P. Palmer, "The Separation of Ownership From Control in Large US Industrial Corporations," *Quarterly Review of Economics and Business,* Vol. 12 (1972), p. 55.

5 See Herbert A. Simon, "The Role of Expectations in an Adaptive or Behavioristic Model," in Simon, *Models of Bounded Rationality* (Cambridge, MA: MIT Press, 1982), pp. 393ff.

6 Sidney G. Winter, "Economic 'Natural Selection' and the Theory of the Firm," *Yale Economic Essays,* Vol. 4 (1964), pp. 224–72.

7 See ibid., pp. 261–62.

8 Ibid., p. 267.

9 Friedman, *Capitalism and Freedom,* p. 110.

10 See George A. Akerlof, "Discriminatory, Status-based Wages among Tradition-oriented, Stochastically Trading Coconut Producers," *Journal of Political Economy,* Vol. 93, No. 2 (1985), pp. 265–76.

11 Herbert A. Simon, "Theories of Decision-Making in Economics and Behavioral Science," *American Economic Review,* Vol. 49 (June 1959), pp. 262–63.

12 Winter, "Economic 'Natural Selection' and the Theory of the Firm," p. 264.

13 Harold Demsetz, "Toward a Theory of Property Rights," *American Economic Review,* Vol. 57 (1967), pp. 358–59.

14 R. Edward Freeman, *Strategic Management: A Stakeholder Approach* (Boston: Pitman, 1984).
15 See ibid., esp. pp. 216ff. and p. 233, as well as Exhibit 1.5 on p. 25 for a sense of Freeman's distinction between "internal" and "external."
16 Ibid., pp. 31–32.
17 See ibid.
18 Ibid., p. 238.
19 Ibid., p. 249.
20 Williamson, *The Economic Institutions of Capitalism*, pp. 298–325.
21 See ibid., pp. 304–307.
22 Ibid., pp. 299–300.
23 Richard Eells and Clarence Walton, *Conceptual Foundations of Business* (Homewood, IL: Irwin, 1969), p. 136.
24 Abram Chayes, "The Modern Corporation and the Rule of Law," in Edward S. Mason, ed., *The Corporation in Modern Society*, pp. 33–34.
25 See, e.g., Freeman, *Strategic Management*, and Thomas J. Peters and Robert H. Waterman, Jr., *In Search of Excellence* (New York: Warner, 1982).
26 Peter A. French, *Collective and Corporate Responsibility* (New York: Columbia University Press, 1984), pp. 41–42.

8. The theoretical impact of a better theory of the firm

1 Mark Blaug, *The Methodology of Economics: Or How Economists Explain* (Cambridge University Press, 1980), p. 178.
2 Boulding, "Implications for General Economics of More Realistic Theories of the Firm," pp. 42, 44.
3 In Kenneth E. Boulding's *Economics as a Science* (New York: McGraw-Hill, 1970), he also reflects the view that marginal analysis is much less central to contemporary economic theory than I have claimed it to be in the preceding chapters. This follows from his characterization of the economy as "that segment of the total social system which deals primarily with exchange and the institutions of exchange and, by extension, with exchangeables or the goods and services which participate in exchange" (pp. 17–18), as opposed to the more common contemporary characterization of the economy as "that segment of the social system which is concerned with the allocation of scarce resources" (p. 18). As I noted in Chapter 3, a central feature of marginalist economics is the claim that allocation is the fundamental problem of economics. Thus, it is not surprising that an author who views economics as fundamentally addressed to problems other than allocation should regard marginal analysis as ancillary to the core of economic theory.
4 Boulding, "Implications for General Economics of More Realistic Theories of the Firm," p. 37.
5 See Mill, *Principles of Political Economy*, Vol. 2, p. 512.

6 John R. Commons, *The Economics of Collective Action* (New York: Macmillan, 1950), p. 35.

7 Papandreou, "Some Basic Problems in the Theory of the Firm," pp. 217–18.

8 See, e.g., David Schweickart, *Capitalism or Worker Control?* (New York: Praeger, 1980).

9 Carl Icahn, "What Ails Corporate America – And What Should Be Done," *Business Week*, No. 2970 (October 27, 1986), p. 101.

10 See, e.g., Williamson, *The Economic Institutions of Capitalism*, pp. 279–81.

11 Jevons, *Theory of Political Economy*, 4th ed. (London: Macmillan Press, 1911), p. 267.

12 Mancur Olson, *The Logic of Collective Action: Public Goods and the Theory of Groups* (Cambridge, MA: Harvard University Press, 1971).

13 Ibid., pp. 1–2.

14 Ibid., p. 48.

15 Ibid., p. 63.

16 Ibid., p. 55.

17 Ibid., p. 177.

18 Richard M. Cyert and Garrell Pottinger, "Towards a Better Microeconomic Theory," *Philosophy of Science*, Vol. 46 (1979), p. 221.

19 See Williamson, *The Economics of Discretionary Behavior*, pp. 147–62.

20 A useful discussion supporting the need for such development is found in "Symposium on Organizations and Economics," *Journal of Economic Perspectives*, Vol. 5, No. 2 (Spring 1991), pp. 15–110.

21 Wendell Gordon, *Institutional Economics: The Changing System* (Austin: University of Texas Press, 1980), p. 17.

22 A decision-making model for the conduct of biomedical research was presented by Herbert Simon in a Symposium on "Models of Biomedical Research," at the 1986 annual meeting of the Philosophy of Science Association, Pittsburgh, PA, on October 24, 1986.

23 Williamson, *The Economic Institutions of Capitalism*, p. 16.

24 Ibid., p. 408.

25 Ibid., pp. 44–45.

26 See ibid., pp. 298–325.

Bibliography

Ackermann, Robert. "Methodology and Economics." *Philosophical Forum,* Vol. 14 (1983), pp. 389–402.

Akerlof, George A. "Discriminatory, Status-based Wages among Tradition-oriented, Stochastically Trading Coconut Producers." *Journal of Political Economy,* Vol. 93, No. 2 (1985), pp. 265–76.

Alchian, Armen A. "Uncertainty, Evolution and Economic Theory." *Journal of Political Economy,* Vol. 58 (June 1950), pp. 211–21.

Alchian, Armen A., and Harold Demsetz. "Production, Information Costs, and Economic Organization." *American Economic Review,* Vol. 62 (December 1972), pp. 777–95.

Aristotle, *The Basic Works of Aristotle,* Richard McKeon, ed. New York: Random House, 1941.

Arrow, Kenneth J. *Social Choice and Individual Values,* 2nd ed. New York: Wiley, 1963.

 Social Choice and Justice. Cambridge, MA: Harvard University Press, 1983.

 "Values and Collective Decision-making." In Laslett and Runciman, eds., *Philosophy, Politics and Society,* 3rd ser., pp. 215–32. Reprinted in Arrow, *Social Choice and Justice,* pp. 59–77.

Baier, Annette. *Postures of the Mind: Essays on Mind and Morals.* Minneapolis: University of Minnesota Press, 1985.

Beauchamp, Tom L., and Norman E. Bowie, eds. *Ethical Theory and Business,* 2nd ed. Englewood Cliffs, NJ: Prentice-Hall, 1983.

Bell, Daniel, and Irving Kristol, eds. *The Crisis in Economic Theory.* New York: Basic, 1981.

Berle, Adolf A., Jr., and Gardiner C. Means. *The Modern Corporation and Private Property.* New York: Commerce Clearing House, 1932.

 Power without Property. New York: Harcourt, Brace, 1959.

Blaug, Mark. *Economic Theory in Retrospect.* Homewood, IL: Irwin, 1962.

 "Kuhn versus Lakatos *or* Paradigms versus Research Programmes in the History of Economics." In Spiro Latsis, ed., *Method and Appraisal in Economics,* pp. 149–80.

 The Methodology of Economics: Or How Economists Explain. Cambridge University Press, 1980.

Boland, Lawrence A. "A Critique of Friedman's Critics." *Journal of Economic Literature,* Vol. 17 (June 1979), pp. 503–22.

Boulding, Kenneth E. *Economics as a Science.* New York: McGraw-Hill, 1970.

 "Implications for General Economics of More Realistic Theories of the

Firm." *American Economic Review Proceedings*, Vol. 42 (May 1952), pp. 35–44.

Bowie, Norman E. "The Moral Contract Between Employer and Employee." In Hoffman and Wyly, eds., *The Work Ethic in Business*, pp. 195–202. Reprinted in Beauchamp and Bowie, eds., *Ethical Theory and Business*, 2nd ed. pp. 150–54.

Bowles, Samuel, and Herbert Gintis. *Democracy and Capitalism: Property, Community, and the Contradictions of Modern Social Thought.* New York: Basic, 1986.

Bray, Jeremy. "The Logic of Scientific Method in Economics." *Journal of Economic Studies*, Vol. 4 (May 1977), pp. 1–28.

Bronfenbrenner, Martin. "The 'Structure of Revolutions' in Economic Thought." *History of Political Economy*, Vol. 3 (1971), pp. 136–51.

Buchanan, James M. "The Economizing Element in Knight's Ethical Critique of Capitalist Order." *Ethics*, Vol. 98, No. 1 (October 1987), pp. 61–75.

Caldwell, Bruce J. "Clarifying Popper." *Journal of Economic Literature*, Vol. 29 (March 1991), pp. 1–33.

Canterbery, E. Ray, and Robert J. Burkhardt. "What Do We Mean By Asking Whether Economics Is a Science?" In Eichner, ed., *Why Economics Is Not Yet a Science*, pp. 15–40.

Chamberlin, Edward H. *The Theory of Monpolistic Competition*, 6th ed. Cambridge, MA: Harvard University Press, 1948.

Chandler, Alfred D., Jr. *The Visible Hand: The Managerial Revolution in American Business.* Cambridge, MA: Harvard University Press, 1977.

Chayes, Abram, "The Modern Corporation and the Rule of Law." In Edward S. Mason, ed., *The Corporation in Modern Society*, pp. 25–45.

Clark, John Bates. *The Distribution of Wealth.* London: Macmillan Press, 1908. *Essentials of Economic Theory.* New York: Macmillan, 1924.

Coats, A. W. "Is There a 'Structure of Scientific Revolutions' in Economics?" *Kyklos*, Vol. 22 (1969), pp. 288–94.

Coleman, Jules. "Competition and Cooperation." *Ethics*, Vol. 98, No. 1 (October 1987), pp. 76–90.

Commons, John R. *The Economics of Collective Action.* New York: Macmillan, 1950.

Copp, David. "Collective Actions and Secondary Actions." *American Philosophical Quarterly*, Vol. 16 (1979), pp. 177–79.

Cyert, Richard M., and Charles L. Hedrick. "Theory of the Firm: Past, Present, and Future: An Interpretation." *Journal of Economic Literature*, Vol. 10 (1972), pp. 398–412.

Cyert, Richard M., and J. G. March. *A Behavioral Theory of the Firm.* Englewood Cliffs, NJ: Prentice-Hall, 1963.

Cyert, Richard M., and Garell Pottinger. "Towards a Better Microeconomic Theory." *Philosophy of Science*, Vol. 46 (1979), pp. 204–22.

Davis, Keith, and Robert L. Blomstrom. *Business and Society: Environment and Responsibility*, 3rd ed. New York: McGraw-Hill, 1975.

188   **Bibliography**

Deane, Phyllis. "The Scope and Method of Economic Science." *The Economic Journal*, Vol. 93 (March 1983), pp. 1–12.

Demsetz, Harold, "Toward a Theory of Property Rights." *American Economic Review*, Vol. 57 (1967), pp. 347–59.

Desai, Meghnad. *Marxian Economics*. Totowa, NJ: Rowman & Littlefield, 1979.

Dillard, Dudley. "Revolutions in Economic Theory." *Southern Economic Journal*, Vol. 44 (April 1978), pp. 705–24.

Donaldson, Thomas. *Corporations and Morality*. Englewood Cliffs, NJ: Prentice-Hall, 1982.

Drucker, Peter F. *Concept of the Corporation*. New York: John Day, 1946.

The New Society: The Anatomy of Industrial Order. New York: Harper & Row, 1950.

Dugger, William. "Methodological Differences Between Institutional and Neoclassical Economics." *Journal of Economic Issues*, Vol. 13 (1979), pp. 899–909. Reprinted in Hausman, ed., *The Philosophy of Economics*, pp. 312–322.

Duhem, Pierre. *The Aim and Structure of Physical Theory*, trans. by Philip Weiner. Princeton, NJ: Princeton University Press, 1954. (Originally published in French in 1906)

Easterbrook, Frank H., and Daniel R. Fischel. "The Proper Role of a Target's Management in Responding to a Tender Offer." *Harvard Law Review*, Vol. 94, No. 6 (April 1981), pp. 1161–1203.

Easterbrook, Frank H., and Gregg A. Jarrell. "Do Targets Gain from Defeating Tender Offers?" *New York University Law Review*, Vol. 59 (May 1984), pp. 277–99.

Eels, Richard, and Clarence Walton. *Conceptual Foundations of Business*. Homewood, IL: Irwin, 1969.

Eichner, Alfred S., ed. *Why Economics Is Not Yet a Science*. Armonk, NY: Sharpe, 1983.

"Why Economics Is Not Yet a Science." In Eichner, ed., *Why Economics Is Not Yet a Science*, pp. 205–41.

Einstein, Albert. "Zur Elektrodynamik bewegter Körper." *Annalen der Physik*, Vol. 17 (1905), pp 132–48.

"Ist die Trägheit eines Körpers von seinem Energieinhalt abhängig?" *Annalen der Physik*, Vol. 18 (1905), pp. 639–41.

Eisenberg, Melvin Aron. "The Legal Roles of Shareholders and Management in Modern Corporate Decisionmaking." *California Law Review*, Vol. 57 (1969), pp. 1–181.

Etzione, Amitai. *The Moral Dimension: Toward a New Economics*. New York: Free Press, 1988.

Ewing, David W. *Freedom Inside the Organization: Bringing Civil Liberties to the Workplace*. New York: Dutton, 1977.

Fama, Eugene F. "Agency Problems and the Theory of the Firm." *Journal of Political Economy*, Vol. 88 (1980), pp. 288–307.

Fishkin, James S. *The Limits of Obligation*. New Haven, CT: Yale University Press, 1982.

Flathman, Richard E. "Convention, Contractarianism, and Freedom." *Ethics*, Vol. 98, No. 1 (October 1987), pp. 91–103.

Frazer, William J., Jr., and Lawrence A. Boland. "An Essay on the Foundations of Friedman's Methodology." *American Economic Review*, Vol. 73 (March 1983), pp. 129–44.

Freeman, R. Edward. *Strategic Management: A Stakeholder Approach*. Boston: Pitman, 1984.

French, Peter A. *Collective and Corporate Responsibility*. New York: Columbia University Press, 1984.

Friedman, Milton. *Capitalism and Freedom*. Chicago: University of Chicago Press, 1962.

Essays in Positive Economics. Chicago: University of Chicago Press, 1953.

"The Methodology of Positive Economics." In Friedman, *Essays in Positive Economics*, pp. 3–43. Reprinted in Hausman, ed., *The Philosophy of Economics*, pp. 210–44.

Galbraith, John Kenneth. *The Affluent Society*, 4th ed. Boston: Houghton Mifflin, 1984.

Georgescu-Roegen, Nicholas. *The Entropy Law and the Economic Process*. Cambridge, MA: Harvard University Press, 1971.

Goldman, Alan H. *The Moral Foundations of Professional Ethics*. Totowa, NJ: Rowman & Littlefield, 1980.

Gordon, D. "The Role of the History of Economic Thought in Understanding Modern Economic Theory." *American Economic Review: Papers and Proceedings*, Vol. 55 (1965), pp. 119–27.

Gordon, Wendell. *Institutional Economics: The Changing System*. Austin: University of Texas Press, 1980.

Hahn, Frank H. "General Equilibrium." In Daniel Bell and Irving Kristol, eds., *The Crisis in Economic Theory*, pp. 123–38.

"The Winter of Our Discontent." *Economica*, Vol. 40, No. 159 (August 1973), pp. 322–30.

Haley, Bernard F., ed. *A Survey of Contemporary Economics*, Vol. 2. Homewood, IL: Irwin, 1953.

Hall, R. L., and C. J. Hitch. "Price Theory and Business Behavior." *Oxford Economic Papers*, Vol. 2 (May 1939), pp. 12–45.

Hands, Douglas W. "The Methodology of Economic Research Programmes." *Philosophy of the Social Sciences*, Vol. 9 (1979), pp. 293–303.

"What Economics Is Not: An Economist's Response to Rosenberg." *Philosophy of Science*, Vol. 51 (1984), pp. 495–503.

Hausman, Daniel M. "Defending Microeconomic Theory." *The Philosophical Forum*, Vol. 15 (1984), pp. 392–404.

"John Stuart Mill's Philosophy of Economics." *Philosophy of Science*, Vol. 48 (1981), pp. 363–85.

ed. *The Philosophy of Economics*. Cambridge University Press, 1984.

Hayek, F. A. von. "The *Non Sequitur* of the 'Dependence Effect'." *Southern Economic Journal,* Vol. 27 (1961), pp. 346–48. Reprinted in Beauchamp and Bowie, eds., *Ethical Theory and Business,* 2nd ed., pp. 363–66.

Hempel, Carl G. *Philosophy of Natural Science.* Englewood-Cliffs, NJ: Prentice-Hall, 1966.

Hobbes, Thomas. *Leviathan,* ed. by C. B. MacPherson, Baltimore: Penguin, 1968.

Hoffman, W. Michael, and Thomas J. Wyly, eds. *The Work Ethic in Business.* Cambridge, MA: Oelgeschlager, Gunn, & Hain, 1981.

Hollis, Martin, and Edward J. Nell. *Rational Economic Man: A Philosophical Critique of Neo-Classical Economics.* Cambridge University Press, 1975.

Hutchison, T. W. *On Revolutions and Progress in Economic Knowledge.* Cambridge University Press, 1978.

Icahn, Carl. "What Ails Corporate America – And What Should Be Done?" *Business Week,* No. 2970 (October 27, 1986), p. 101.

Jensen, Michael C. "Takeovers: Folklore and Science." *Harvard Business Review,* Vol. 62 (1984), pp. 109–21.

  "When Unocal Won over Pickens, Shareholders and Society Lost." *Financier* (November 1985), pp. 50–52

Jenson, Michael C., and William H. Meckling. "Theory of the Firm: Managerial Behavior, Agency Costs and Ownership Structure." *Journal of Financial Economics,* Vol. 3 (October 1976), pp. 305–60.

Jevons, W. Stanley. *The Principles of Science,* 2nd ed. New York: Macmillan, 1924.

  Theory of Political Economy, 4th ed. London: Macmillan Press, 1911. (Originally published in 1871)

Kavanagh, John P. "Ethical Issues in Plant Relocation." In Beauchamp and Bowie, eds., *Ethical Theory and Business,* 2nd ed., pp. 106–15.

Kaysen, Carl. "The Corporation: How Much Power? What Scope?" In Mason, ed., *The Corporation in Modern Society,* pp. 85–105.

Keynes, John Maynard. *The General Theory of Employment, Interest, and Money.* New York: Harcourt, Brace & World, 1935.

Keynes, John Neville. *The Scope and Methods of Political Economy,* 4th ed. New York: Kelley & Millman, 1955. (Originally published in 1891)

Knight, Frank H. *The Economic Organization.* New York: Augustus Kelley, 1951. (Originally published in 1933)

  The Ethics of Competition and Other Essays. London: Allen & Unwin, 1935.

  Risk, Uncertainty, and Profit. Boston: Houghton Mifflin, 1921.

  " 'What Is Truth' in Economics?" *The Journal of Political Economy,* Volume 48, No. 1 (February 1940), pp. 1–32.

Kuhn, Thomas. *The Structure of Scientific Revolutions,* 2nd ed. Chicago: University of Chicago Press, 1970.

Lakatos, Imre. "Falsification and the Methodology of Scientific Research Programmes." In Lakatos and Musgrave, eds., *Criticism and the Growth of Knowledge,* pp. 91–195.

Lakatos, Imre, and Alan Musgrave. *Criticism and the Growth of Knowledge.* Cambridge University Press, 1970.

Landsburg, Steben E. *Price Theory and Applications.* Chicago: Dryden, 1989.

Laslett, Peter, and W. G. Runciman, eds. *Philosophy, Politics and Society,* 3rd ser. New York: Barnes & Noble, 1967.

Latham, Earl. "The Body Politic of the Corporation." In Mason, ed., *The Corporation in Modern Society,* pp. 218–36.

Latsis, Spiro. "A Research Programme in Economics." In Latsis, ed., *Method and Appraisal in Economics,* pp. 1–42.

ed. *Method and Appraisal in Economics.* Cambridge University Press, 1976.

Laudan, Larry. *Progress and Its Problems.* Berkeley & Los Angeles: University of California Press, 1977.

Science and Values. Berkeley & Los Angeles: University of California Press, 1984.

Lazear, Edward P. "Labor Economics and the Psychology of Organizations." *The Journal of Economic Perspectives,* Vol. 5, No. 2 (Spring 1991), pp. 89–110.

Leijonhufvud, Axel. "Schools, 'Revolutions', and Research Programmes in Economic Theory." In Latsis, ed., *Method and Appraisal in Economics,* pp. 65–108.

Lester, Richard A. "Marginalism, Minimum Wages, and Labor Markets." *American Economic Review,* Vol. 37 (March 1947), pp. 135–48.

"Shortcomings of Marginal Analysis for Wage-Employment Problems." *American Economic Review,* Vol. 36 (March 1946), pp. 63–82.

Levitt, Theodore. "The Danger of Social Responsibility." *Harvard Business Review,* Vol. 36 (September–October 1958), pp. 41–50.

Levy, David M. "The Impossibility of a Complete Methodological Individualist: Reduction When Knowledge is Imperfect." *Economics and Philosophy,* Vol. 1 (1985), pp. 101–108.

Lipsey, Richard G., and Peter O. Steiner. *Economics,* 3rd ed. New York: Harper & Row, 1972.

Loasby, B. J. "Hypothesis and Paradigm in the Theory of the Firm." *Economic Journal,* Vol. 81 (December 1971), pp. 863–85.

Long, Norton E. "The Corporation, Its Satellites, and the Local Community." In Mason, ed., *The Corporation in Modern Society,* pp. 202–17.

Machlup, Fritz. "Marginal Analysis and Empirical Research." *American Economic Review,* Vol. 36 (September 1946), pp. 519–54.

"Professor Samuelson on Theory and Realism." *American Economic Review,* Vol. 54 (1964), pp. 733–36.

"Rejoinder to the Antimarginalist." *American Economic Review,* Vol. 37 (March 1947), pp. 148–54.

"Theories of the Firm: Marginalist, Behavioral, Managerial." *American Economic Review,* Vol. 57 No. 1 (March 1967), pp. 1–33.

MacMahon, Thomas F. "Models of the Relationship of the Firm to Society." *Journal of Business Ethics,* Vol. 5, No. 4 (August 1986), pp. 181–91.

Marshall, Alfred. *Industry and Trade*. London: Macmillan Press, 1919.

Principles of Economics, 8th ed. London: Macmillan Press, 1920.

Marx, Karl. *Economic and Philosophical Manuscripts of 1844*, Martin Milligan, trans. Moscow: Foreign Languages Publishing House, 1961.

Mason, Edward S., ed. *The Corporation in Modern Society*. Cambridge, MA: Harvard University Press, 1960.

Masterman, Margaret. "The Nature of a Paradigm." In Lakatos and Musgrave, *Criticism and the Growth of Knowledge*, pp. 60–65.

May, Larry. *The Morality of Groups: Collective Responsibility, Group-Based Harm, and Corporate Rights*. Notre Dame, IN: University of Notre Dame Press, 1987.

Mayer, Thomas. "Economics as a Hard Science: Realistic Goal or Wishful Thinking?" *Economic Inquiry*, Vol. 18 (April 1980), pp. 165–78

Mill, John Stuart. "On the Definition of Political Economy; and on the Method of Investigation Proper to It." In *Collected Works of John Stuart Mill*, Vol. 4. Toronto: University of Toronto Press, 1967, pp. 308–39. (Originally published in 1836)

Principles of Political Economy, 2 vols., 5th ed. New York: D. Appleton & Company, 1894.

A System of Logic, 2 vols., 8th ed. London: Longmans Group, 1974.

Mises, Ludwig von. *Epistemological Problems of Economics*, trans. by G. Reisman. Princeton, NJ: Van Nostrand, 1960.

Mitchell, Wesley C. *Business Cycles: The Problem and its Setting*. New York: National Bureau of Economic Research, 1927.

Mongin, Philippe. "The Early Full-Cost Debate and the Problem of Empirically Testing Profit Maximization." *Journal of Post Keynesian Economics*, Vol. 13, No. 2 (Winter 1990–91), pp. 236–51.

Monsen, R. Joseph, Jr., and Anthony Downs. "A Theory of Large Managerial Firms." *The Journal of Political Economy*, Vol. 73, No. 3 (June 1965), pp. 221–36.

Mulligan, Thomas. "A Critique of Milton Friedman's Essay 'The Social Responsibility of Business Is to Increase Its Profits'." *Journal of Business Ethics*, Vol. 5, No. 3 (June 1986), pp. 265–69.

Naughton, John. "The Logic of Scientific Method in Economics: A Response to Bray." *Journal of Economic Studies*, Vol. 5 (November 1978), pp. 152–65.

Nelson, Alan. "Average Explanations." *Erkenntnis*, Vol. 30 (1989), pp. 23–42.

"New Individualistic Foundations for Economics." *Nous*, Vol. 20, No. 4 (December 1986), pp. 469–90.

Nozick, Robert. *Anarchy, State, and Utopia*. New York: Basic, 1974.

O'Brien, D. P. "The Evolution of the Theory of the Firm." In Frank H. Stephen, ed., *Firms, Organization and Labor: Approaches to the Economics of Work Organization*, pp. 25–68.

Olson, Mancur. *The Logic of Collective Action: Public Goods and the Theory of Groups*. Cambridge, MA: Harvard University Press, 1971.

The Rise and Decline of Nations. New Haven, CT: Yale University Press, 1982.

Palmer, John P. "The Separation of Ownership From Control in Large US Industrial Corporations." *Quarterly Review of Economics and Business,* Vol. 12 (1972), pp. 55–62.

Papandreou, Andreas G. *Economics as a Science.* Chicago: Lippincott, 1958.

"Some Basic Problems in the Theory of the Firm." In Haley, ed., *A Survey of Contemporary Economics,* Vol. 2, pp. 183–219.

Parsons, Talcott. *The Structure of Social Action,* 2nd ed. New York: Glencoe, 1949.

Peters, Thomas J., and Robert H. Waterman, Jr. *In Search of Excellence.* New York: Warner, 1982.

Pigou, A. C. "An Analysis of Supply." *The Economic Journal,* Vol. 38, No. 150 (June 1928), pp. 238–57.

 ed. *Memorials of Alfred Marshall.* New York: Kelley & Millman, 1956.

Plato. *The Republic of Plato,* F. M. Cornford, trans. Oxford University Press, 1945.

Popper, Karl R. *Conjectures and Refutations.* London: Routlege & Kegan Paul, 1963.

The Logic of Scientific Discovery. New York: Harper & Row, 1965.

Objective Knowledge: An Evolutionary Approach. Oxford University Press, 1972.

Quine, W. V. *From a Logical Point of View.* Cambridge, MA: Harvard University Press, 1980.

"Two Dogmas of Empiricism." In Quine, *From a Logical Point of View,* pp. 20–46.

Rawls, John. *A Theory of Justice.* Cambridge, MA: Harvard University Press, 1971.

Reeder, Melvin W. "Chicago Economics: Permanence and Change." *Journal of Economic Literature,* Vol. 20 (March 1982), pp. 1–38.

Ricardo, David. *Principles of Political Economy and Taxation.* London: George Bell & Sons, 1891.

Robbins, Lionel. "The Representative Firm." *The Economic Journal,* Vol. 38, No. 151 (September 1928), pp. 387–404.

Robinson, Joan. *The Economics of Imperfect Competition.* London: Macmillan Press, 1938.

Roemer, John E. *Analytical Foundations of Marxian Economic Theory.* Cambridge University Press, 1981.

Rosenberg, Alexander. "If Economics isn't Science, What is it?" *The Philosophical Forum,* Vol. 14 (1983), pp. 296–314.

Microeconomic Laws: A Philosophical Analysis. Pittsburgh: University of Pittsburgh Press, 1976.

Rostow, Eugene V. "To Whom and for What Ends Is Corporate Management Responsible." In Mason, ed., *The Corporation in Modern Society,* pp. 46–71.

Sah, Raaj K. "Fallibility in Human Organizations and Political Systems." *The Journal of Economic Perspectives,* Vol. 5, No. 2 (Spring 1991), pp. 67–88.

Samuelson, Paul A. "Out of the Closet: A Program for the Whig History of

Economic Science." *History of Economics Society Bulletin,* Vol. 9, No. 1 (1987), pp. 51–60.

Samuelson, Paul A., and William D. Nordhaus. *Economics,* 12th ed. New York: McGraw-Hill, 1985.

Sappington, David E. M. "Incentives in Principle–Agent Relationships." *Journal of Economic Perspectives,* Vol. 5, No. 2 (Spring 1991), pp. 45–66.

Schrader, David E. "The Corporation and Profits." *Journal of Business Ethics,* Vol. 6 (1987), pp. 589–600.

Schumpeter, Joseph A. *History of Economic Analysis.* New York: Oxford University Press, 1954.

Schweickart, David. *Capitalism or Worker Control?* New York: Praeger, 1980.

Scott, John. *Corporations, Classes and Capitalism,* 2nd ed. London: Hutchinson, 1985.

Sen, Amartya K. "The Impossibility of a Paretian Liberal." *Journal of Political Economy,* Vol. 78 (1970), pp. 152–57.

Sensat, Julius. "Methodological Individualism and Marxism." *Economics and Philosophy,* Vol. 4 (1988), pp. 189–219.

Shackle, G. L. S. *The Years of High Theory: Invention and Tradition in Economic Thought 1926–1939.* Cambridge University Press, 1967.

Simon, Herbert A. *Administrative Behavior,* 2nd ed. New York: Free Press, 1957.

Models of Bounded Rationality, 2 vols. Cambridge, MA: MIT Press, 1982.

"Organizations and Markets." *The Journal of Economic Perspectives,* Vol. 5, No. 2 (Spring 1991), pp. 25–44.

"The Role of Expectations in an Adaptive or Behavioristic Model." In M. J. Bowman, ed., *Expectations, Uncertainty, and Business Behavior.* New York: Social Science Research Council, 1958. Reprinted in Simon, *Models of Bounded Rationality,* Vol. 2, pp. 380–99.

The Shape of Automation for Men and Management. New York: Harper & Row, 1965.

"Theories of Decision-Making in Economics and Behavioral Science." *American Economic Review,* Vol. 49 (June 1959), pp. 253–83. Reprinted in Simon, *Models of Bounded Rationality,* Vol. 2, pp. 287–317.

Untitled contribution to "PSA Symposium: Models for Biomedical Research," at the annual meeting of the Philosophy of Science Association, Pittsburgh, PA, October 24, 1986.

Simon, John G., Charles W. Powers, and Jon P. Gunnemann. *The Ethical Investor: Universities and Corporate Responsibility.* New Haven, CT: Yale University Press, 1972.

Smith, Adam. *An Inquiry into the Nature and Causes of the Wealth of Nations,* 2 vols. Oxford University Press, 1976.

Spiegel, Henry William. *The Growth of Economic Thought.* Durham, NC: Duke University Press, 1983.

Steiner, George A. *Business and Society,* 2nd ed. New York: Random House, 1975.

Stephen, Frank H., ed. *Firms, Organization and Labor: Approaches to the Economics of Work Organization.* New York: St. Martin's, 1984.

Stigler, George J. "The Development of Utility Theory I." *Journal of Political Economy,* Vol. 58 (August 1950), pp. 307–27.

"The Development of Utility Theory II." *Journal of Political Economy,* Vol. 58 (October 1950), pp. 373–96.

"The Economics of Minimum Wage Legislation." *American Economic Review,* Vol. 36 (June 1946), pp. 358–65.

"Professor Lester and the Marginalists." *American Economic Review,* Vol. 37 (March 1947), pp. 154–57.

Stiglitz, Joseph E. "Symposium on Organizations and Economics." *The Journal of Economic Perspectives,* Vol. 5, No. 2 (Spring 1991), pp. 15–24.

Symposium: Organizations and Economics. *The Journal of Economic Perspectives,* Vol. 5, No. 2 (Spring 1991), pp. 15–110.

Thomson, Judith Jarvis. "A Defense of Abortion." *Philosophy and Public Affairs,* Vol. 1 (1971), pp. 47–66.

Veblen, Thorstein. "The Limitations of Marginal Utility." *Journal of Political Economy,* Vol. 17 (1909), pp. 620–36. Reprinted in Hausman, ed., *The Philosophy of Economics,* pp. 173–86.

"Why Economics Is Not an Evolutionary Science." *Quarterly Journal of Economics,* Vol. 12 (July 1898), pp. 373–97.

Watkins, J. W. N. "Ideal Types and Historical Explanation." *British Journal for the Philosophy of Science,* Vol. 3 (1952), pp. 22–43.

Weintraub, E. Roy. *General Equilibrium Analysis: Studies in Appraisal.* Cambridge University Press, 1985.

Microfoundations. Cambridge University Press, 1979.

Stabilizing Dynamics: Constructing Economic Knowledge. Cambridge University Press, 1991.

Werhane, Patricia H. *Persons, Rights, and Corporations.* Englewood Cliffs, NJ: Prentice-Hall, 1985.

Westin, Alan F., and Stephan Salisbury, eds. *Individual Rights and the Corporation.* New York: Pantheon, 1980.

Williams, Philip L. *The Emergence of the Theory of the Firm.* New York: St. Martin's, 1978.

Williamson, Oliver E. *Corporate Control and Business Behavior.* Englewood Cliffs, NJ: Prentice-Hall, 1970.

The Economic Institutions of Capitalism. New York: Macmillan, 1987.

The Economics of Discretionary Behavior: Managerial Objectives in a Theory of the Firm. Chicago: Markham, 1967.

Winter, Sidney G., Jr. "Economic 'Natural Selection' and the Theory of the Firm." *Yale Economic Essays,* Vol. 4 (1964), pp. 224–72.

Wolff, Robert Paul. *Understanding Rawls: A Reconstruction and Critique of "A Theory of Justice."* Princeton, NJ: Princeton University Press, 1977.

Wong, Stanley. "The F-Twist and the Methodology of Paul Samuelson." *American Economic Review,* Vol. 63 (June 1973), pp. 313–25.

Index